This way to check in ──────▶

The MONOCLE *Guide to*
Hotels, Inns and Hideaways

A manual for everyone from holidaymakers to hoteliers. We sidestep
the humdrum haunts in favour of stays with substance.

For more information,
please visit gestalten.com

———

Bibliographic information published by the
Deutsche Nationalbibliothek. The Deutsche
Nationalbibliothek lists this publication in
the Deutsche Nationalbibliografie; detailed
bibliographic data is available online at
dnb.d-nb.de

FSC MIX
Paper from
responsible sources
www.fsc.org FSC® C006655

This book was printed on paper certified
according to the standards of the FSC®

Edited by *Josh Fehnert*
Monocle editor *Andrew Tuck*
Books editor *Joe Pickard*
Foreword by *Tyler Brûlé*

———

Designed by *Monocle*
Proofreading by *Monocle*
Typeset in *Plantin & Helvetica*

———

Printed by *Nino Druck GmbH,
Neustadt an der Weinstraße*

Made in Germany

Published by *Gestalten*, Berlin 2018
ISBN 978-3-89955-952-1

© Die Gestalten Verlag GmbH & Co. KG,
Berlin 2018

Cover images:

TOP LEFT: Hôtel Les Roches Rouges
(*see pages 78 to 79*)
by *Anthony Lannertonne*
TOP RIGHT: The Ned (*see page 68*)
by *Jason Larkin*
BOTTOM LEFT: 1898 The Post (*see page 37*)
by *David De Vleeschauwer*
BOTTOM RIGHT: Miramonti (*see page 97*)
by *Tiberio Sorvillo*

Contents

Foreword, introduction and how to use this guide

Part 1: Monocle 100

Our editors are often quizzed for tips that we've gleaned from a decade-plus on the road (and those weeks we while away relaxing come summer), so we've decided to share. Read on for our 100 favourite hotels, inns and hideaways from around the world.

Part 2: Trade secrets

We proffer smart tips from hoteliers who've made it and dispense the advice they wish they'd known when they started. Then we visit four classy hotel schools and mull over the merits of learning on the job. Plus we dream up an imaginary hotel and attendant staff to keep the show running smoothly. All the guidance you need for starting out, or honing your hospitality venture.

Part 3: Here to stay

There's more to hotels than a bed for the night. The best ones embellish the cities in which they reside and bear witness to life, love and even war.

Part 4: Eating and drinking

The hotel restaurants and bars worth hunkering down in.

Foreword

Tyler Brûlé: *thoughts on what makes a good hotel great*

"When is MONOCLE opening its first hotel?" is a question that frequently crops up when we're out and about meeting our readers. It's also a line of enquiry that ends up tugging at our imagination as we stroll through the streets of a favourite city or drift high above the clouds. Would it be a city-centre bolthole or a handsome retreat on a remote coast? How many rooms and how would they be decorated? Would it be a renovation of a faded classic or a new build designed by a respected firm of young architects? What would the staff wear and would the service be familiar or formal? Would the branding be discreet or punchy? Yes, dear reader, we think about hotels all the time and we'd venture that you do the same.

It's for this reason that we decided to pour our energy and experience into a book that chronicles our favourite properties around the world. It also serves as a textbook to help further the dreams of so many of us who one day would like to open a B&B on Waiheke Island, renovate a modernist hotel on the Oregon coast or buy a petite 60-key property in the heart of Marseille. Our starting point was to think of all the places we've visited over the past decade that succeed from a hospitality perspective and then analyse why they work, how they've sustained themselves and, most importantly, how they stand the test of time. In order to capture the entrepreneurial spirit that has seen some hoteliers transform entire neighbourhoods and whole cities, we've spoken to the GMs, chefs and property owners who've ventured out on their own and filled gaps in markets both crowded and fresh for the taking.

Our book isn't just a collection of five-star and designer properties. It's as much about the three-star hostel that gets everything just right as it is about grand hotels that keep us coming back because they don't fall victim to culinary or technology trends. From a MONOCLE perspective, a good hotel still has proper light switches, and a phone with real buttons and a receiver tethered to a cord. There should be low lighting, a good bar that stays open late and a hearty breakfast that veers to the Germanic end of the food spectrum: fresh bread, cheese, smoky ham, and eggs from the chickens that live out the back. Our top hotels are also owned and staffed by people who are proper hosts, passionate about service and proud of their communities. GMs are on hand to greet us and keep an eye on the details, the cabana boys remember us season after season and the woman running the kiosk in the lobby always saves us a copy of *Handelsblatt*, no matter how late we check in.

If you're looking to plot out a year of long weekends, short city hops and greater escapes then we're confident this book will deliver the goods. If you're hoping to dip into your savings or raise money to open a lodge of your own then there are plenty of interviews, design cues, anecdotes and lessons to inform your business plan and fill your rooms. As for that MONOCLE hotel, let's just say we've put most of our thoughts and fantasies into these pages to help the industry raise its game and inspire the next generation. — (M)

Introduction

Just as video didn't kill the radio star, apartment-sharing apps haven't scuppered our enduring need for hotels. Instead the increased competition that these companies have offered has done much to galvanise the good ones and clear out the clutter. In truth, sleek platforms and apps promise hospitality, humanity and convenience but often miss the smile on arrival, a humming bar and the help with bags that can gladden the weariest of wanderers.

Our favourite 100 hotels – old, new, itsy and ample – form the first part of our tale, which takes us from lofty pensions and seaside resorts to rural inns and revelrous city boltholes. And, of course, to those grander stays that will always mean business.

Over the past decade-plus of reporting we've heard our share of remarkable revival stories and seen new openings shape neighbourhoods. We've met entrepreneurs who have hung out their shingles – some building new, others augmenting existing places that were short on ideas, and a fair few rethinking what hotels should be altogether. In Part 2 we seek counsel from the success stories, enrol in the schemes and hospitality schools worth knowing and have a little fun with a few tips we've learned along the way.

The third and perhaps most politically pressing part of the book delves into the stories of hotels that have borne witness to history, change and coups, from Cairo and Cuba to the Côte d'Azur. Plus three survivors worth celebrating in Chile, Japan and Russia.

We also shake hands with the scions of hotel dynasties, meet the maids who make stays worth celebrating and recommend a few secluded spots for dinners and drinks along the way. We apologise for any omissions. (Though when was the last time you actually caught yourself feeling cosy in a glass tower on the Arabian Gulf?) Our collection can't ever be exhaustive but consider this book a modest manifesto and contemplation on the finer points of hospitality and where to enjoy it. It's also something of a manual: for the first-timer considering giving the hotel game a go or the group owner seeking a little inspiration. Additionally we tender a footnote on renovating too hastily: our hotels celebrate *where* and *what* they are admirably, and the majority found their own way rather than aping what they thought the laptop-toting next generation fancied that weekend (but might not want the next).

We're sure that hotels are here to stay and are keen to celebrate that fact – now it's just a case of furnishing you with the finest ones we've found. The hotel industry isn't giving up, it's turning a page. Speaking of which, isn't it time you did the same?

Can we take your bags? ———▶

How to use this guide

Monocle 100
For recommendations of our favourite hotels
From seaside to mountaintop and with plenty of fantastic city options to boot, we unveil our top 100 hotels around the world. They're not all new (though plenty are) and don't expect glitzy five-star affairs or big-box chains. We've plumped for the honest, charming and interesting hotels that have offered us a warm welcome, comfy bed and an elevated version of home away from home on our travels.

Trade secrets
For those starting a business or looking to refresh an existing one
We meet the owners behind the brands we like and the one-offs doing delightful work and breaking new ground. We also head to four hospitality schools and dream up an ideal hotel of our own. Consider this a call to arms for those mulling over a career in hospitality, or some inspiration for those looking to spruce up an old gem.

Here to stay
For lessons from the hotels that made it
Apartment-sharing apps may have seized some ground from hotels but it's far from the end for the good ones – and just the beginning for others. We show how life has unfolded (and demonstrate why it will continue) in both grandes dames and new arrivals. We talk to those whose lives have taken place in hotels, profile three timeless survivors and see how hotel architecture has mirrored the societies they've hosted. Plus a note on the danger of hasty renovation.

Eating and drinking
For a square meal and something to sip on
Our list of 25 hotel restaurants and 25 bars worth checking out wherever you are in the world. We meet the F&B folk drawing crowds that aren't even staying the night, creating spaces that are also destinations for locals.

Part 1:

Monocle 100

I.

Our favourite 100 hotels

For 10-plus years, MONOCLE's editors and correspondents have interviewed everyone from presidents and prime ministers to architects and entrepreneurs the world over. And, more often than not, hotels – big and small, stately and spare – have formed the backdrop. We've amassed a little black book of boltholes to which we'd be more than happy to return and in which we've often taken time to escape.

The first thing you'll notice is that our taste is usually for the independent, the unusual and the characterful – and not always for the new. From seaside stopovers and mountaintop retreats to business-minded behemoths and pensions with a handful of guest rooms, we have – at great length and not without a few editorial squabbles over what merited inclusion and what narrowly missed it – corralled a collection of our favourite hotels. May we offer you a tour?

1

Hotel Albergo
Beirut

Initially this Beirut stop-in may seem frenetic: its rooms, reception and restaurants are all decorated differently and crammed with oddities and objets d'art. But after a fortified pink lemonade it's hard not to appreciate the frantic genius of Lebanese-born, London-based designer Tarfa Salam.

"Lebanon was ruled by the Ottomans and the French but also had Italian influences; we've translated this in the decor," says general manager Jihane Khairallah. "We don't want to rival other hotels in town."

Besides the impressive collection, two of the main draws here are the outdoor Lebanese breakfasts on the roof terrace, affording views onto the sun-drenched capital below, and a bartender who won't retire for the night until you're ready to do the same. This commitment to hospitality makes the Albergo a spot frequented by ambassadors and locals alike.

The cosy Monot-based venture opens a twin building next door in 2019, increasing its rooms to more than 50. The hotel's updated offering includes two restaurants (including Beirut's first Italian), a gym, spa, hamam and rooftop pool.
37 Rue Abdel Wahab El Inglizi
+961 (0)1 339 797
albergobeirut.com

In numbers

1930s originally built

1998 opening of the city's first Italian restaurant, Al Dente

222 steps to the rooftop terrace

 2

The Drifter Hotel
New Orleans

The boom in refurbishing dilapidated hotels that has swept the US arrived in New Orleans with a bang in 2017 upon Jayson Seidman's (*see page 200*) opening of The Drifter. Located in the Mid-City neighbourhood, this mid-century beauty first built in 1956 was restored to its full glory by Nicole Cota Studio. It's a great place to stay for people who like a good yarn.

Set around an open-air swimming pool, the 20-room space was spruced up with the aim of staying true to the heritage while rehabilitating the relic. The building retains its basic form but there are added shocks of pink, murals and plenty of wood to give it a homely feel.

Key to the reboot is the tropical vegetation planted around the outdoor space, plus modern comforts such as La Colombe coffee in the café and Aesop products in the bathrooms. Bedrooms are simple but smart with custom wooden furniture, trowelled-concrete walls and a flourish by way of the Oaxacan floor tiles. Nola was crying out for a place like this.
3522 Tulane Avenue
+1 504 605 4644
thedrifterhotel.com

 ●

In numbers

1956	originally built
20	bedrooms
15	staff
20,000	guests a year

3
Trunk Hotel
Tokyo

Small independents have never made much of an impression in Tokyo but Trunk, which opened in 2017, has proved to be an imaginative addition to Shibuya. With 15 rooms, wooden decking and a 13-metre-tall zelkova tree, this four-storey building designed by Mount Fuji Architects Studio is a welcome departure from the city's many soulless business hotels.

The hotel shop – designed by Tokyo-based Torafu Architects – sells snacks from small businesses around Shibuya, while the Trunk-branded goods include mugs and towels that are made in Japan. The team was keen to use environmentally friendly products where possible: aprons are made from deadstock denim, T-shirts from recycled cotton and even the flip-flops in the room are fashioned from recycled rubber. Toiletries in the rooms come from Caring Japan and the bicycles for guests' use are built from others that have been found abandoned. The restaurant and bar are open to non-residents from dawn to dusk, with an outdoor terrace for sunny days.
5-31 Jingumae, Shibuya-ku
+81 (0)3 5766 3210
trunk-hotel.com

►
In numbers

2017 opened
15 bedrooms
4 floors
13-metre-tall zelkova tree

Casa Bonay
Barcelona

"This is a place for me to learn and collaborate," says Inés Miró-Sans (*see page 161*), the young entrepreneur who opened Casa Bonay in Barcelona's well-heeled Eixample. She gestures towards Satan's Coffee Corner, a timber-table-filled café that shares the ground floor with Southeast Asian restaurant Elephant, Crocodile, Monkey, a small bookshop and the lively Libertine bar; the basement hosts cultural and party space Salon Bonay. Miró-Sans prides herself on having charmed the locals while luring visitors: Libertine teems as much with young Barcelonans enjoying post-work drinks as hotel guests.

In the hotel part of the converted 1869 townhouse, original mosaic floors and terracotta tiles have been spruced up by Brooklyn-based interior-design firm Studio Tack (*see page 190*). The guest rooms are capacious, with spare but smart wooden decor from Barcelonan firm AOO, a well-stocked minibar and outdoor rain showers in the terrace rooms. Topping it all off is the rooftop Chiringuito bar and lounge, decked with flora by horticulturalist Alejandra Coll.
700 Gran Via de les Corts Catalanes
+34 93 545 8050
casabonay.com

▶

In numbers

2016 opened
67 bedrooms
250 wines in the cellar
18 plant species on the roof

5

Ett Hem
Stockholm

Keep a thesaurus of superlatives handy during your stay at Ett Hem (which literally means "at home"). Stockholm's best hotel was designed by Ilse Crawford and mingles modern fittings with antiques, tasteful furniture and tactile finishes. Its restaurant, meanwhile, is the best-conceived in the Swedish capital: wander into the kitchen and pop your head in the fridge before you strike up a conversation with the chef about what you're after.

Owner Jeanette Mix (*see page 164*) bought the brick-built corner plot in 2006 and opened Ett Hem in 2012. Today both she and her button-bright staff hold themselves to the highest standards. Each of the 12 rooms is unique and accented variously with Swedish oak, sheepskin throws, parquet floors and colourful rugs, plus planters, Scandinavian chairs and sink-in sofas that conspire to create superb stays.

Swedish landscape gardener Ulf Nordfjell's outdoor terrace is a lovely and leafy place in which to unwind. If you'd like to stretch your legs, however, the Lärkstaden area – where the hotel is located – is just a 20-minute amble from the city proper.
2 Sköldungagatan, 11427
+46 (0)8 200 590
etthem.se

◀

In numbers

2012	opened
12	bedrooms
2006	the former home was acquired

6

The Old Clare Hotel
Sydney

Since it opened in late 2015, The Old Clare Hotel has taken a lead in shaping up the once down-at-heel Chippendale neighbourhood. The lobby sits where a bank of "pokies" (slot machines) once entertained the punters of the rowdy pub that sat here from 1939. Throughout the space, weathered tiles, original poster-clad walls and exposed bricks allude to the building's old occupiers – a drinking den up front and the HQ of a brewery behind.

Sydney architects Tonkin Zulaikha Greer deftly converted the two buildings into a 62-room stopover with an attractive bar and two restaurants: Jason Atherton's Kensington Street Social and Asian-influenced Automata. The rooms are smart and include Triumph & Disaster amenities, prints from Sydney-based designer Eloise Rapp and industrial lamps by The Rag And Bone Man. The best suites are in the former boardrooms.

The Old Clare was Singapore-based Loh Lik Peng's sixth hotel under the Unlisted Collection, not to mention an impressive Australian debut.
1 Kensington Street
+61 2 8277 8277
theoldclarehotel.com.au

▶

In numbers

2015	opened
62	bedrooms
1939	pub built here
2	restaurants

 7

Pera Palace Hotel
Istanbul

From a lofty spot overlooking the Golden Horn, Pera Palace Hotel has witnessed a tumultuous century and weathered the overthrow of the Ottoman Empire. Today it may be a grand memento of former days but it shines as resplendently as ever.

Built by the French-Ottoman architect Alexander Vallaury in 1892, the hotel was one of the most advanced buildings of its day, boasting electricity and lifts – something found only in royal palaces. It has long been a beacon for writers and artists too: Agatha Christie was among the regulars.

Though it's owned by Turkey's Demsa Group, the Pera was refurbished by Dubai-based Jumeirah, which spruced up the historic building but left the character in place. The Orient Bar – perfect for a pre-lunch martini – and the domed Kubbeli Saloon have been artfully styled by designer Anouska Hempel with rich fabrics and antiques.

The rooms overlooking the Golden Horn are the best. Make sure you ride up in the cage lift – the oldest in Turkey.
52 Mesrutiyet Caddesi
+90 (0)212 377 4000
perapalace.com

In numbers

115 bedrooms	
2010 refurbished	
€23m spent on renovations	
411 is the room where Agatha Christie wrote 'Murder on the Orient Express'	

8

Marktgasse Hotel
Zürich

Nestled in the heart of Zürich's old town, the 39-room Marktgasse Hotel opened in 2015 after careful restoration that focused on simplicity and clean finishes. Forget floral wallpaper and needless knick-knacks: homegrown interior designer Karsten Schmidt balanced historical substance with mid-century furniture and a few contemporary flourishes. Hardwood floors hug the curves of the 15th-century building, which retains original architectural touches such as tiled stoves and wall panelling.

A spacious reception and lobby on the first floor provide space to work and wait, while the sedate library can be rented for events or meetings. The building dates back to 1291 and has been a guesthouse since 1425. In the 1900s the former stables played host to raucous *variété* nights. Today they house Baltho Küche & Bar, which serves hearty Swiss fare. The bar quickly made a name for itself with its dusky demeanour.
17 Marktgasse
+41 (0)44 266 1010
marktgassehotel.ch

In numbers

1291	originally built
1425	became a guesthouse
2015	opened
39	bedrooms
407	is our favourite room

 9

Nobis Hotel
Copenhagen
Copenhagen

Stockholm-based Nobis Hospitality Group settled on the former Royal Danish Academy of Music site for its fifth hotel and first (long-awaited) foray outside Sweden; it has 77 rooms and is but a few pedal pushes from Tivoli Gardens. The interiors are by Swedish firm Wingårdhs, with lighting by Wästberg and carpets from Kasthall; the Alexander Calder-inspired mobile lighting and inkblot rugs are high points of this otherwise ever-so-Scandinavian place.

Having begun in restaurants, Nobis CEO Alessandro Catenacci *(see page 172)* takes food seriously. Head chef Casper Sundin brings experience from Michelin-starred restaurants Søllerød Kro, Formel B and Kadeau.

"When we found this building it felt right," says Catenacci, the Italian behind Stockholm hotels such as Miss Clara and Hotel Skeppsholmen *(see page 279)*. "We may have nice designer chairs and my 1950s lamp collection but when we open the design ceases to be so important," he adds. "For us the major challenge is to deliver every day, 24 hours a day."
1 Niels Brocks Gade
+45 7874 1400
nobishotel.dk

In numbers

2017	opened
77	bedrooms
210	is our favourite room
€21.2m	renovation in 2017

A Day in Khaki
Kyoto

Situated close to Nijo Castle, A Day in Khaki is a rare 120-year-old *machiya* (traditional Japanese townhouse) that you can actually stay in. The two-storey former kimono-shop-cum-residence was given a refreshing renovation by a Kyoto designer-and-architect duo and opened its doors in 2017.

Available for one group of guests a night, the slender building features a mix of old and new features. The well-aged *tsuchikabe* (mud walls) and original double-height ceiling are still firmly in place, while the kitchen and bathroom have been modernised to fit the building's warm charm and irregular footprint.

The main building hosts two tatami rooms upstairs, where guests sleep on futon mattresses, and there is a western bedroom in the annex. The *tsuboniwa* (courtyard garden) and tranquil terrace, where you can kick back on the lounge chairs after pounding the pavement, are delightful additions to this characterful little guesthouse.
310 Yawata-cho, Nakagyo-ku
+81 (0)75 744 6326
adayinkhaki.com

In numbers

1898	originally built
2017	opened
3	bedrooms
4	metres wide
18.5	metres long

11

Hotel Locarno
Rome

Hotel Locarno, a belle époque-era gem, appeals to the romantic in most guests. It conjures up a bygone Rome and exudes that Italian charm many seek when visiting the Eternal City.

It was a guesthouse under the same name long before interior designer Maria Teresa Celli took ownership in 1969 and spruced up each room with Liberty prints, Tiffany lights and the best of the family's antiques. Ever since, it's been a hotspot for artists, painters, film directors and the city's intelligentsia. "Hotel Locarno has an unbreakable bond with the world of art and culture," says Celli's daughter Caterina Valente, who's given the hotel a welcome touch-up.

The renovation was as much to restore original features as to bring in modern amenities – the rooms still boast 19th-century wallpaper. Monk-sized quarters have gone in favour of 66 larger rooms and suites spread across two buildings. But one thing hasn't changed: the garden bar is as idyllic as it was a century ago. Reserve a bench under the trees for aperitivo hour and observe the local cognoscenti at leisure.
22 Via della Penna
+39 06 361 0841
hotellocarno.com

In numbers

2018 renovations completed

4 suites

605 is our favourite room

5 authors have written books about the hotel

The Warehouse Hotel
Singapore

This hotel on the banks of the Singapore River was a storied spot even before the developers broke ground. The area was first a furtive meeting place for bootleggers and later a *godown* (warehouse) for stockpiling spices shipped across the Strait of Malacca in the 19th century.

Inside, a custom-made pulley-and-wheel lighting system by Singapore firm Asylum – the group responsible for most of the venue's furnishings – spans the length of the lobby's vaulted ceiling. Its design is a nod to the machines that once lugged sacks of spices and grain through the former warehouse.

The sunken bar on the lobby's left lends proceedings a film-noir feel, while the bartenders' inventive cocktail list conjures flavours that guide guests through the building's history. Think peppery concoctions to evoke the tastes of its role in the spice trade, moonshine-based highballs to signify its darker days of unlawful distilling and a few fruitier numbers to celebrate its time as a disco in the early 1990s.
320 Havelock Road
+65 6828 0000
thewarehousehotel.com

In numbers

1898	originally built
2017	opened
37	bedrooms
2	floors

13

The Fleming
Hong Kong

Hotels in Hong Kong's Wan Chai district generally come in two shapes and sizes: big international chains take care of business travellers while local love hotels host other business – by the hour. In the middle, there's The Fleming.

Reopened in 2017, the hotel has moved its lobby upstairs to make room for a new centrepiece: Italian restaurant Osteria Marzia. Deep-blue tiles and fresh seafood displays offer a taste of the Amalfi Coast on Victoria Harbour and an introduction to the maritime theme that runs throughout the hotel. Further nautical nods come from the use of brass and the curved teak door frames that give the feeling of being below deck.

Tropical hardwoods and rattan furniture speak to the hotel's Asian location but it's the visual cues of Hong Kong that firmly place the hotel in this city. Among them is the ubiquitous bamboo scaffolding referenced in the exterior lighting and the narrow entrance that evokes the alleyways between Hong Kong's walk-up housing.
41 Fleming Road
+852 3607 2288
thefleming.com

In numbers

66 bedrooms
16-month refit
750 metres from Wan Chai pier

 14

1898 The Post
Ghent

"When you open a new hotel, you can't just do the same thing a bit better or a bit cheaper – you have to bring a different story." These may sound like the words of a man talking from experience but Arnaud Zannier, the founder of Zannier Hotels, only appeared on the hospitality scene in 2011. First came venues in the French Alps and Cambodia and then this, in the Belgian city of Ghent.

You'll find 1898 The Post on the upper floors of a former post office. The building had stood empty from 2001 to 2014, at which point developers bought it. After adding shops and restaurants on the ground floor, they then turned their attention to creating a hotel and called upon a French hotelier who, having married a Belgian, had lived in the country for more than a decade.

"I like to create products or places that will last, not ones that are trendy," says Zannier, who also owns a shoe brand. The result is a moody venue with characterful duplex rooms, interiors decorated with antique furniture picked out at flea markets, a cocktail bar called The Cobbler (try the Silky Smooth) and a kitchen serving breakfast and afternoon tea.
16 Graslei
+32 9 391 5379
1898thepost.com

In numbers

2017	opened
38	bedrooms
1	beehive

15

Hotel Sanders
Copenhagen

Alexander Kølpin, a one-time dancer in the Royal Ballet, saw something special in his former stomping ground around the Danish capital's heart, next to the Royal Danish Theatre. Sashaying from his dancing career into hospitality, Kølpin opened Hotel Sanders – his third but most personal project. "When I was a kid and performing we would come here after shows," he says.

The 19th-century spot (formerly the 92-room Hotel Opera) was acquired in 2015 by Kølpin, who set about transforming it from a fusty pension into a leading light of the booming city's hotel scene. Interiors come courtesy of London-based studio Lind + Almond, which kitted out every cranny with specially made fittings, from rattan panelling and textured linen cupboards to marble flooring and laser-cut grills. There's even a covered courtyard and a log fire by the rooftop terrace.

"It's like a theatre production: you have a stage, you have a space and someone is buying a ticket," says Kølpin. For our part, we think that the price of admission is well worth the show.
15 Tordenskjoldsgade
+45 4640 0040
hotelsanders.com

In numbers

54 bedrooms
404 is our favourite room
6 fireplaces
200 spirits behind the bar

 16

Maison Borella
Milan

Unassuming and discreet, this hotel overlooking the Naviglio Grande is an intimate affair and the only hotel on this 12th-century canal. Given its location – the neighbourhood of Navigli exists in a perpetual cocktail hour – Maison Borella is space of welcome calm. Four years of sensitive restoration under the eye of the Ministry of Cultural Heritage were needed to turn the 18th-century *casa di ringhiera* – a typical Milanese apartment block with a shared balcony – into the noble quarters that stand today.

The main part of the hotel wraps around an internal courtyard, with each floor's railings covered in sweetly scented jasmine. Those seeking a little more privacy, however, can opt for the Maison Privée: a nearby outbuilding that houses just seven rooms. The hotel is tasteful and quietly eclectic throughout thanks to the vintage furnishings chosen by Milanese furniture collector Raimondo Garau.

If you can wrest yourself from the comfort of the rooms head to the ground-floor restaurant Bugandè, where chef Davide Brovelli serves a delicious take on Lombard classics, such as *cotoletta* (veal cutlet) and creamy risotto.
8 Alzaia Naviglio Grande
+39 02 5810 9114
hotelmaisonborella.com

In numbers

2011	opened
30	bedrooms
12th-century	canal outside

17

Hotel V Fizeaustraat
Amsterdam

Run by 12th-generation Amsterdammers (*see page 170*), the Hotel V group now offers three design-minded places to stay across the Dutch capital. It may be a little further afield, in the southeast's developing district of Watergraafsmeer, but the boxy Fizeaustraat branch is only a 10-minute taxi ride from the canal ring and in our opinion the best of the bunch.

The modernist pile by Dutch architect Piet Zanstra was abandoned for 12 years before being transformed into a hotel. In-house designer Mirjam Espinosa and her husband Tom blended 1970s furniture with modern pieces and chose furnishings that echo the area's surrounding greenery. All 91 rooms are finished with hexagonal-tiled solid-oak floors, pebble-grey linens and woollen tapestries.

The ever-friendly staff are on hand to assist with requests, including bike rental, international newspapers, laundry and in-room massages. Then there's chef Jeroen van Spall's always-humming restaurant, The Lobby Fizeaustraat, which also features a casual café, well-stocked bar and sunny terrace.
2 Fizeaustraat, 1097 SC
+31 (0)20 662 3233
hotelvfizeaustraat.nl

●
In numbers
10-minute taxi ride to the canal ring
40 plants in the lobby and restaurant
1,308 lengths of bike chain in
the chandelier

 18

Michelberger Hotel
Berlin

When Tom and Nadine Michelberger (*both pictured*) opened their hotel in Berlin's late-night neighbourhood in 2009, a steady stream of music-industry heavyweights and high rollers rolled in. Nights were debauched and guests rarely roused before noon.

"The band thing was a pleasant accident," says creative director Azar Kazimir. "We've grown up a little now and so has the hotel." You'll still spot bleary-eyed musicians who have been holed up in the band rooms (yes, there are purpose-built ones) but today families and business travellers also populate the homely hotel.

Its best attribute, however, is an absence of stuffiness. Staff are friendly and accommodating; the café, courtyard and restaurant are relaxed; and rooms, although petite, are playful and cleverly configured, with a few vast suites bucking the trend. Leave space in your luggage for a bottle of Michelberger schnapps or the brand's coconut water, adorned with its playful monkey mascot.
*39-40 Warschauer Strasse
+49 (0)30 2977 8590
michelbergerhotel.com*

In numbers

2009 opened

119 bedrooms

Rooms 204 and 304 designed by Sigurd Larsen

19

Petit Ermitage
Los Angeles

The Petit Ermitage seems to have one foot in Europe and the other in the US, with a refined old-world charm and the glamour that comes with the territory in West Hollywood. Brought to life by hotelier Stefan Ashkenazy, the hotel is clad in ivy. Its rooftop – which opened as a private members' club in 2009 – is where a large chunk of the action happens. There's a saltwater pool, a dining area and, adding to the surreal quality of the hotel, a hummingbird and butterfly sanctuary. The sunken "Firedeck" also hosts classes and outdoor film screenings.

The rooms – all suites – are brimming with colour, fun and all the amenities you might expect (and a few you might not: kitchenettes, anyone?). If art is your thing then this place is also a winning bet because Ashkenazy has sprinkled his collection around the hotel. Check out the annual April Bombay Beach Biennale that he helps to organise too.
8822 Cynthia Street
+1 310 854 1114
petitermitage.com

In numbers

80 bedrooms
100 staff
25,000 guests a year
Dozens of hummingbirds and butterflies call the sanctuary home
2009 rooftop opens as private members' club

 20

The Upper House
Hong Kong

The Upper House was not the first of the House Collective to open its doors but the Hong Kong flagship certainly sets the standard for this expanding group of distinctive hotels. Contemporary Asian design comes courtesy of British-educated, Hong Kong interior designer André Fu; impeccable service continues to win international plaudits and each of the 117 rooms – palatial by local standards – has a bird's eye view over the city's harbour.

From its hillside perch, the Upper House is both apart from hectic Hong Kong and very much a part of the bustle below. You'll find Admiralty MTR station nearby, which takes travellers to all four compass points: beach, mountains, skyscrapers and sundowners.

Nearly 50 floors above, Café Gray Deluxe commands the top floor of the hotel. This modern European restaurant and bar is an important meeting place for hotel guests and well-heeled Hong Kongers. Meanwhile, the adjacent sky lounge and, downstairs, The Lawn play host to salon-style talks and canapés served among the city's awe-inspiring skyline.
88 Queensway
+852 2918 1838
upperhouse.com

In numbers

2009 opened
117 bedrooms
10-floor atrium
2nd property in the House Collective

21

Ham Yard Hotel
London

The Ham Yard Hotel is a village-like oasis in the heart of London's Soho, wrapped around a courtyard and lined with a cluster of handpicked independent shops. It's one of 10 Firmdale Hotels across New York and London, run by the group's ambitious founders Tim and Kit Kemp.

Just like New York's Crosby Street Hotel and London's Charlotte Street premises, no bedroom or suite in the 91-room hotel feels the same. From the bespoke patterned wallpaper to the colourful textiles of the curtains and upholstered furniture, Kit has lovingly designed every last detail of this townhouse-style abode.

With no shortage of entertainment, the busy establishment also includes a gym, a 190-seat cinema, a bar and a restaurant showcasing the best of British produce. There's also a fully functioning maple bowling alley, as well as a rooftop terrace – a rare amenity in often-rainy London – with views of the city. The hotel also features an event space that's bookable seven days a week and has a dance floor, lounge and bar.
1 Ham Yard
+44 (0)20 3642 2000
firmdalehotels.com

●

In numbers

2014	opened
24	apartments
13	boutiques
2	beehives
1	bowling alley

22

Micasaenlisboa
Lisbon

A prime position at the top of a steep hill grants this nine-room guesthouse unbeatable views across a rambling park to the crenellations of the Castelo de São Jorge. The work of Spaniard María Ulecia (*pictured; see page 204*), Micasaenlisboa's name reflects the owner's philosophy towards hospitality: a view that prides character and individuality over and above prescriptive decor or matching rooms. "There are books and interesting objects in every room," says Ulecia. "It's as if you are at a friend's house surrounded by things that have their own lives and stories."

Pared-back interiors come courtesy of Madrid firm Ábaton Architects and are pepped up by Ulecia's flea market finds (expect mid-century furniture and quirky one-off pieces, such as the sculptural submarine lightbulbs), as well as her own ceramic tiles in the bathrooms and fresh flowers from the nearby market. The experience is compounded by Ulecia's personal touches: homemade breakfast and leisurely chats over aperitifs in the small sun-trapping courtyard below.
48 Calçada do Monte
+351 919 090 595
micasaenlisboa.com

In numbers

2006	opened
9	bedrooms
2018	year renovated

㉓

The Miami Beach Edition
Miami

There are few better places to see the success of hotelier Ian Schrager's (*see page 174*) collaboration with Marriott than the Miami Beach Edition. The Florida city represents the mixture of opulence and sophistication that Schrager seems so good at tapping (he started in New York after all).

Located in the middle of the beach strip, the Edition is on the spot of the former Seville Hotel and cast in white and gold. Dominated by a forest of greenery, its lobby boasts a heady atmosphere and is where you'll also find the lively Market restaurant.

The 294 bedrooms are pristine, elegant and warm and there are two swimming pools to choose from if it's too much effort to make it to the ocean. But this is a place that really comes into its own at night when you head down to the basement. Even if you're not in town during the high jinks of Art Basel Miami Beach, there's still plenty of entertainment: from a funky bowling alley with multicoloured lights to an ice rink and a club with a couple of different music rooms.
2901 Collins Avenue
+1 786 257 4500
editionhotels.com

In numbers

2014	opened
294	bedrooms
175,000	guests a year
525	staff
5	restaurants/bars

Handpicked Hotel & Collections
Seoul

This 10-storey stopover in Seoul's southern neighbourhood of Sangdo-dong rises above the site of owner and general manager Sean Kim's former family home. He had lofty dreams for the property, which included revitalising the area in which he grew up. That's why the casual basement restaurant, Ballroom, welcomes walk-ins, blurring the line between guests and local residents.

Kim's brief for South Korean architecture firm L'eau Design was inspired by the Wythe Hotel in Brooklyn – hence the red-brick façade, which blends with the neighbourhood's 1970s low-lying architecture – and the Claska Hotel in Tokyo. Handpicked's version of Claska's design shop stocks "Made in Korea" products by homegrown brands such as Firemarkers, Cosmic Mansion and Green Bliss.

"I hope people take away the experience of everyday Korean life," says Kim of the space, which has a small library of design and travel books and magazines. He also keeps bees on the roof, which produce small batches of honey. He tends to give it to (ahem) honeymooners.
120 Sang-doro, Sango-dong
+82 (0)2 2229 5499
handpicked.kr

In numbers

2016	opened
43	bedrooms
3	business rooms
1	flower shop

㉕

Orania
Berlin

"I like to leave things as they are, with rough surfaces," says hotelier Dietmar Müller-Elmau (*pictured*) as his hand glides over the faint grooves of a tabletop. "If you leave people and things as they are, they work together very well. It's only when you try to make them the same that they don't fit anymore."

Müller-Elmau is a master of making spaces in which people love to linger – see his fêted property Schloss Elmau in the Bavarian Alps (*see page 100*). The hotelier's 2017 project Orania Berlin, however, in rough-around-the-edges Kreuzberg, is another beast entirely – and not one that our host plans on taming.

Opening a high-profile hotel in such a spit-and-sawdust neighbourhood didn't go unnoticed by the locals. "We were threatened by some radical leftists who said that we don't fit here," he says, pointing to a few paint splats on the wall outside. "Our managing director and chef are from here. We provide jobs and pay taxes but we are non-conformists too. It's very Kreuzberg that we don't fit. We don't want to fit."
40 Oranienstrasse
+49 (0)30 695 39680
orania.berlin

In numbers

1913 originally built
41 bedrooms
5 floors

 26

The Pilgrm
London

We've consciously skipped some of London's grander hotels in favour of small, honest and interesting options. This recent addition to Paddington, just a 15-minute train link to London Heathrow, is a case in point. With the Regent's Canal and Notting Hill's shops within easy reach (not to mention our own Kioskafé concession close by), it's surprising that Paddington's hotels have been found wanting for so long.

The man behind this welcome new spot facing Norfolk Square is Jason Catifeoglou (*pictured*), formerly of the Zetter Group. The finishes by Sheffield design agency 93ft reveal the care that's gone into The Pilgrm's refit. The rooms feature custom steel-worked fittings, lamps salvaged from former hospitals, schools and military facilities, and some extraordinarily comfy beds. The bar is lively without being brash and the café is an appealing nook in which to enjoy breakfast with the papers before hopping on the express train to the airport.

25 London Street
+44 (0)20 7354 0100
thepilgrm.com

In numbers

4 Victorian townhouses united to form a hotel

200-year-old parquet flooring

100 metres from Paddington Station

93ft the Sheffield-based agency behind the refit

27

Mama Ruisa
Rio de Janeiro

In 2004, when Frenchman
Jean Michel Ruis bought a
19th-century colonial mansion
that once belonged to the
Bulhões de Carvalho family, the
Santa Teresa neighbourhood
was just turning around. This
elevated part of town had been
overlooked for more than half
a century as the beachfront
districts of Copacabana and
Ipanema enjoyed their time
in the sun.

Ruis was part of a wave
of people bringing new
life and investment to the
neighbourhood. His is easily
the nicest small hotel in the
city and one of our favourites
for its capacity to make you
feel far from the crush and
chaos despite being resolutely
within it.

There are just seven airy
rooms, each themed around a
famous historical personality
(Carmen Miranda, for instance),
with floor-to-ceiling windows to
capitalise on those rolling views.
Ruis prides himself on giving
each guest a unique experience
and regularly recommends
personalised itineraries to visitors.
132 Rua Santa Cristina
+55 21 2508 8142
mamaruisa.com

In numbers

1800s originally built
2005 opened
7 bedrooms

㉘
Villa Terminus
Bergen

This heritage-listed former rest-home in Bergen, Norway, is today a spritely city centre hotel with something of the charming rural cottage about it. It's designed to feel distinctly domestic, with bookshelves that aren't just for looks, unfussy furniture and lighting, plus spaces created to prompt conversations and encourage interaction among the guests.

Danish painter Vilhelm Hammershøi's neutral colour palette, meanwhile, inspired Swedish trio Claesson Koivisto Rune's interior designs. The halls, kitchen, bar area and anterooms to the small library are all dark grey. To complement it, the guest rooms, dining room, lounge and library feature lighter shades of grey and tan, making all the rooms feel airy despite the typically overcast Bergen weather.

Each room boasts literature by a different Norwegian author. The social feel at the heart of this joint is also aided by the coffee and pastries served in communal areas that are flanked with furniture from the likes of David Chipperfield, Ilse Crawford and Josef Frank.
Gate 6, Zander Kaaes
+47 5521 2500
villaterminus.no

In numbers
1770	originally built
2017	opened
18	bedrooms

29

The Tilden
San Francisco

The Tilden took a punt when it came to location: eschewing San Francisco's easier neighbourhoods in favour of the gritty Tenderloin area. That shouldn't scare off prospective guests, however; this is one of the most tasteful places you could choose to stay in the City by the Bay. Plus, it's right in the thick of it, just a few blocks from Union Square.

Open since the start of 2017 and designed by Brooklyn's Studio Tack (*see page 190*), the hotel has a mid-century feel, with plenty of wood in the lobby and a skylight (long covered during the building's previous incarnation as the Hotel Mark Twain). The team behind The Tilden also strive to engage the community, supporting nearby organisations and inviting artists to give talks.

The in-house café serves brews from San Rafael native Equator Coffee and pastries from nearby bakery Jane. There's also art by San Francisco painter Daniel Phill. As for the rooms, they're smartly decked out in black, white and grey with plenty of storage space, faucets by Waterworks and toiletries from Malin + Goetz.

345 Taylor Street
+1 415 673 2332
tildenhotel.com

► **In numbers**

118 bedrooms	
1 shop	
122 Jenny Kiker watercolours	
15-minute walk from SFMOMA	

 30

The Greenwich Hotel
New York

Located in a seven-storey curved corner building in Tribeca, The Greenwich Hotel (owned by Robert De Niro) is designed to offer guests every comfort expected from a decent hotel without the stultifying trappings that many hotels fall into. You still get the impression that you're staying in someone's guest room thanks to unique spaces, with changing textiles from hand-loomed silk to English leather, and marble finishes in the roomy bathrooms.

From the Japanese-inspired Shibui spa to the guest-only drawing room, staying at the rustic-style hotel will make you forget that you're on the bustling island of Manhattan – the lusciously green internal courtyard helps as well.

If searching for a premium stay, opt for the Tribeca Penthouse. The rooftop sanctuary, designed in the Japanese spirit of wabi-sabi, has three bedrooms as well as a huge expanse of outdoor space. Hungry for more? There's an excellent Italian restaurant from noted chef An Carmellini.
377 Greenwich Street
+1 212 941 8900
thegreenwichhotel.com

In numbers

2008 opened

88 bedrooms

12 fireplaces

(31)

Baur au Lac
Zürich

When Austrian Johannes Baur opened his second hotel in 1844, it was to provide a more intimate alternative to his first establishment Baur en Ville in Zürich's city centre. The Baur au Lac has been the address of choice for decades for those enjoying the benefits of a discreet, personal refuge with lovely views of the lake. The ample park is a backdrop for balmy summer drinks and the restaurant in the pavilion is the place to continue a decadent evening.

However, it's not the grandeur or old-world decor that have kept this hotel a standout; instead, it's the mastery of detail. The well-looked-after kiosk with a wide selection of international newspapers and treats for spontaneous gifts makes its mark as soon as guests arrive. An in-house laundry and wine shop cover a few essential services. And family ownership has resulted in judicious development and a few clever refreshes, while the staff (often a stumbling block that lets down great hotels) are eagle-eyed and solicitous.

1 Talstrasse
+41 (0)44 220 5020
bauraulac.ch

►

In numbers

1844 opened

119 bedrooms

CHF160m (€133.5m) spent on renovations in recent decades

32

Muji Hotel
Shenzhen, China

Some people were stumped when Muji – the Japanese retailer known for its simplicity and lightness of touch – opened its first hotel in Shenzhen, a city full of loud-looking skyscrapers, in early 2018. Located next to leafy Lianhuashan Park, the 79-room stop-in sits atop a two-storey Muji shop and restaurant within a mixed-use complex called UpperHills.

With rooms starting at €120 a night, the hotel is made for business travellers who are looking for a comfy bed that doesn't break the bank. Muji had an all-star team at its disposal, including Tokyo-based Super Potato for the interior and Kenya Hara for the graphics. Hunks of hinoki and walnut-wood blocks in the lobby were recycled from lodgings in the Henan and Zhejiang regions, while pale wood and low lighting set a calm tone throughout.

The outpost in Mainland China's southern tech hub is a pilot programme for subsequent openings – and one we think future hoteliers aiming at the middle of the market can learn plenty from.
5001 Huanggang Road
+86 755 2337 0000
hotel.muji.com

In numbers

79 bedrooms
650 books in the library
50 per cent of wood used is recycled
15-minute walk to Lianhuashan Park
418 is our favourite room

 33

Rosewood London
London

The Edwardian courtyard of the Rosewood London, which once accommodated horse-drawn carriages, is a fittingly grand introduction to this High Holborn hotel that opened in 2013 as the first European outpost of the Rosewood Hotels and Resorts group (*see page 209*).

Inside, porters dressed in tweed uniforms from British fashion designer Nicholas Oakwell clip across the marble-floored foyer and gilded cages house budgies and lovebirds at the hotel's reception. A seven-storey marble staircase leads up to 44 suites and 262 rooms, each individually furnished and sealed behind hefty Cuban-mahogany doors.

Next to a spa area are three bar-cum-restaurants to suit any occasion. A traditional afternoon tea can be had at the Mirror Room, while the Scarfes Bar not only serves cocktails inspired by the caricaturist after which it's named (we recommend the Bubble & Shrubs with notes of elderflower) but also hosts great jazz, soul and blues musicians seven days a week. For a private getaway there's the Manor House Suite and Wing, which has its own entrance, lift and, strangely, its own postcode too.
252 High Holborn
+44 (0)20 7781 8888
rosewoodhotels.com

In numbers

1914 originally built (Grade II-listed)

2013 opened

12 event spaces

34

Soho House Barcelona
Barcelona

Anyone whose eyes rolled when they heard that UK-based hospitality firm Soho House & Co had opened a members' club in Barcelona in 2016 probably did so because they thought they weren't eligible to visit – but luckily the hotel is open to everyone. The on-point conversion of this residential building is a high watermark of hospitality where original mosaic floors and parquet pathways give way to vaulted red-brick ceilings (common in Catalonia). The downstairs restaurant Cecconi's does a brisk trade in Venetian dishes while the rooftop offers an enviable view towards the Port Vell marina and the sea beyond.

Among the trappings that are available to guests are an old-school gym, a 36-seat cinema and a horseshoe-shaped terrazzo bar on the fifth floor. Plus, all eyes are on the mooted Soho House & Co beach club. The Plaça del Duc de Medinaceli (where the club and hotel's entrance lies) is also the setting for a scene in Pedro Almodóvar's 1999 film *Todo sobre mi madre*.
Plaça del Duc de Medinaceli
+34 93 220 4600
sohohouse.com

In numbers

2016 opened
36 seats in cinema
5 floors (plus a rooftop bar)

Grand Hyatt Erawan
Bangkok

Few hotels in Bangkok are better situated than the Grand Hyatt. BTS lines (the city's mass transit system, commonly known as the Skytrain) run alongside the hotel and some of Bangkok's best shopping can be found a short stroll away – from independent designers at Siam Center to big brands at Central Embassy.

The Grand Hyatt's attention to detail is what makes it Bangkok's best for those visiting on business. The smart staff remember guests' names, most rooms are equipped with large desks nestled into corner windows and the gym and spa provide travellers with a top-notch jet lag cure.

We would suggest a room in the Grand Club. Spread across eight floors, it has the feel of a separate, even more seemly hotel atop the main building. Alternatively, the six spa cottages on the fifth floor offer a resort-style experience in the heart of the capital. This oasis features private terraces with views of the tropical garden and the swimming pool, as well as a private spa treatment room.

Head chef Pholwut Phetnae's *khao phad kai dao* (fried chicken rice) in the ground-floor dining room is a must too *(see page 276)*.
494 Rajdamri Road
+66 (0)2 254 1234
bangkok.grand.hyatt.com

In numbers
380 bedrooms
503 is our favourite spa cottage
25-metre-long pool
9 restaurants

36

The Dewberry
Charleston

This intimate 155-room hotel was eight years in the making. It's the result of John Dewberry's vision of the American South reimagined – a selling point that's helped put Charleston, South Carolina, on the map as a gateway to Dixie.

The Dewberry is housed in the former L Mendel Rivers Federal Building, built in 1964 and commissioned by President John F Kennedy, and has been restored to its mid-century glory by Dewberry's in-house design team (with a little elbow grease and a few ideas from Brooklyn's Workstead studio too). While the façade has remained unchanged, the refurbished inside features period furniture and custom metalwork.

Besides its prime downtown location, the Dewberry is known for its spa – with rooms lined in cypress wood and hand-painted wallpaper. Its most recent restoration is the rooftop Citrus Club, which boasts commanding views of the oldest and largest city in South Carolina. But be sure to check out the lobby Living Room with its beautiful full brass bar too.

334 Meeting Street
+843 558 8000
thedewberrycharleston.com

In numbers

1964	originally built
2016	opened
155	bedrooms

 37

Paramount House Hotel
Sydney

Rising two storeys above the brick-built roofline of its neighbours in Surry Hills sits a surreal, copper crown-like extension. The contemporary façade was added to what was once the Sydney outpost of the Paramount Picture Studios.

For several years the site has been home to Paramount Coffee Project, a café and collaboration between Russell Beard, Mark Dundon (*both pictured, Beard on left*) and Ping Jin Ng. Together they run the coffee shop, as well as a string of café projects, and each spends a lot of time travelling when sourcing beans to roast.

"We wanted to build a place where you feel at home and looked after," says Beard. There are Australian-designed furnishings throughout – such as plump Jardan sofas, bold textured rugs and wall hangings – that soften the concrete walls and the recycled-timber floor. There's also art from the nearby China Heights Gallery. The bathrooms feature terrazzo walls and floors and in some suites local blackbutt timber (eucalyptus) has been fashioned into vast Japanese-style baths.
80 Commonwealth Street
+61 9211 1222
paramounthousehotel.com

In numbers

2018	opened
29	bedrooms
4	floors

38

Hotel Henriette
Paris

Former fashion stylist and
interior designer Vanessa
Scoffier is the creative spirit
behind the refurbishment
of this intimate hotel in
Paris's up-and-coming 13th
arrondissement. The bedrooms
and communal spaces are filled
with vintage furniture – much
of it Scandinavian – sourced
by Scoffier from flea markets
in Paris and abroad. Textured
natural materials such as vintage
pressed-tin panels and rope-light
fixtures are playfully combined
with patterned wallpapers and
bright paintwork.

"The overall idea was to
make it like a family home,"
says Scoffier. "I hadn't planned
anything. It was all about
feeling." The courtyard is a
lovely place to sit with a coffee
in the sun and breakfast is
served each morning in the
communal canteen. Expect a
warm welcome, fresh flowers
in your room and a croissant
on your plate in the morning.
Staff pride themselves on
enabling guests to experience
the city "like real Parisians" and
will help you build an itinerary
to get the most from your stay.
9 Rue des Gobelins
+33 (0)1 4707 2690
hotelhenriette.com

►

In numbers
32 bedrooms
07.00 to 23.00 room service available
13th arrondissement

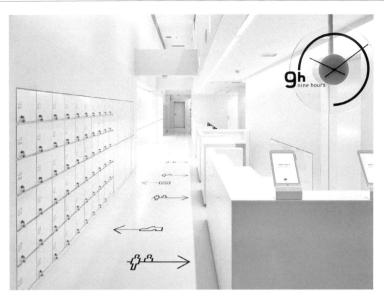

39
Nine Hours
Kyoto

Keisuke Yui (*see page 166*) reinvented the capsule hotel concept with Nine Hours. He now has seven in Japan but the nine-storey, 125-pod location in Kyoto is where it all began in 2009.

It gets its name from Yui's idea of the typical stay – seven hours sleeping, one hour showering and one hour relaxing – and is meant for travellers who prefer to do without the standard hotel extras. And yet everything at Nine Hours is carefully considered: graphic designer Masaaki Hiromura was behind the easy-to-follow icons on the walls and floors; Gunze supplied the pyjamas; and Design Studio S founder Fumie Shibata created the sleeping pods, which have Panasonic control panels, pillows by Kitamura and comfortable Nishikawa mattresses.

Sleeping quarters – separate for men and women (as are the lifts) – are upstairs and every guest is assigned a locker and given pyjamas, toothbrush, towel and shower amenities. Each room has 25 pods stacked in two rows and closed off with nylon shades. Many capsule hotels have TVs but not Nine Hours: pods are solely for sleeping.
588 Teianmaeno-cho, Shijo, Teramachi-dori, Shimogyo-ku
+81 (0)75 353 7337
ninehours.co.jp/kyoto

In numbers

2009 opened
125 pods
1-hour-minimum stay

40

Imperial Hotel, Tokyo
Tokyo

In Tokyo, a city that has been destroyed by earthquakes and bombs, history doesn't always come in the most obvious packaging. So it is with the Imperial Hotel, Tokyo, which has been in business since 1890 but today largely resides in a 1970s building. The pedigree of this Tokyo classic – which spent 45 years in a building designed by Frank Lloyd Wright – is all there in the detail though: the Viking buffet restaurant, the shopping arcade and the Old Imperial Bar (*see page 292*), which is overseen by top barmen.

It's in the service too: the staff, who bow to guests even after a door has been closed; the laundry, where the team transforms party-worn clothes; and long-serving members such as Setsuko Tanaka, who has been looking after the serene tea ceremony room for 47 years, and housekeeper Yukiko Koike (*see page 207*). It helps that the president, Hideya Sadayasu, spent more than 30 years in the hotel working his way up from bellboy.

As other hotels in the city are being demolished or remodelled, the Imperial rolls on, offering another perspective on 21st-century luxury entirely.
100-8558 Chiyoda
+81 (0)3 3504 1111
imperialhotel.co.jp

◗
In numbers

1890	opened
931	bedrooms
2,000	staff
26	wedding venues

41

Fasano
São Paulo

Opened in 2003, this was the first hotel venture from the Fasano family. Before, the tribe was better known in the city as restaurateurs – their first establishment opened in 1930.

Designed by fêted Brazilian architects Isay Weinfeld and Marcio Kogan, Rogério Fasano's (*see page 169*) first property (to which he's added considerably over the years) remains the most sophisticated stay in the city. The hotel is all about elegance, starting with the impressive lobby-bar. But the stand-out features are its two restaurants (Fasano and Nonno Ruggero).

As part of the hotel's 15-year anniversary celebrations, which kicked off in 2018, its Baretto bar created a whole new music programme (ranging from jazz to bossa nova) and launched a new cocktail menu. Luckily very little about what makes this hotel great has changed and we recommend the classic dry martini from the tried-and-tested side of the drinks list.
88 Rua Vittorio Fasano
+55 11 3896 4000
fasano.com.br

●

In numbers

2003	opened
60	bedrooms
160	staff

Two Bedroom Suite, with Persian rugs and Murano vases, is our favourite

 42

The Hoxton
Paris

It's a shame that not all of Paris's ramshackle architecture is as thoughtfully restored as the Hoxton in the fast-gentrifying 2nd. Opened in mid-2017, the four-storey space dates back to the 18th century, when it was built for an advisor to Louis VX, and features cobbled courtyards decked out with smart Roda chairs and Tuuci parasols.

The suave Rivié restaurant and Jacques Bar are fine places from which to watch cool customers convene while the airy lobby sees as many dapper walk-throughs as the average Parisian catwalk. There are 172 rooms – each at a fair price, in keeping with the brand's ethos – and there's been no skimping on the looks (think reclaimed herringbone parquet floors) thanks to Parisian firm Humbert & Poyet.

The UK-based Hoxton brand is owned by Sharan Pasricha (*see page 173*) and already has spots in London and Amsterdam, with more openings mooted for the US. Inside there are green walls that brim with pothos, tropical maranta plants and glossy split-leaf philodendrons.
30-32 Rue du Sentier
+33 (0)1 85 65 75 00
thehoxton.com

◣

In numbers

2017	opened
172	bedrooms
4	floors
190-seat	restaurant

43

The Ned
London

With nearly 40 restaurants, members' clubs, cinemas and spas across three continents, it's hard to imagine a hospitality hurdle Nick Jones of Soho House & Co couldn't clear. So imagine our glee when the invite arrived to the brand's first venture with Sydell Group: a grand and regally revived former Midland Bank building by Edwin ("Ned") Lutyens in the City of London. A penny's toss from the Bank of England and Royal Exchange, the imposing pile is fashioned out of the same white-grey Portland stone from which nearby St Paul's Cathedral was hewn.

Not short on ambition, this hotel has six restaurants, bars and endless plushly panelled rooms in which to retire. The pan-shaped atrium has entrances on both Poultry and Princes Street and is decked with 92 soaring verdite marble columns in parakeet green. Keep your eyes peeled for the listed oak and walnut former banking counters in some of the restaurants.

27 Poultry
+44 (0)20 3828 2000
thened.com

●

In numbers

€235m spent on renovations
1,200-plus covers in the restaurants
92 verdite marble pillars on the ground floor
2 pools

 44

The Principal
Madrid

Within a palatial 1917 Spanish renaissance-style building, The Principal spans seven floors that overlook the always-lively Gran Vía – studded with the city's best bars, shops and galleries – and a stone's throw from Buen Retiro park. Its rooms and suites exude old-world charisma appropriate to the architecture, topped with modern furnishings and fittings.

Designer Pilar García-Nieto and the team at Barcelona-based studio Luzio put together the smart interiors, preserving the building's original high ceilings, large windows and impressive ironwork. "We wanted to create a mix of styles," says García-Nieto. "A classic British club, the flamboyance of a French palace and the masculinity of a Manhattan loft." No shortage of ambition then.

Equal thought has gone into restaurant and bar Ático, where chef Ramón Freixa serves an elevated European menu. If the weather is blissful (it almost always is in Madrid) ask the maître d' for a spot on the balcony. Better yet, take dessert onto La Terraza for sweeping views of the capital: it's all about the rooftop terraces in Madrid and The Principal's is by far our favourite.

1 Calle Marqués de Valdeiglesias
+34 915 218 743
theprincipalmadridhotel.com

In numbers

1917 originally built
2015 opened
76 bedrooms
7 floors

45

Cortiina Hotel
Munich

One of Münchners' favoured maxims is dubbing the Bavarian capital "Italy's northernmost city" – this adage is said to have inspired Cortiina's name and ethos. "There are so many Italians moving to Munich, bringing their talent and influencing our culture," says co-founder Rudi Kull. "It's really part of our city's fabric."

The 75-room stop-in near Marienplatz was the original hotel in restaurateurs and hoteliers Kull and Albert Weinzierl's stable (Louis Hotel opened in 2009). The well-oiled service helps peg Cortiina as one of Munich's best business options. Its rooms span three buildings and include two two-bedroom apartments and a maisonette. The stone-tiled bathrooms and velour textiles are plush but understated and it will take some coaxing to drag guests out of bed in the morning, what with the spring-free mattresses and silky-soft bed linen.

Once they do emerge it's only a short hop across the lane to Weinzierl and Kull's coffee house Bar Centrale: an ideal place to drink an espresso while catching the morning sun.
8 Ledererstrasse
+49 (0)89 242 2490
cortiina.com

►

In numbers

2001 opened
70 sq m maisonette for two
35-minute drive from Munich International Airport

 46

Ghion Hotel
Addis Ababa

As the home of the African Union and dozens of non-governmental agencies, Addis Ababa has its share of swanky stays aimed at diplomats and dignitaries with expense accounts. But nothing beats the Ghion for pure character.

One of the last hotels still in government hands (a hangover from the communist regime that ruled Ethiopia for nearly 20 years from the 1980s), it has the elegant, tranquil atmosphere of a bygone era. This impression is accentuated by the fact that the property sits within 12 hectares of well-kept gardens, a rare treat in a city short on both greenery and serenity.

Yet what makes staying here such a joy is that, come the weekend, the grounds are taken over by the denizens of Addis itself. During the unofficial marriage season in January, barely a day goes by without a wedding party commandeering the lawns. On weekends, people come from across the city to enjoy the 50-metre-long swimming pool, outdoor café and red-clay tennis courts. In Africa, where hotels are so often compounds walled off from their cities, the Ghion is a welcoming oasis that's open to all.
Ras Desta Damtew Avenue
+251 11 551 3222
ghionhotel.com

In numbers

1951 opened
195 bedrooms
1 club, the African Jazz Village

47

The High Line Hotel
New York

The brick façade of The High Line Hotel might fool unsuspecting passers-by: a former seminary, it has a naturally modest appearance. The hotel itself is a slice of old-school New York in the Chelsea neighbourhood that has become increasingly peppered with samey-looking glass-and-steel towers. The front courtyard is dotted with bistro tables and planters and is a great spot to sit and have a cortado from the vintage Citroën truck turned Intelligentsia coffee bar.

In the summer the patio sheds its daytime caffeine crowd and becomes a restaurant with a seasonal menu – allowing a full display of the city's culinary talents. The seminary's former refectory has also been turned into a great hall, kitted out for an array of artsy events.

The property has become a de facto retreat from the glitzy establishments in the nearby Meatpacking District. The hotel's 60 rooms are understated yet well-kept and offer a smart mix of accents from classic to mid-century. This place reminds you that a stay in New York doesn't have to be all pomp; it can be about quirk and charm too.
180 10th Avenue
+1 212 929 3888
thehighlinehotel.com

▶

In numbers

1895 originally built

60 bedrooms

225 seats in the refectory

2013 The High Line opened

 48

Grand Ferdinand Hotel
Vienna

The stately Grand Ferdinand is a tasteful gear change from the team behind Hotel Daniel, who specialise in design-minded accommodation where the frills are optional. This hotel opened in 2015 after a careful year-and-a-half refit of the 1950s building.

As you enter, you're greeted by a Viennese 18-candle crystal chandelier from glass specialist J & L Lobmeyr. But this is where the stuffy ceremony ends. The reception and lobby are spare but homely – and patrolled by attentive staff. Hang a left for a 150-seat restaurant dotted with wooden Thonet chairs and ruby-red leather booths. Upstairs there are 188 well-appointed rooms and up top there's a bright eighth-floor terrace (guests only, mind).

It's perched on the Ringstrasse so expect views towards the city's twinkling Donaukanal (Danube Canal). An attractive cocktail crowd forms come nightfall. The Viennese tend not to frequent hotels as they do restaurants or bars but the tall windows that showcase the hotel's inviting restaurant to the street outside may yet change this.
10-12 Schubertring
+43 (0)1 91 880
grandferdinand.com

In numbers

2015	opened
188	bedrooms
8th-floor	rooftop
6-minute walk	to Vienna State Opera

49

Raffles
Singapore

Established in 1887 by two Armenian brothers, this is one of Singapore's oldest and rightly most recognisable hotels. Declared a national monument 100 years after it first opened its doors, the iconic mansion retains much of its original architecture and has hosted guests as different and disarming as Rudyard Kipling, the Duke and Duchess of Cambridge and Karl Lagerfeld.

The opulent, airy suites are replete with period furniture and whirling ceiling fans, giving guests a taste of colonial excess and splendour in the 21st century. In 1915 the hotel's Long Bar became the birthplace of the Singapore Sling – the pink (too-sweet for some) gin-based concoction is the unofficial national cocktail and is still best enjoyed while on the premises.

Even if you're not staying at the hotel, its breezy courtyard restaurants and shopping arcade are open to the public. Almost as recognisable as the building are the Sikh doormen decked out in smart turbans and military garb.
1 Beach Road
+65 6337 1886
raffles.com/singapore

►

In numbers
1887 opened
103 bedrooms
3 floors
1942 year of Japanese invasion, in which troops were said to have encountered guests dancing a final waltz when they arrived

Hotel Santa Clara
Cartagena

You can't miss this vast hotel in the Colombian city of Cartagena. Part of the complex dates back to 1621 and it boasts an impressive mixture of colonial architecture and modern fittings.

Each of the 123 rooms, including 20 suites, is unique but none are as special as the Botero suite. Named after Colombia's famous artist, this sprawling room is adorned with the master's works and equipped with mod cons such as the NightCove system, which tweaks the light according to the time of day. Speaking of arts and culture, there are plenty of other references: the hotel has a hall named after novelist Gabriel García Márquez, who died in 2014 and drew inspiration from the place back when it operated as a convent; elsewhere look out for sculptures by Hugo Zapata.

All this discovery warrants a drink and you should consider the stunning El Coro bar – also part of the old convent – for a cocktail. The grounds are also unbeatable for a wander: it happens to have the largest garden inside Cartagena's walls, brimming with lush flora.
39 Calle del Torno
+57 5 650 4700
sofitel.com

In numbers

1995	opened
60,000	guests a year
300	staff
240 sq m	pool

51

Chiltern Firehouse
London

Its bar may be a headline-grabbing watering hole and its restaurant beloved for business lunches but MONOCLE's near neighbour in Marylebone is also a hotel par excellence. The 26 rooms spread across four floors of this Victorian red-brick building guarantee a quiet spot for a kip – regardless of what riotous party may be brewing downstairs. Capacious closets can hold gifts from nearby menswear shop Trunk (part of the MONOCLE family) and the minibar comes stocked with ready-to-pour cocktails that have been whisked at the lower-ground-floor bar.

Room details that make the difference: the international plug sockets and tactile Bakelite switches. It's the work of hotelier extraordinaire André Balazs, who chose pretty Chiltern Street for his first hotel venture outside the US. Despite Balazs's reputation for place-making, few could have predicted the success that followed. The former ladder shed has been converted into a bar and in the restaurant chef Nuno Mendes (who has previously worked at El Bulli) has created a hearty, filling and reliable menu.

1 Chiltern Street
+44 (0)20 7073 7690
chilternfirehouse.com

In numbers

1889 originally built
2013 opened
26 bedrooms
115 covers in the restaurant

The Peninsula Hong Kong
Hong Kong

The Peninsula Hong Kong gets its name from the location of the group's first hotel on the southern tip of the Kowloon Peninsula. Its iconic white-stone façade is a little more hidden from view in today's crowded Tsim Sha Tsui district but a visit to the hotel continues to be the jewel in the crown of any trip across Victoria Harbour.

When it opened in 1928, the only way to get from Hong Kong Island to Kowloon was by taking the Star Ferry or paying a fisherman to cross the harbour. Fortunately for hoteliers Lawrence and Horace Kadoorie, the construction of a five-star hotel flanked by shopping arcades was a matter of right place, right time: the hotel prospered from the growth in international travel and continues to do so to this day.

Bridges and tunnels bring most hotel guests in by car and metro, while a well-heeled few arrive by air. The Peninsula's helipad – one of only two private ones in Hong Kong – sits on top of a 30-storey tower block that was added to the back of the original building in 1994.
Salisbury Road
+852 2920 2888
peninsula.com

In numbers

1986 opening of Spring Moon restaurant

1941 to 1945 occupation of the hotel by the Japanese army

14 Rolls-Royce Phantoms in the hotel's fleet

80-plus shops in Peninsula Arcade

53

Hôtel Les Roches Rouges
Côte d'Azur

Along the glittering shores that connect Cannes and St Tropez, the coastal terrain takes a dramatic turn where the reddish rocks of the Esterel mountain range meet the sea. It's here that Valéry Grégo, owner of several hotels in the Alps and Paris, has gambled on transforming a tumbledown motel into the sort of lively premises that this stretch of the Riviera lacked.

Paris-based practice Festen Architecture has returned the 50-room hotel to its Côte d'Azur glory, inspired by the straight lines and chalky hue of Eileen Gray's E-1027 villa in Roquebrune-Cap-Martin. The architects blended terracotta, oak and plastered walls and added vintage rattan furniture, brass lamps and farmhouse tables. Contemporary accents come in the form of Guy Bareff lights, cement garden armchairs by Willy Guhl and a De Sede leather sofa.

Activity-wise, there's a 30-metre-long seawater pool with a swimming lane carved into the cliffs. Christian Mentozzi also teaches pétanque (with a strong Provençal twang) once a week and fisherman Olivier Bardoux will happily entertain you on his boat too.
90 Boulevard de la 36e Division du Texas
+33 (0)4 8981 4060
hotellesrochesrouges.com

●

In numbers

50 bedrooms and suites
2 restaurants
3 bars

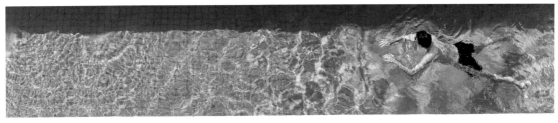

54
Belmond Copacabana Palace
Rio de Janeiro

Long considered the grandest of the hotels in Rio de Janeiro, the Belmond Copacabana Palace (simply "Copa" to Cariocas) remains one of the most sophisticated addresses in the city and an interesting counterpoint to the newer but less interesting hotel developments that have sprung up in its wake.

Since opening its doors in 1923, it has remained connected to Rio's party scene, hosting legendary pre and post-carnival revelry. The hotel was even the backdrop of a 1933 Hollywood musical featuring Ginger Rogers and Fred Astaire, and illustrious guests have ranged from Marilyn Monroe to Bill Clinton.

The art deco hotel has some 239 rooms, with furniture made from Brazilian teak and mahogany. It also boasts a lauded (and recently renovated) outdoor pool, with an army of assistants on hand to adjust loungers or proffer stacks of fresh towels. Sip a cocktail, or sneak a game of tennis, and take in this slice of Rio's still-raging golden age, overlooking the Avenida Atlântica and the sandy reaches of Copacabana beach beyond.

1702 Avenida Atlântica
+55 (21) 2548 7070
belmond.com/
copacabana-palace-rio-de-janeiro

In numbers

1923	opened
3	restaurants
590	staff
€2.5m	for the latest renovation

Hotel San Cristóbal
Todos Santos, Mexico

The southern part of Mexico's Baja California state has a sun-soaked, surfy feel and the Hotel San Cristóbal, with its easy-on-the-eye 1970s look, ticks these boxes nicely too.

The hotel, by Texas-based hospitality group Bunkhouse, sits on the edge of a beach in Todos Santos, 76km north of the over-boozed madness of Cabo San Lucas. The 32 guestrooms are kitted out with cotton bedspreads and Amethyst Artisan tiles, as well as modern Mexican furniture and light fixtures from Guadalajara. "One of the most important things to us for this project was to create opportunities in this community," says Bunkhouse founder Liz Lambert.

There's a 5km bicycle trail linking the hotel directly with the town so you can escape it all without cutting yourself off. After an excursion, enjoy a plate of Mexico-meets-Europe cuisine at the hotel's Benno restaurant – and maybe sip a cocktail by the pool while you're at it.

19 Carretera Federal
+52 612 175 1530
sancristobalbaja.com

In numbers

32 bedrooms	
14,200 guests a year	
71 employees	
11 dogs adopted	

56
Guntû
Seto Naikai, Japan

Guntû, if it's a hotel at all, is unique: a wooden boat built by the finest carpenters from Hiroshima and designed by one of Japan's top architects, Yasushi Horibe. It was conceived as a way to bring people into the Setouchi area and celebrate the heritage of the homegrown shipbuilding giant, Tsuneishi.

Guntû (pronounced "gantsu" and meaning "blue crab" in the local dialect) carries passengers through the Seto Naikai (also known as the Seto Inland Sea), a beautiful part of Japan with blue waters peppered with islands. Passengers enjoy spacious, wood-lined berths, cedar baths on outdoor terraces, a spa, and food overseen by chef Kenzo Sato from Tokyo restaurant Shigeyoshi. There's even a tea master, Akihiro Nakamura, who makes guests whisked matcha and traditional *rakugan* sweets.

There are six routes, stretching from Okayama to Yamaguchi. The boat leaves from a small dock next to the shipyard in Onomichi. It doesn't port anywhere but guests can go on fishing excursions, tour one of the islands on a smart motorboat (also designed by Horibe) or set forth on a *yakatabune* cruise boat.
Bella Vista Marina
+81 (0)3 6823 6055
guntu.jp

►
In numbers

38 passengers maximum
46 crew
81 metres long
90 sq m Guntû Suite

Oyster Inn
Waiheke Island,
New Zealand

When Jonathan Rutherford Best and Andrew Glenn (*pictured, Glenn on left*) looked through the windows of what was then an abandoned restaurant on the island of Waiheke, an idea fell into place. "We wanted an environment where you came up the stairs and left the world behind," says Glenn.

The result is part restaurant, part inn on the white shores of Oneroa village. Across a fern-filled atrium the Kiwi duo built a private dining room, three guestrooms and a small shop selling beachwear from the likes of The Waihetian and Saturdays Surf, as well as their own line of kaftans, beach bags and towels. From the shop you can catch a whiff of chef Christian Hossack's fresh seafood, served in an airy space by local designer Katie Lockhart.

In the rooms are 19th-century Turkish rugs and works by local artists such as Dan Arps and Shane Cotton. At the bar you'll be presented with a bottle of Oyster Inn's own riesling from the Two Paddocks vineyard.
124 Oceanview Road
+64 (0)9 372 2222
theoysterinn.co.nz

▶

In numbers

2011 opened

35 minutes by ferry from Auckland

90 seats at the restaurant

28 brands in the shop

58

Hotel Parco dei Principi
Sorrento, Italy

Entering Parco dei Principi feels like stepping back into the 1960s. This boxy white building perched on a cliff a few kilometres from Sorrento was designed by Italian modernist Gio Ponti and his original vision remains unchanged. Everything from the overall structure to the smallest detail (including bed frames, wardrobes and furniture) bears Ponti's signature touch – and strictly adheres to a palette of white and blue.

All 96 rooms feature tiled floors, each with a different geometric pattern. At the bottom of the cliff a sunbathing jetty and a restaurant on stilts are accessible via a tunnel excavated into the rock, while a free-form salt-water pool sits on the upper level.

"A hotel is not just a place where you sleep and eat – this place has great character," says manager Fiorella Vecchia. "Ponti imagined it as a diamond set in the cliff, as a point in between the park and sea. That's what I think our hospitality needs to represent too: a moment of pause, an experience that Gio Ponti tried to express through this space."
44 Via Bernardino Rota
+39 (0)81 878 4644
royalgroup.it/parcodeiprincipi

In numbers

1962	opened
96	bedrooms
3 hectares	of botanical gardens

 59

Casa Mãe
Lagos, Portugal

In the breezy coastal town of Lagos in southern Portugal lies Casa Mãe, a hotel built to celebrate some of the things the country does best. "It's about connecting every guest with the region and giving something back," says owner and founder Veronique Polaert (*pictured*), who traded France for the Algarve in 2016.

To achieve this community spirit, she tasked a team of Portuguese craft-and-design companies with kitting out the space. Everything is made especially for the hotel, from the notebooks in the bedrooms to the bathroom amenities.

Tucked away by the old city walls, the hotel spans three buildings and plenty of green space, which includes an organic garden that supplies the restaurant. Canny design informs every aspect of the property. The original 19th-century estate house even has a heritage classification due to its anti-seismic architecture. There are also three bungalows, each with a private courtyard surrounded by greenery, plus the more contemporary wing, complete with warm terracotta floors and white wooden screens enclosing balconies.

41 Rua do Jogo da Bola
+351 (0)282 7800 80
casa-mae.com

In numbers
33 bedrooms
24 Portuguese brands
22 co-working spaces available
1 national monument

60

Halekulani
Honolulu

Everyone in Honolulu seems to have a story about this historic beachfront hotel, which opened as Hau Tree in 1907. A decade later it was taken over and renamed Halekulani ("house befitting heaven") and gradually expanded to include more cottages and, in 1932, a larger main building designed by one of Hawaii's great architects, Charles William Dickey.

Japanese property developer Mitsui Fudosan bought the hotel in 1981 and remodelled it, replacing the old bungalows and restoring the Dickey building with its verandahs and eucalyptus floors. Today the property is probably the best in Hawaii and run with a thoughtful blend of Japanese service and Hawaiian aloha.

The sunset hula show in the House without a Key bar (immortalised in Earl Derr Biggers' 1925 Charlie Chan novel of the same name) has been a fixture for years, while L'Aperitif bar is the best in town. Try a smoke-infused Red Nichols Manhattan by veteran head barman, Henry Kawaiaea. Waikiki may have changed over the years but Halekulani remains a beacon of continuity.
2199 Kalia Road
+1 808 923 2311
halekulani.com

▶

In numbers

1907	opened
453	bedrooms
308 sq m	Royal Suite
3	bars

61

Habitas Tulum
Tulum, Mexico

During the past decade the electric-blue waters of Tulum in Mexico's Yucatán have seen some unsightly hotel openings. But Habitas Tulum is a handsome haunt that treads the right line between modern comfort and bohemian design, complements the natural beauty and respects the local flora.

Habitas' tent-style rooms with palapa roofs are either tucked away inside a jungle of palms and sea-grape trees or overlooking the Caribbean waters. Hardwood floors, furniture fashioned from local Tzalam wood, kilim rugs and natural cosmetics are just some of the thoughtful touches that elevate the hotel beyond a hippie-chic retreat.

There's also a roof terrace and chef Federico Cappi's restaurant Moro, where guests enjoy Spanish fare with Moorish flair at candlelit communal tables made from reclaimed indigenous wood. The glass-and-steel pavilion hosts a cabana-style bar, hammocks, film screenings by celebrated Mexican directors, yoga sessions and a DJ most nights, should you wish to shake a tail feather.
Carretera Tulum-Boscapaila
+52 (0)1 984 182 3124
habitastulum.com

In numbers

2017	opened
32	bedrooms
3,000	palm trees planted before opening
3	resident DJs

62
Katamama
Seminyak, Bali

"We spent two years working with artisans in the Balinese village of Penglipuran to hand-press these bricks," says Ronald Akili (*pictured; see page 162*), co-founder of the Potato Head Family, the firm behind the stunning Katamama hotel in Seminyak, Bali. The bricks in question are a clear example of the care and commitment that Akili and his team have put into the design of this postcard-pretty 58-room place, which opened in 2016.

The five-storey building has an Andra Matin-designed exterior that takes its cues from the Balinese building practice of *tri angga* (a system of keeping buildings in proportion with the humans that inhabit them), with flourishes informed by pioneering US architect Frank Lloyd Wright. The interiors are skirted with warm teak finishes.

"Building the Katamama felt more like we were building a house," says former product and interior executive Sashia Rosari. "Ronald's design is driven by his passion for the mid-century look. Sometimes the reference wasn't just furniture: it might have been a Bauhaus room. It's a particular vibe or particular feel."
51B Jalan Petitenget
+62 (0)361 302 9999
katamama.com

In numbers

58 bedrooms

5 floors

1.5 million handmade bricks used in construction

63

Sound View
Greenport
Long Island, USA

On the North Fork of Long Island, Erik Warner, the co-founder of hospitality firm Eagle Point, has refurbished the Sound View motel with breathtaking results. This isn't a first for the group, which has enlivened locations from Hawaii to Napa Valley. While not as famous as its South Fork cousin (home of the heady Hamptons), the northern reaches of Long Island makes up for a lack of prestige and celebrity endorsements with pretty wineries and organic farms.

To honour the former motel's 60-odd-year history, the team took inspiration from the ferries that chug past on Long Island Sound. Outside are wooden benches by Evan Z Crane, while inside restored lights by Early Electrics illuminate chamfered nooks in the lobby lounge, which serves breakfast and cocktails.

Each of the 55 rooms and suites features either a private balcony or shared patio. In the restaurant, The Halyard, award-winning chef Galen Zamarra of New York's Mas serves dishes such as lobster beignet. But the real stars of the show are the secluded private beach, sound views and fresh air.

58775 Route 48
+1 631 447 1910
soundviewgreenport.com

▶
In numbers

1953	opened
90	staff
19,000	guests a year

64

Il San Pietro di Positano
Positano, Italy

It's surprising that the Il San Pietro di Positano wasn't designed by a famous architect. Rather, the building owes its spectacular structure to founder Carlino Cinque, who opened the venture in 1970.

At the time, this was one of two five-star hotels along this ribbon of coast – and the only one to feature an elevator that would ferry guests down to a private beach. Many of the devoted clientele return every year (often booking their next stay at check-out) under the care of the Cinque clan.

Third-generation Vito Cinque now heads operations but his mother Virginia Attanasio remains an unflappable presence in the hotel lobby. "We've always seen this as a house, not a business," says Vito. "This hotel gives us emotions that we feel every day. It's a place that has defined and changed our existence. We have lived through its many transformations." Vito himself has spearheaded a series of timely evolutions, including the addition of a spa and the spectacular seafront restaurant, Il Carlino. "Everything needs to change for everything to stay the same," he says.

2 Via Laurito
+39 (0)89 812 080
ilsanpietro.it

In numbers

1970	opened
57	bedrooms
146	employees
48	fridges in Carlino's kitchen
23	is our favourite room

(65)

Villa Flor
S-chanf, Switzerland

Villa Flor is, just as the name suggests, very much owner Ladina Florineth's home. The model, photojournalist and gallerist is above all a splendid host, who knows all the best ski routes and even cooks for her guests every once in a while. She and her dog Kalua make visitors feel at home as soon as they arrive in the mosaic-tiled lobby.

Located in the village of S-chanf in Upper Engadine, Villa Flor is a 1904 art nouveau mansion converted in 2009 into a cosy Alpine inn. Florineth has accessorised the classic Swiss pine interiors with mid-20th-century furniture galore. Its seven guestrooms and public areas double as a gallery for Florineth's art collection and include pieces by Swiss photographer Albert Steiner and German artist Karin Sander. A large canvas by the US artist (and patron) Julian Schnabel can be found in the reception. The visual feast continues at breakfast, when colourful homemade mountain-berry preserves are served.
19 Somvih
+41 (0)81 851 2230
villaflor.ch

●

In numbers

2009	opened
7	bedrooms
1	is our favourite room
19km	from St Moritz

Gasthof Bad Dreikirchen
Barbiano, Italy

Perched on a hillside above Barbiano in South Tyrol, the Bad Dreikirchen hotel is in an isolated spot with stunning views across the Valle Isarco and some of the cleanest air you'll find in Europe – cars aren't allowed in this quaint village. "The inn has existed since 1315 and has been in the family since 1811, so it's a tradition to continue the family business," says Matthias Wodenegg, who runs the 26-room hotel together with his wife Annette.

The main building is 600 years old and takes its name from the three ancient churches clustered on the historic Roman site; it was renovated by Rome-based Lazzarini Pickering Architetti. "The hotel takes you on a journey into the past: the rooms have no TVs but there is a well-stocked library," says Wodenegg, noting that they couldn't get around installing wi-fi. "The panoramic view of the Dolomites soothes the spirit and the scent of the forests and fields helps our guests to get away from it all." The regional capital Bolzano is only a 45-minute drive away (and is easily accessed from Innsbruck in Austria and Verona).
12 Dreikirchen
+39 (0)471 65 0055
baddreikirchen.it

In numbers

1315	opened
19 and 26	are our favourite rooms
1	pool
1,120	metres altitude

⓪67

Nest Inn Hakone
Hakone, Japan

Although a mere 90-minute drive from Tokyo, Hakone could hardly feel further away from the busy city. With Mount Fuji as its backdrop, it's a town of 11,000, famous for its hot springs, ryokan and cool climate.

Nest Inn Hakone opened in 2016. A renovated 48-room hotel set in a generous swathe of unspoiled nature, it lures weary city dwellers who want to switch off and recharge. There are freshly revamped rooms in the main hotel, 11 newly built wooden villas, a large natural hot-spring spa and an outdoor hinoki-wood tub filled with water from the nearby volcanic valley of Owakudani. Villas come with a hot-spring bath (indoor or open-air) while rooms in the main hotel are refreshingly minimal (there are no TVs), with plenty of natural light and warm wooden furniture.

Sheltered from the road, the hotel is surrounded by mountain cherry trees, Japanese maple and hydrangeas. A natural spring gurgles in the background, rainbow trout swim and pheasants stroll past the villas. The lighting is kept low, inside and out, allowing for an unobstructed view of the moonlit sky.
1290 Sengokuhara
+81 (0)460 83 9090
nestinn-h.co.jp

●
In numbers

1914 original Japanese lounge built
60 staff
B23 is our favourite suite
55,000 sq m site

 68

Brücke 49
Vals, Switzerland

Swiss-born Ruth Kramer (*pictured*) and her Danish husband Thomas Schacht opened this idyllic bed and breakfast in the Vals Valley of the Swiss Alps in 2011. She was a fashion designer and he had been working in communications and business development before they upped sticks.

The duo sensitively restored the early 20th-century structure, retaining the granite slabs on the ground floor and the chunky wooden beams supporting the stone roof. Each of the four rooms (including a suite) has a Scandinavian sensibility, with a neutral palette and modern classics by designers such as Finn Juhl and manufacturers including Minotti.

Guests can look forward to home-cooked meals made from produce that's delivered to the doorstep. "We are butlers for our guests," says Schacht, who takes care of visitors' needs, from renting skis and bikes to making reservations for massages, thermal baths and restaurants. "We also make sure they have a hot tea, a bun or a piece of chocolate when they take off for a hike."
49 Poststrasse
+41 (0)81 420 4949
brucke49.ch

In numbers

1902	originally built
1,000	sheep graze in the valley
4,500	Danish bread rolls made each season
6	mountain peaks surround the hotel

(69)

Hotel Jungfrau Wengernalp
Wengernalp, Switzerland

It may be in the middle of nowhere but trains have trundled through the mountain village of Wengernalp since 1893 on their way from Lauterbrunnen to Grindelwald in the Bernese Alps. Illustrious visitors to this 19th-century guesthouse included Mark Twain, Lord Byron, Goethe and Karl Marx. Carefully renovated over the years, it now features 24 one-of-a-kind rooms that are both charmingly historic and contemporary in varying degrees.

The hotel is open to travellers for the winter season only, from mid-December to early spring. The ski slope in front of the hotel makes for a simple descent towards the region's 200km of pistes, while the sunny terrace is a great spot in which to unwind.

Another reason to visit this Alpine refuge is that it has one of the best-stocked wine cellars in the region and an ever-changing five-course menu. The Von Almen family, who have been looking after the hotel since 1865, know how to maintain a healthy balance.
Wengernalp, Berner Oberland
+41 (0)33 855 1622
wengernalp.ch

●

In numbers

1865 the Von Almen family started operating the hotel

24 bedrooms

50 covers in the restaurant

3 fireplaces

 70

Miramonti
Avelengo, Italy

Before buying their beloved Miramonti in 2012, owners Carmen and Klaus Alber managed this hotel for seven years. "We had a dream of creating our own business," says Klaus, "but we had left our heart here." They were very aware of its potential – mainly owing to its unparalleled, panoramic position on a hill overlooking the South Tyrol town of Merano.

Surrounded by a thick wood, the 1932-built structure featured spacious rooms that looked out over the valley. But the couple knew it could be improved. "We didn't want to build something beautiful but something unique," adds Klaus.

Having enlisted South Tyrolean architects Arch-Tara, the duo set out to expand the original structure by adding a larch-panelled house next door with an extra nine rooms, as well as transforming the original space with Scandi-inspired, minimalist-yet-warm interiors styled by local designers Harry Thaler and duo Daniel Debiasi and Federico Sandri. The most impressive addition, though, is the swimming pool: a narrow basin, flanked by a top-to-bottom window, that seemingly protrudes from the mountain.
14 Via Santa Caterina
+39 (0)473 27 93 35
hotel-miramonti.com

In numbers

43 bedrooms
€10m spent on renovations
16-metre-long pool
1,230 metres altitude

71

Foxfire Mountain House
Mount Tremper, USA

The 101-year-old Foxfire Mountain House, nestled into the Catskill Mountains in upstate New York, was bought in 2013 by husband-and-wife team Tim Trojian (*pictured*) and Eliza Clark. A TV producer and chef respectively, the couple combined their skills to bring the derelict hotel back to life – but the resuscitation wasn't a snappy process. They took four years to painstakingly renovate it, designing custom furniture and laying the tiles themselves.

"We wanted a project that we could do together since the hours are long in both our industries," says Clark of her and Trojian's previous jobs. Less than a three-hour drive from New York, the 11-room Foxfire is perfect for a weekend away from the big smoke. And once you're settled in, there's little need to leave. The Bar Room's brunch and dinner service feature farm-fresh produce and homemade preserves.

The hotel's verdant grounds are the perfect place to catch a mountain breeze – or engage in a friendly game of *bocce*. And if you really like the digs, Clark and Trojian have turned their DIY chops to taking on residential and commercial design commissions too.
72 Andrew Lane
+1 845 688 2500
foxfiremountainhouse.com

◣
In numbers
57 vintage sand-glass windows
5,000 handmade Moroccan tiles
6 species of frog in the pond

 72

Hotel Piz Linard
Lavin, Switzerland

The Wes Anderson-worthy Hotel Piz Linard rose from the ashes – literally. A fire in 1869 destroyed much of the village of Lavin and it was rebuilt in the following years by Italian architects who weren't afraid of injecting some colour into the traditional townscape.

The candyfloss-pink building served many purposes in the town before becoming a hotel but was in a shameful state of disrepair when entrepreneur Hans Schmid took over in 2007. He depleted his pension fund to do so but the gamble paid off. The former cultural director of the canton of Sankt Gallen invited artists to decorate the eclectic rooms. Photographer Cécile Wick's winter landscapes adorn Room One.

The downstairs restaurant, which serves hearty mountain staples such as pork sausages with polenta and fennel, was once a stable and maintains its original rustic architecture, as does most of the hotel. Some of the luckier locals even have keys to the restaurant when the hotel is closed off-season and are welcome to treat the pantry and cellar as an honesty bar.
2 Plazza Gronda
+41 (0)81 862 2626
pizlinard.ch

In numbers

1871 originally built	
23 bedrooms	
9 staff	
CHF5.4m (€4.6m) spent purchasing and renovating	

73

Schloss Elmau
Krün, Germany

There's a reason why Schloss Elmau was selected to host the 41st G7 summit of world leaders. Nestled in the forested valleys of the Bavarian Alps, the retreat offers an escape from the trappings of city life.

The spacious lobby welcomes guests with furniture designed by proprietor Dietmar Müller-Elmau, also of the Orania Berlin (*see page 48*). "The lobby is one enormous room that includes a bar, library, restaurant and lounge; it's intended to be like a large living room," says Müller-Elmau, who opened the retreat in 2015 in the 20th-century castle that has been in his family for generations. The halls are furnished with dark wood panelling from Brazil, Germany and the US, Chinese tapestries and lamps from Italy. "The whole concept is to celebrate the diversity of materials and of the world," says the hotelier.

Every year, the hotel hosts some 200 concerts headlined by the likes of Mercury Award-winner Gregory Porter or big names from the world of chamber music, as well as 40 literary events with international authors. All that, plus a chance to unwind in its enviable spa.
2 In Elmau
+49 (0) 882 3180
schloss-elmau.de

►
In numbers

1916	castle originally built
9	restaurants, including the Michelin-starred Luce d'Oro
6	pools
100km	from Munich

Miyamasou
Kyoto

In the days before cars, Miyamasou was where pilgrims stayed after the day-long walk from central Kyoto to Bujo-ji, a 12th-century wooden temple at the foot of Mount Daihi. Today it's run by fourth-generation owner Hisato Nakahigashi and his wife, Sachiko, as a ryokan and restaurant par excellence.

For many, Miyamasou is a chance to return to simplicity. Guests sleep on futons spread out on tatami mats in the six traditional quarters, much as weary travellers would have done in centuries past. For others it's an opportunity to sample the region's finest *tsumikusa ryori*, a type of haute cuisine that relies on fish from nearby streams and plants and fruits foraged from the surrounding forest.

The pampering is discreet, with staff preparing bedding while guests bathe and delivering the multi-course meals in perfectly timed batches with brief explanations of the ingredients. From April to November, Sachiko recommends you start the morning with a climb to the top of the temple Bujo-ji for the view from the wooden observation deck above the ancient forest.
375 Daihizan, Hanaseharachi, Sakyo-ku
+81 (0)75 746 0231
miyamasou.jp

▶

In numbers

Late 19th century opened

6 bedrooms

35km from Kyoto

75

Fasano Las Piedras
La Barra, Uruguay

Fasano Las Piedras is perched among 490 hectares of rolling hills in Uruguay. The hotel reopened in 2016 following a regal refit by Brazilian architect Carolina Proto, who added apartments to the 20 existing bungalows.

The addition is eye-catching in the extreme and comprises three overlapping Jenga block-shaped structures with 10 apartments that range from roomy to palatial. Run by hotelier Rogério Fasano (*see page 169*), the hotel is 20km from the seaside resort of Punta del Este, a favourite summer spot for South Americans of all stripes.

Both outside and in, warm materials and dark woods are coupled with modernist furniture hand-picked from antiques shops by Fasano and the architects. "We try to work with materials that speak to the surroundings," says Proto. Outside, a sundeck features eight loungers and seating looking out towards the horizon.

The hotel shares the space with the Fasano restaurant, formerly accessible only by a (charming yet dangerous) stairway built directly onto the jagged rocks.
Camino del Cerro Egusquiza and Paso del Barranco
+598 (0)4267 0000
fasano.com.br

In numbers

10 apartments and 20 bungalows
490-hectare estate
5,931 visitors a year
9 holes of golf

Scribner's Catskill Lodge
Hunter, USA

Perhaps it's Scribner's relative proximity to the Big Apple – the former is about two-and-a-half hours north by car – that makes it feel like such an escape from the city crush. But far from seeming remote, this smart 38-room lodge in the Catskill Mountains transplants something of New York's vitality to its alpine surrounds.

Found high in the mountains frequented by keen skiers and hikers, Scribner's originally opened its doors to adventurous holidaymakers in 1966. The latest incarnation by Marc Chodock and Glennon Travis was unveiled in 2016.

Some of the rooms are fitted with gas-burning fireplaces while modern touches from those talented souls at Brooklyn-based Studio Tack (*see page 190*), coupled with the staff's properly outdoorsy Fjällräven uniforms, are well-considered additions throughout. The lodge also has an in-house restaurant. All of which combines to make for a rustic but refined stay within striking distance of New York.
13 Scribner Hollow Road
+1 518 628 5130
scribnerslodge.com

In numbers
9-hectare property
53, the Scribner Suite, is our favourite room
580 metres altitude

77

Azerai
Can Tho, Vietnam

The scenery during the 10-minute boat ride from the Vietnamese city of Can Tho to Azerai's private island changes quickly. It flits from a busy strait crowded by traditional wooden *sampans* and *ghes* (small boats) to still mangroves and banyan forests. Located in a sheltered cove on a tributary of the Mekong River, the islet of Au was transformed by hotelier Adrian Zecha (*see page 208*).

The 30 villas (each contains two rooms) were designed by Thailand-based architect Pascal Trahan, who was inspired by the lively clusters of traditional boats at the floating markets in Cai Rang, a district in the Mekong Delta. Bamboo, rattan and timber feature, bringing earthy outdoor tones inside, and each villa has a wide terrace overlooking the lake, river and gardens beyond. There are also two breezy restaurants and a bar with an arresting view of the long infinity pool and lotus pond in the central courtyard.

Evenings are best spent winding down at one of the property's eight spa rooms, with massages and scrubs using Mekong rice and sweet almond oil.
Au Islet
+84 (0)292 362 7888
azerai.com/can-tho

In numbers

60 bedrooms
31-metre-long pool
3 dining pavilions
2 boats used to ferry guests

Jackalope
*Mornington Peninsula,
Australia*

A daring response to a broadly
boring hotel scene down
under, the Jackalope hotel is in
Mornington Peninsula, a top
wine region south of Melbourne.

"Not a lot of high-end hotels
have a strong narrative," says
owner Louis Li of his idea to
concoct a design-led story with
the 46-room hotel via sculptures
and dazzling light fixtures.
Opened in 2017 and forged by
a dream cast of Aussie artists
and creative talent, Li's brief
was, of all things, to pay
homage to the ancient practice
of alchemy. The response is
felt in the large, lab-like glass
vessels that line the bar and the
smattering of gold, silver and
bronze that dot the hotel.

Despite pouring on the
glamour inside, effort has
been made to ensure that the
exterior suits its surroundings.
The hotel's sloped roof takes
cues from an adjoining winery
and a low-profile construction
helps it harmonise with the
rolling sylvan hills that surround
this most seemly of sites.
*166 Balnarring Road
+61 (0)3 5931 2500
jackalopehotels.com*

In numbers

46 'terrace/vineyard' (bedrooms)
and 'lairs' (suites)

11-hectare vineyard

30-metre-long infinity pool

79

Sumahan on the Water
Istanbul

Perched on the Asian side of the Bosphorus just beyond the neighbourhood of Cengelkoy, the Sumahan is a family-owned hotel in a former distillery that once produced *suma* – a spirit made from figs that's then used to produce raki. The mid-19th-century building was inherited by Turkish-US architect couple Mark and Nedret Butler, who transformed it into a peerless riverside hotel while retaining the building's quirks, history and character.

The Butlers' daughter, Yasha, took care of the interiors, combining Turkish marble and kilims inside with Adirondack chairs in the garden. All 13 rooms have fireplaces and enjoy fishermen-filled views from wide, arched windows. Book a suite with French doors opening onto the garden and watch the sunset over Istanbul's old town – dotted with domes and minarets – from bed.

The Sumahan also has a shoreline restaurant that serves both Turkish and international food, as well as a white-marble hamam decorated with turquoise Iznik tiles.
43 Kuleli Caddesi
+90 (0)216 422 8000
sumahan.com

▶

In numbers

1905	Bosphorus naval map in the lobby printed
13	wild plum trees in the garden
1,000	books in the library
52,000	ships pass through the Bosphorus every year

La Colombe d'Or
Saint-Paul de Vence, France

A sign at the entrance of this stone auberge in Saint-Paul de Vence once read: "*Ici on loge à cheval, à pied ou en peinture*" (Here we lodge those on horses, on foot or in paintings). La Colombe d'Or started life as a bar and dance spot called Chez Robinson. But its enterprising owner Paul Roux expanded it, changed the name and began amassing a collection of paintings, sculptures and murals, often by inviting artists to lunch in exchange for their work.

The hotel displays its artworks with an impressive nonchalance: the dining room features a stunning Picasso still life and a cubist lobster by Braque. On the terrace is a ceramic mosaic by Fernand Léger, and a sculpture by Alexander Calder flanks the swimming pool. Despite its haul, the hotel has the spirit of a bohemian farmhouse, with rustic wooden furniture and unfussy local food. "People are at ease," says Daniele Roux (who is married to François, the grandson of Paul Roux).

Pillow menus and other five-star fads have bypassed this place. Instead, rooms are furnished with antiques, Persian rugs, snowy white linen and, of course, artworks galore.
1 Place du Général de Gaulle
+33 (0)4 9332 8002
la-colombe-dor.com

In numbers
1920 Chez Robinson opened
1950 terrace lighting installed
1952 ceramic mosaic by Fernand Léger

81

L'Horizon Resort and Spa
Palm Springs

Set against a backdrop of the San Jacinto Mountains, L'Horizon Resort and Spa in Palm Springs reopened in 2015 after a full and thorough renovation by Steve Hermann. Originally designed in 1952 by William F Cody, the mid-century jaw-dropper was the family retreat for oil tycoon and TV producer Jack Wrather, of *The Lone Ranger* fame.

Situated on a patch of well-groomed desert, the 25 modernist bungalows are fitted with furnishings that bring to mind a large home rather than a hotel, albeit one with marble bathrooms, Frette linen and exposed wooden beams that are offset by plush seating covered in graphic fabrics. There are also plenty of glass walls that allow you to drink in the mountain views.

The spa features four treatment rooms, a serene outdoor space, a juice bar and a number of pristine white canvas cabanas. You can also take to the poolside, which features a serene asymmetrical design that complements the hotel's mid-century chops fetchingly. Mediterranean-inspired dishes are served outdoors under Lindsey Adelman lights.
1050 E Palm Canyon Drive
+1 760 323 1858
lhorizonpalmsprings.com

In numbers

1952	originally built
2015	opened
25	bungalows

82
Bisma Eight
Ubud, Bali

"Having the forest right here lets us bring the trees and the landscape into our building," says Suraj Melwani, co-owner of Bisma Eight in Ubud, Bali. "I wanted it to be as natural as possible; as contextual as possible." So despite Bisma Eight's brutalist-inspired structure, sketched by Balinese studio Arte Architects, the hotel's concrete design has not detracted from the greenery.

Most of the modernist retreat's suites open to views of the dense jungle. Some have gardens, and a pool pavilion offers an outlook over the jungle canopy. Comforts amassed by interior designers from Singaporean firm FUUR include cedar-wood Japanese bathtubs that sit alongside walls decorated with Indonesian *tegel kunci* tiling.

Situated within the Tegalalang region, known for its stacked rice fields, Ubud – and, more widely, Indonesia – provided the team with a pool of skilled artisans to help furnish the joint. The rooms come complete with terracotta-coloured throws made from the fabric of the Central Java region of Tumanggal, ikat pillows, and scents and toiletries from Balinese brand Republic of Soap.
68 Jalan Bisma
+62 361 479 2888
bisma-eight.com

In numbers

38 bedrooms
331 Forest Suite is our favourite
18-metre-long pool
90 to 100 local craftsmen employed

83

Toukouen
Tottori, Japan

Japan's Yumigahama peninsula curves like an archer's bow, with the fishing port of Sakaiminato at one end and the hot-spring resort of Kaike at the other. Kaike has several hotels but the best is Toukouen, which has occupied a beachfront berth here for more than a century. The hotel was once a simple wooden structure (now an annexe to the main building) popular for its salty therapeutic baths (the water is still a scalding 80c).

Change came in the early 1960s, when the owner called on the sculptor Masayuki Nagare to bring the hotel up to date. Nagare invited the architect Kiyonori Kikutake to design a new seven-storey building, while he took care of the bathhouse and Japanese garden; the new hotel opened in time for the Tokyo Olympics in 1964.

Five decades on, little has changed. Guests choose between retro Japanese or western rooms, eat healthy food and soak in the mineral-rich water. Many regulars come back year after year. The open fourth-floor garden offers a close-up of Kikutake's thoughtful 1960s intervention and the room where the Japanese royals have stayed is a wood-panelled gem.
3 Chome-17-7 Kaikeonsen
+81 (0)859 34 1111
toukouen.com

In numbers

1964	opened
70	bedrooms
60	staff
24	visits by the royal family

84

Villa Sorgenfrei
Radebeul, Germany

What was once a vineyard has been transformed into a charming hotel nestled among vines and beech trees in the hilly suburbs of the German city of Dresden. The house isn't called Sorgenfrei (literally, "carefree") for nothing. Its expansive gardens offer a tranquil escape from the city and its Versailles-style architecture is reminiscent of Frederick the Great's Sanssouci Palace in Potsdam.

Having gone through two meticulous renovations, the hotel combines all the comforts of a modern affair with the historic patina befitting an estate dating from the 1780s. Each of the 16 guestrooms is individually furnished and decorated with historic murals.

For a personal touch, host Antje Kirsch delivers daily home-baked treats from the kitchen of chef Marcel Kube's restaurant Atelier Sanssouci. Here, regional food is served upon Hering Berlin porcelain plates and paired with local wines as fine as the crystal chandeliers suspended from the ceiling above.

48 Augustusweg
+49 (0)351 795 6660
hotel-villa-sorgenfrei.de

In numbers

1783	originally built
2004	opened
16	bedrooms, including 2 suites
30	covers in the restaurant
600	wines on the menu

85
Troutbeck
Hudson Valley, USA

Country lodges don't come much finer than Troutbeck, a storied property in upstate New York. Easily accessible by train (a rarity in these parts), Troutbeck's 18 hectares once played host to a private home and then an inn that was frequented by the likes of Mark Twain and Ernest Hemingway.

Recently revamped by interior designer Alexandra Champalimaud, the 36 light-filled rooms are spread across four buildings. Each room retains elements of the original building while modern conveniences prevent them from feeling too rustic. Don't forget to take a dip in the pristine swimming pool, lounge in one of the hammocks scattered about the grounds and visit the 1916-built walled garden.

Dining at Troutbeck reflects the abundance of the Hudson Valley, with local produce on full display in the restaurant. And if you want to take some goodies home, the pantry is overflowing with food from nearby producers and shores.
515 Leedsville Road
+1 (845) 789 1555
troutbeck.com

In numbers

2017	opened
36	bedrooms
76	seats in the restaurant
14	hammocks in the grounds

86

Villa Antoinette
Semmering, Austria

Perched above green valleys rolling towards Austria's craggy Rax mountain range is Villa Antoinette, a 1912 residence renovated by Michael Niederer and partner Andreas Wessely into a luxurious retreat. It sits in the town of Semmering, once a focal point of 19th-century Mitteleuropa's champagne-soaked summer culture. The Habsburg heyday is long gone but the architectural splendour of the period is very much alive – especially at Villa Antoinette, which features patterned tiling with the flamboyant colours of Gründerzeit grandeur and delicate art deco chandeliers in the bedrooms that capture the golden evening light.

"We've stepped into big footprints," says Wessely, with unnecessary modesty. The magic of old Semmering has been wonderfully reimagined at this mountain haunt, which offers panoramic views and luxurious facilities at 900 metres above sea level (the perfect altitude for fresh air, apparently). With a plunge pool and Jacuzzi, Finnish sauna and Turkish bath, this retreat is designed for small groups to enjoy weekends or longer stays as the well-heeled Habsburgs did so delightfully.
9 Gläserstrasse
+43 699 1900 7079
villa-antoinette.at

In numbers

2015	reopened
6	bedrooms
550	people live in Semmering
17	types of cake served

 87

Beit al Batroun
Thoum, Lebanon

Sunlight pours through two soaring porticoes that illuminate ivory-white sofas in the lobby of Beit al Batroun, 40 minutes north of Beirut. This hideaway is part of a growing crop of smaller family-run hotels and guesthouses in Lebanon: places offering a glimpse of life in a real Lebanese *beit* (home).

Previously a rarity here, these ventures are now booming, particularly as the rest of the market is largely made up of similar-looking business-oriented establishments and five-star extravaganzas catering to wealthy Gulf tourists.

"I want guests to feel at home," says owner Colette Kahil as she strokes her French bulldog, Kloe. "This is the important thing. I'm not here as a manager; in fact sometimes it feels like I'm a mother to my guests."

Kahil built the hotel for her family and she herself lives in one of the rooms – and is always on hand to advise guests or share a bottle of wine and some conversation. Visitors read, doze and natter on the balcony, or lounge by the plunge pool with a sweeping view of the eastern Mediterranean.
Thoum
+961 (0)3 270 049
beitalbatroun.com

In numbers

2013	opened
5	double rooms
1	plunge pool
3-minute drive to the sea	
1	French bulldog

88
The Craftsman's Cottage
Semley, UK

Amanda Bannister's passion project opened in the Wiltshire village of Semley in 2017. This brick-built guesthouse, nestled in a valley a two-hour drive from London, is more than just another holiday let.

"I wanted to create a more immersive offering," says Bannister (*pictured*), who is a talented potter and whose love of William Morris's arts and crafts movement gives the cottage its name. "The industrial revolution spun the movement and now it's thanks to a digital revolution that we're experiencing a revival of handicraft. The Craftsman's Cottage encourages people to turn away from their screens and everyday life."

The three-bedroom, 19th-century home has British furniture, wallpaper by Morris, art by the likes of London-based Danny Rolph and pottery by ceramicists including Malene Hartmann Rasmussen, Nicola Tassie and Bannister herself.

She turned to local carpenter Wardour Workshops to design and build the kitchen's corner-seating unit and table, and to Semley-based furniture-maker Philip Hawkins for the shelves by the heartening hearth.
Semley Lodge
thecraftsmanscottage.com

In numbers

1800s	originally built
2017	opened
3	bedrooms

 89

Fogo Island Inn
Fogo Island, Canada

Only about 2,400 people live on Fogo Island, a lake-studded territory off the rugged coast of Newfoundland, and among them is Zita Cobb (*pictured*). Born into a family of fishermen, the entrepreneur grew up in a house with no running water – and scarce contact with the mainland – before moving to Silicon Valley and eventually becoming the CFO of a publicly traded tech firm. "I've lived in three different centuries," she says, laughing.

Memories of this place, however, pulled Cobb back to the island, where the fishing industry had long stopped providing a reliable income for many. Opening a hotel, though, could become a new way to sustain – and kick-start – this community. "The drive to do anything comes from a love of place," says Cobb. Her Fogo Island Inn was born with a dedication to staying true to its context. "It's not about whether you have the latest design of sofa in your lobby. Who cares? We're past that now," she says.
210 Main Road
+1 709 658 3444
fogoislandinn.ca

In numbers

29 bedrooms	
2001 Cobb retired from Silicon Valley to start a hospitality business	
45 minutes to the island from Newfoundland by ferry	
35km × 24km size of the island	

90

Mitchelton Hotel
Nagambie, Australia

Situated on a crook in the Goulburn River, the Mitchelton Wines estate has about 115 hectares of riesling and shiraz vines. The building's swooping roofs create dramatic shapes against the gumtrees and, at the centre, a 55-metre tower presides peacefully over the rolling countryside.

By 2011 the winery, a 1970s affair 90 minutes north of Melbourne, had gone through a series of ownership changes and felt tired. But Melbourne-based entrepreneur Andrew Ryan and his father Gerry were so impressed by the passion of the staff and the quality of the wine that they became determined to take the business over.

With the help of architects Hecker Guthrie, the Ryans transformed the winery from a crumbling relic into a tasteful destination, complete with a new hotel, spa and gallery. The revamp has been an economic boost for the nearby town of Nagambie and has encouraged new interest in the estate's overlooked architecture. "For years, people have talked about the Mitchelton's potential," says Andrew. "And when I came here I just had a great feeling. It's important to listen to your gut."
470 Mitchellstown Road
+61 (0)3 5736 2222
mitchelton.com.au

In numbers

1974 originally built
58 bedrooms
1969 first vines planted

 91

Hotel Rantapuisto
Helsinki

Looking out of Rantapuisto's vast windows onto the peaceful views around the hotel, it's hard to imagine that Helsinki city centre is only a 20-minute drive away. Surrounded by birch trees and the placid banks of the Baltic Sea, this squat structure hidden in the woods is a wilderness hideaway to match any other.

Built in 1963 as a training centre for PYP bank by architects Ragnar and Martta Ypyä, the building was inspired by the work of Finland's vaunted mid-century architect Alvar Aalto. With its modernist lights, wooden-beam ceilings and light-filled corridors, it displays a peculiarly mid-century brand of warm minimalism.

Over the years, the hotel eventually began to open to customers beyond the corporate world. But it's still an excellent bet for a company retreat: an impeccably designed auditorium can host some 300 spectators, while the Finnish restaurant, saunas and diving pier make for excellent after-hours entertainment.
3 Furuborginkatu
+358 (0)9 319 1110
rantapuisto.fi

In numbers

1963	originally built
70	bedrooms
10	meeting rooms
15km	from the city centre

92

Hotel Bachmair Weissach
Tegernsee, Germany

"My travels around Japan inspired the *onsen* spa," says Korbinian Kohler (*see page 185*), director of the Hotel Bachmair Weissach in the picturesque lakeside town of Tegernsee, an hour's drive from Munich. The hotel's Japanese-style hot springs and bathing facilities were the first in Germany. "Many spas create a foreign, artificial world as an escape from reality. We want to do the opposite," says Kohler, adding that the onsen's design is deliberately pared-back so that it isn't distracting for guests. Walnut and local limestone form a backdrop for the gently lit pools and the only sound is the trickle of crystal-clear water.

The rustic hotel offers tailor-made treatments for visitors who want to make the most of the spa. It's furnished with loungers, treatment rooms and baths filled with water that ranges in temperature from a bracing 2C to a balmy 42C. There are also daily fitness classes and an on-site equestrian centre offering lessons for both beginners and accomplished riders.
1 Wiesseer Strasse
+49 (0)84 246 000
bachmair-weissach.com

In numbers

1862	opened
146	bedrooms
200	employees
44	horses in the hotel's stable

93

Ceylon Sliders
Weligama, Sri Lanka

"We agreed that a dream life would be to live somewhere in the sun, surfing and eating good food together," says Linn Lundgren, who moved to Sri Lanka with partner Petter Toremalm after graduating from Malmö University in 2014. That year they founded the Sunshinestories retreat in a colonial villa close to the town of Ahangama. And in late 2016 they added another property to the portfolio: Ceylon Sliders.

From a pristine beachfront berth in nearby Weligama, on the island's southernmost tip, the three-storey abode caters to surfers and sport-lovers. "We work with local trades and craftspeople," says Lundgren. "There is no Ikea here," adds Toremalm. "If you want a table someone has to cut down a tree and actually fashion a table from it."

The main building houses seven whitewashed rooms with ocean views and four-poster beds, while three more suites occupy a restored colonial building out back. The rooftop is an excellent vantage point from which to take in the sand and gentle roll of the waves.
9 New Galle Road
+94 (0)76 359 4734
ceylonsliders.com

In numbers

5 bedrooms

120 years – age of original building

25 local makers enlisted

20 steps from nearest surfable wave

10 beaches nearby

94

The Slow
Canggu, Bali

Australian designer George Gorrow's plans for The Slow were the result of interests cultivated during more than two decades working in fashion. The space, designed by Gorrow with help from architect Rieky Sunur, also hosts 114 works from his personal art collection.

Although it's just 300 metres from a popular beach, the feeling here is as the name suggests: slow-moving and secluded. A light *bangkirai*-latticed screen (made from Balinese timber) rolls from wall to ceiling and shields the small reception-cum-restaurant and bar from Canggu's scooter-choked streets.

Gorrow points proudly to the green lounge chairs he made from Indonesian military tents, the hand-woven hyacinth-fibre rugs and the staff uniforms. "All locally made," he says. The same goes for the bright, sizeable suites with their floor-to-ceiling windows and private plunge pools (for those on the ground level). Mid-century furniture is offset by pillows, curtains and tapestries made from hand-dyed fabric from the nearby islands of Timor, Sumba and Sumbawa. Scrubs and facial mists are concocted with a scent designed by Gorrow's wife, Cisco.
97 Jalan Batu Bolong
+62 (0)361 209 9000
theslow.id

●

In numbers

12 bedrooms	
11 is our favourite suite	
114 original artworks	

95

Hoshinoya Fuji
Yamanashi, Japan

Hoshinoya Fuji is a getaway for people who enjoy the outdoors but aren't too keen on roughing it. Perched on a hill near the shore of Lake Kawaguchi in central Yamanashi prefecture, the resort has 40 sparsely furnished, concrete-walled cabins with large sofas on covered balconies (some with outdoor wood-burning stoves) and floor-to-ceiling windows that frame Mount Fuji.

Tokyo-based Azuma Architect & Associates designed the site with a tiered wooden terrace under a canopy of red pines, where guests lounge on hammocks during the day and sit around bonfires at night. The moment guests arrive they're handed backpacks stuffed with essentials for a hike: head-lamps, a steel drinking flask, a blanket, an inflatable cushion, a map and binoculars to spot migratory birds and flying squirrels.

The hotel's staff can arrange small group activities, from chopping wood and learning how to smoke food to canoeing and horseback riding. Chef Takaaki Tagawa's meals combine local wild boar and deer with mushrooms, wild herbs and other foraged ingredients.
1408 Oishi, Fujikawaguchiko-machi, Minami Tsuru-gun
+81 (0)50 3786 1144
hoshinoyafuji.com

In numbers

2015	opened
40	bedrooms
1	spectacular mountain view
2.5	hours drive from Tokyo

Grand Hotel des Iles Borromees
Stresa, Italy

Despite its French-sounding name, the Grand Hotel des Iles Borromees sits on the banks of Italy's Lake Maggiore. But with its backdrop of lush, forest-covered hills, turreted roof and neat rows of geranium-edged balconies, this building certainly suits its grand hotel moniker.

First built in 1861, it retains all the grandeur of a bygone era. The extravagantly furnished rooms, featuring everything from velvet daybeds to lacquered bedframes, still evoke the time when this hotel was a stop-off on the Orient Express route from London to Istanbul. From George Bernard Shaw to John Steinbeck, Clark Gable to Ernest Hemingway (who described the Grand Hotel in *A Farewell to Arms*), the continent's high society flocked here for rejuvenating sojourns.

Aside from its peaceful garden planted with magnolias, the spa was always one of the hotel's main draw cards. Nowadays its three pools (one of which is heated), sauna and steam room are still reason enough to check in for an old-school wind-down.
67 Corso Umberto I
+39 (0)323 938 938
borromees.com

In numbers

1861 originally built

172 bedrooms

8 golf courses nearby

1945 to 1946 hotel served as a casino

97

São Lourenço do Barrocal
Monsaraz, Portugal

Surrounded by undulating plains and cork trees, São Lourenço do Barrocal lies in the heart of the Alentejo, Portugal's big-sky country and agricultural heartland. Close to fortified Roman towns, Moorish ruins and the vast Alqueva Lake, the hotel is part of a 200-year-old farming estate that's replete with vineyards and olive groves.

Its whitewashed stone buildings with terracotta-tiled roofs have been refurbished by Pritzker Prize-winning architect Eduardo Souto de Moura, who has carved out an idyllic collection of rooms, cottages and a spa for guests in former stables and barns.

Hotel spas are often over-designed (it's time to rethink mood lighting) and under-deliver on what matters: treatments to keep you feeling fresh. Hats off to founder José António Uva for getting it right. The vaulted ceilings and natural light create a serene setting. The massages and facials on offer use oils and lotions developed by Austria's Susanne Kaufmann, who sources the ingredients from the Alps.
7200-177 Monsaraz
+351 266 247 140
barrocal.pt

◗

In numbers

200 years in the same family
2,020 hectares vineyard
2006 first wine harvest
75 bird species on the property

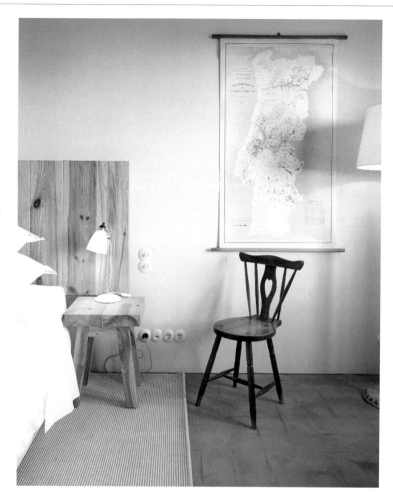

Grand Hotel a Villa Feltrinelli
Lake Garda, Italy

It's not often a 20-room establishment can edge itself into the grand hotel category. "We are a small but great hotel," says general manager Markus Odermatt. Built in 1892 as a holiday home for the Feltrinelli family (renowned in Italy for its eponymous publishing house), this residence was confiscated by the fascist army during the Second World War so it could be enjoyed by Benito Mussolini.

Reclaimed by the Feltrinellis, it hosted many a literary and artistic bash before 1997, when it was sold to entrepreneur Bob Burns who turned it into a hotel. A four-year restoration yielded rooms that are distinct from one another and maintain much of the original furniture. "Our philosophy is not the same as a 'normal' hotel," says Odermatt. "Everything is made specifically for Villa Feltrinelli, as if it's still a private home."

Centuries-old magnolias are the garden's centrepiece. The expansive green patch on the banks of Lake Garda is also planted with cypress, linden, fig, orange, olive and lemon trees. There are fresh herbs, too, many of which end up in chef Stefano Baiocco's signature salad.
38 Via Rimembranza
+39 0365 798 000
villafeltrinelli.com

►

In numbers

2001	opened
80	employees
30	seats in the restaurant
80	lemon trees in the garden

99

The Ritz-Carlton, Kyoto
Kyoto

It used to be that western-style hotels announced their arrival in Japan by being as big and obtrusive as possible. When The Ritz-Carlton, Kyoto opened in 2014 it did the opposite, taking its cues from the city's discreet ryokan (inns) and occupying a low-rise building on the Kamogawa River.

The hotel is close to busy shopping districts and famous temples but guests are enveloped in a bubble of serenity. Local craftsmen added their touches to the modern Japanese interior. Many of the rooms and suites have views over the river and the Higashiyama mountains.

This is top-level hospitality, with 600-thread count linen, handmade Kyoto soaps and crisp cotton *yukata* (casual kimonos). The Garden Suite looks onto its own zen garden and the spa offers Japanese treatments such as heated bamboo massages and a beautifully lit indoor pool.

The private dining room, Ebisugawa-tei, is housed in a century-old structure that was restored in the hotel. Celebrated French patissier Pierre Hermé oversees the baking and has a shop selling pastries, chocolates and macarons. It's well worth dropping by for afternoon tea.
Kamogawa Nijo-Ohashi Hotori
+81 (0)75 746 5555
ritzcarlton.com

●

In numbers

2014	opened
134	bedrooms
409 works by	80 artists

100

Four Seasons Hotel Ritz
Lisbon

In a culture that venerates youth, it's hard to become a grande dame without a few nips and tucks along the way. But Lisbon's Four Seasons Hotel Ritz is a noteworthy exception.

The hotel, which opened in 1959, has survived the decades intact. Outside, the 10-storey modernist façade retains its simple, geometric lines; inside, the public spaces are an enthralling throwback. The Portuguese art and classic French furniture are also redolent of another age.

Rather than instigate any major renovations, the management has contented itself with simple additions such as bouquets of fresh orchids hanging from the ceiling. Apart from a new spa that opened in 2003, Four Seasons has had the good sense to leave this beauty be.

The hotel also houses a remarkable secret. In place of worn-down treadmills or ill-advised routes over city sidewalks, runners can enjoy a rooftop athletics track. The 400-metre-long U-shaped lane on the top floor allows you to work up a sweat and get an early start on sightseeing in the Portuguese capital.
88 Rua Rodrigo da Fonseca
+351 21 381 1400
fourseasons.com/lisbon

In numbers

1959 opened
282 bedrooms
273 bedrooms with private terraces
10 floors

Part 2:

Trade secrets

2.

All you need to open a hotel of your own

So you've sampled the singular experiences that we've recommended for a visit but what about the components that transform a good hotel into a great one? How about the entrepreneurs who struck out on their own to create new businesses to benchmark? We meet the folk behind our favourite brands – big and small, novel and time-tested – and attend classes at the institutions worth enrolling in. We proffer the advice we've gleaned on running a tight ship (with windows that actually open, eventful event spaces and plug sockets that you needn't remodel your room to reach).

So whether you're considering jacking in your nine-to-five to take over a property on New Zealand's North Island, or in Bali or Barcelona, here are the folk you should hear from and the things to consider before hanging out the welcome sign.

Canny lodgings

Our take on the aspects of hospitality worth, ahem, checking out. Plus a lighthearted layout for an imaginary but ideal stopover.

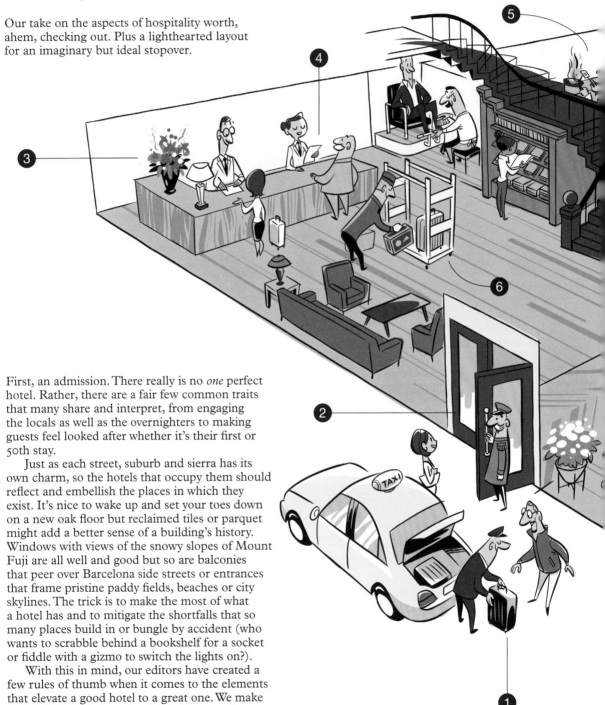

First, an admission. There really is no *one* perfect hotel. Rather, there are a fair few common traits that many share and interpret, from engaging the locals as well as the overnighters to making guests feel looked after whether it's their first or 50th stay.

Just as each street, suburb and sierra has its own charm, so the hotels that occupy them should reflect and embellish the places in which they exist. It's nice to wake up and set your toes down on a new oak floor but reclaimed tiles or parquet might add a better sense of a building's history. Windows with views of the snowy slopes of Mount Fuji are all well and good but so are balconies that peer over Barcelona side streets or entrances that frame pristine paddy fields, beaches or city skylines. The trick is to make the most of what a hotel has and to mitigate the shortfalls that so many places build in or bungle by accident (who wants to scrabble behind a bookshelf for a socket or fiddle with a gizmo to switch the lights on?).

With this in mind, our editors have created a few rules of thumb when it comes to the elements that elevate a good hotel to a great one. We make a case for what a great hotel should comprise. Speaking of which, can we help you with yours?

Checklist: Ground floor

1. Street-to-suite service is a nice start
2. A warm welcome sets the tone
3. Hire receptive receptionists
4. Ensure a speedy check-out
5. Cook up a scrummy scent
6. Have porters to help with haulage
7. Provide an elevating experience
8. Invest in a beloved restaurant
9. Find a barman who shakes it all night
10. Sit back and watch the fun unfold

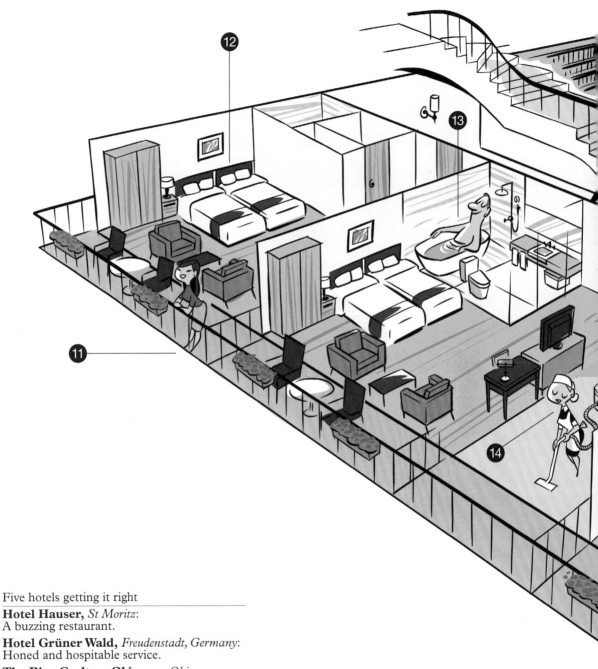

Five hotels getting it right

Hotel Hauser, *St Moritz*:
A buzzing restaurant.

Hotel Grüner Wald, *Freudenstadt, Germany*:
Honed and hospitable service.

The Ritz-Carlton, Okinawa, *Okinawa*:
A lobby that makes an impression.

Tawaraya-Ryokan, *Kyoto*:
Just-so interiors.

Park Hyatt Tokyo, *Tokyo*:
A brilliant bar.

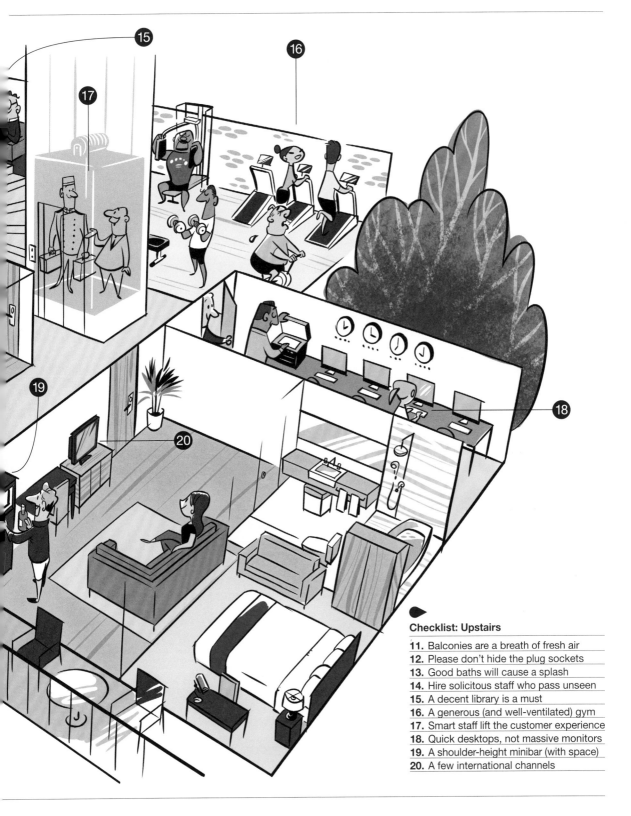

Checklist: Upstairs

11. Balconies are a breath of fresh air
12. Please don't hide the plug sockets
13. Good baths will cause a splash
14. Hire solicitous staff who pass unseen
15. A decent library is a must
16. A generous (and well-ventilated) gym
17. Smart staff lift the customer experience
18. Quick desktops, not massive monitors
19. A shoulder-height minibar (with space)
20. A few international channels

Checking in

Our checklist of everything you need to ensure
your guests have the smoothest of stays.

Warm welcome

A dapper doorman to greet you, a solicitous concierge and a GM who doesn't hide in a back office
paper-pushing, all help to get a guest's visit off on the right foot.

Lobby group

Every hotel needs an entrance space with a sense of occasion. It's a fallacy that hotels should always be a "home away from home" – stay at home if you choose but we think hotels should provide an elevated experience, from the hum of activity as you enter to the fireside nooks in which to hunker down later.

Meet and greet

So now you know, a hotel's worth isn't measured by the volume of its lobby – triple-height ceilings create a din and feel overblown and unwelcoming. Human-scale is better. Also, keep the check-in desk away from the bar – neither wants to see the other.

Beware of over-branding

A strong name and understated logo inspire confidence and set the tone before guests arrive. Hotel names with the word "design" in the title or scrawled beneath it are usually making up for a dearth of ideas and lack of an interesting crowd.

Touching sentiment

On the subject of sound as well as aesthetics, an array of textiles and upholstery (try Kvadrat or Kasthall) will help to hush the ruckus.

Read all about it

Invest in a well-stocked lobby newsstand and a library teeming with international titles. A spot of print provides endless diversions.

7
Silver service

Tip: employ 20 40-year-olds rather than 40 20-year-olds. Too many too-young helpers lolling around looking awkward feels more like immersive theatre than a fitting welcome. Seasoned hands tend to steady the ship more diplomatically – and deal better with finicky customers.

8
Silent treatment

Staff should be attentive, not finishing up with personal chit-chat while you're waiting around with your luggage.

9
Telling tales

Fulfilling folklore adds to the excitement of checking in but hotels should convey this without mentioning it every five minutes.

10

Hot desks

Writing desks have become an endangered species and we'd suggest more stringent conservation efforts. Smart stationery is also advised.

 11

Key purchase

Woeful is the red dot warning you that your plastic keycard doesn't work. The satisfying click of a key, though, speaks convincingly of security.

 12

Dim view

Late-night arrivals make early mornings hard enough. Curtains and blinds that leave you in the dark will help inspire a restful night's kip.

 13

Sound investment

Soundproofing keeps rooms feeling private and ensures a good long slumber. Customers won't come back if they're kept up by next door's antics.

High beams

A sense of humour should be conveyed by wry but friendly staff – not natty catch-phrases, themed rooms or poor puns.

Mean business

Yellowing monitors and pay-per-page printing are naff in the extreme. Plump for quick printers and sleek computers on wooden desks.

Heavy petting

Not a cat sanctuary for mangy moggies or a place for fruitcakes to take hamsters on holiday. But how about a pup salon or dog-walker for Fido?

Scent opportunity

Forget commissioning smelly chemists in Grasse to make a house scent. What about a downstairs bakery that turns out delicate pastries instead?

Eyes on stalks

Fresh flowers (in fresh water) show the care that goes into the upkeep of the place. They also add a little olfactory lift, dash of colour and sense of occasion that can reflect the season and support nearby florists (keep their cards behind reception for guests in need of emergency "thank yous" too).

Glass act

Spotless windows speak volumes. It sounds simple but gleaming glass is a great reflection of a rigorous cleaning routine, brightens the outside world a touch and increases the natural light within.

Dress the part

Uniform sets a tone and should fit the atmosphere
– you shouldn't be mistaken for a customer rather
than a member of staff, or vice versa.

Follow suit

Create subtle dress codes to discourage people
wearing flip-flops in smart city-centre affairs
or dressing like Gatsby at a beach resort.

Step up to the plate

Hotel restaurants should be places for guests and locals to mingle (with preferential bookings for the former, of course). Having trouble finding a chef to fill your kitchen? Why not recruit a few budding talents from the local pop-up scene and see how they fare?

Stay up late

A bar that makes you want to stay the night does wonders for occupancy. It should be open late with a barman who doesn't mind manning it until the final drop is drunk. No dry ice or cocktail umbrellas – ours is a savvy barman and a dab hand with the classics, not a self-dubbed "mixologist".

Discrete dining

Tucked-away booths and snug banquettes are perfect for private meetings, whispered words or tender trysts. No more, mind.

Get trolleyed

We usually eschew frippery and ceremony in service but hotel restaurants are one of the few places where cloches and trolleys should reign.

Adapt to change

Bin the DVD players and docks – we can all do with fewer useless bells and whistles. Technology should mean fast wi-fi and a universal charger.

Channel positivity

A radio with a few upbeat presets and a TV with international channels will keep visitors content, informed and entertained.

Day-long dining

A fold-down table is preferable to a desk or, worse, eating a sad sandwich off your lap because you had the bad grace to arrive after midnight.

Sturdy choices

Solid furniture and a few one-off pieces (for personality) set the tone and show you're invested in the service you offer. No cheap veneers.

Flattering light

Too-bright LEDs are everywhere, as are unfathomable gizmos labelled "control centres". Try sconces and shades that cast a flattering light.

Socket to 'em

Investing in design isn't about mad, glassy chandeliers or avant garde furniture. Well-placed plugs are still a rarity – keep them in view.

Flush finish

Stock covetable amenities in proper quantities, no sad single-serve sachets. Plus a shower and bath (ideally in a wet-room setting) and a Toto Washlet.

Chill out

Minibars should sit at shoulder height and offer plenty of drinks and snacks, as well as extra room for a bottle of crisp white and any other purchases.

Roll with it

A concierge should have good taste (and not fob you off to the most expensive place in town), a full Rolodex of contacts and a healthy dose of discretion. Optional – but excellent – extras in his or her arsenal include the ability to connect like-minded guests and insulate those seeking solace.

Hit the right note

A decent crooner and a jazzy pianist set a good tone for proceedings, as the never dull nor too-noisy New York Grill in Tokyo's vertiginous Park Hyatt proves. A changing line-up of interesting local musicians trumps a shoddy playlist on tinny speakers and will attract walk-ins.

Porter call

Our hale porters may look muscular but they never break a sweat hauling heavy cases to and from rooms – let alone dent them by overestimating their own strength. Instead, luggage in our imagined stopover is borne from roadside to room on silent, fast-moving wood-hewn trollies.

Total stitch-up

A tidy tailoring service such as Lim's in Seoul's Grand Hyatt is indispensable for quick fixes if hems need crimping or jackets tweaking before formal occasions. A sensibly priced laundry service with a quick turnaround is also a rare thing worth celebrating and investing in.

Head start

The last thing you need after a long flight is to spell out your name 10 times. Guests should be whisked upstairs upon arrival.

Means to an end

Questions about what you had from the minibar shouldn't hamper a speedy departure. Payments can be taken and city taxes totted in a jiffy.

 40

Easy sell

Neighbourhood-focused retail adds life and a sense of place. Renting out space for a coffee shop or florist lures life and locals into the foyer.

 41

Cut above the rest

Out on the town tonight or chairing an AGM this afternoon? A first-rate shoe-shining business in the lobby and sharp barber are both crucial.

Turn of events

Event spaces are often stuffy afterthoughts or ways of trying to monetise dank and useless rooms or windowless basements. Dedicated areas for book signings, talks, art classes or the like will add life and reel in a lively crowd.

Elevating experience

An uplifting lift with a crisp whoosh on the doors is an excellent thing – but without the boring beeping that can be heard from rooms, please.

Novel idea

An in-room read is a must – a few thoughtfully chosen novels and magazines that lure you in and allow you to escape.

45
Flexible entry

Too many hotels still employ anachronistic arrival and departure slots. Not all schedules adhere to a 15.00 check-in or midday exit so systems should allow for block-booking rooms during desired hours.

46
Into the fold

A single, tastefully typeset directory espousing the hotel's services is infinitely preferable to a wodge of promotion cards stuffed in a top drawer. Why not offer a few tips for under-the-radar restaurants and independent shops in the area too?

47
Learn the lingo

How about 20-minute morning language lessons? Just the basics, mind – how order a drink, toast a deal and apologise profusely (just in case).

48
Route finder

A good city map can help guests get their bearings, describe the lay of the land and highlight a few much-needed points of interest.

49
Waiting game

Hatches, anterooms and dumbwaiters all work well when it comes to depositing goods without disturbing guests.

On a roll

A calm and efficient car service saves a mad scramble for a taxi and the anxiety-inducing airport dash. Bikes and vintage cars are fine for exploring but we think a small but stately fleet of German-made motors with capacious back seats make for an excellent send-off. See you again soon.

Meet the team

Great hotels are a puzzle, partly because what makes them great is hard to fathom but also because the big picture is made up of hundreds of small but essential pieces. Enter the staff. Our imagined bunch is a mix of seasoned campaigners and keen-to-please dilettantes. They're drilled, of course, and could quote protocol if they needed to, but mostly they're humane, fun and here to help. Let us introduce you.

1. Receptionist
João Buenvenida

Smiles don't come wider than that of our swarthy front-desker João. His lilting Carioca accent soothes the weariest of travellers. He's composed, calm and well turned out despite the weight of inquiries (we get a fair few), phone calls, hubbub and the comings and goings of the always-lively lobby.

3. Head barman
Jin Toniku

The reliable rudder of our renowned bar is a veteran of the cocktail game who can free-pour to the millilitre and judge by sight the guests who are thirsty (and the ones who've had enough). Tokyo-born Jin's cabinet is stocked with fine spirits and he's more than happy to keep the night watch.

2. Reliable regular
Dowager Dandie Dinmont

So she's not really staff but she's been visiting longer than most here have served (and since before the younger members were born). Some say she's a spy, others a novelist, others still a racing driver. All we know for sure is that she's perpetually dressed for a Viennese ball.

4. General manager
Klara Abel

Our unflappable Swiss-German GM doesn't spend her days hiding away in the back office. Her two decades in the industry mean she's tried her hand at most jobs – menial to managerial – and brings her easy air from lobby to lift and street to suite. It's her calm influence that keeps the hotel ticking.

5. Porter
Shane Goodaye

Smiley Shane fell in love with hotels back in his native Antipodes and, although he'd relish the GM job one day, he's happily learning the ropes, hauling cases and lugging the luggage trolley. He's obliging, easy on the eye and usually appears from thin air to help as soon as the car boot clicks open.

6. Housemaid
Grace Poppin

As well-mannered as the Dickensian mould from which she seems to have soundlessly sprung, our British housekeeper manages a team of taciturn and dexterous house staff. With an expert inkling for when curtains need drawing or pillows fluffing, she's known for her dulcet tones and discreet manner.

7. Spa manager
Ella V Rubdøwn

Ella's spa treatments tempt punters, whether they're hotel guests or not. The word "wellness" and all the associated whale song and wispiness have been banned in favour of firm massages, a seemly Swedish-style sauna and a well-equipped gym complete with on-hand and handsome trainers.

8. Head chef
Vito Buonogusto

French food can be fussy and too filling but our Italian-trained cook (who's larger than life – and most Fiat hatchbacks) has a light touch and uses a small number of fresh ingredients to sumptuous effect. The menu is reliably robust and, although service comes with a sense of occasion, it's never stuffy.

9. Concierge
Constance Durand

Our charming Parisian concierge can second-guess a guest's taste at 20 paces. She has a reliable book of contacts for sorting seats at lesser-known restaurants, queue-hops at popular museums and fuss-free taxi-transfers to the train station or airport (naturally, the hotel has a fleet of roomy BMWs too).

10. Handyman
Tapio Hänninen

Tool-in-hand Tapio ("Tap" for short) cut his teeth as an engineer in the Finnish military – or so he says. There's no problem that he can't identify, weigh up and fix. He may not have the glitziest job but woe betide the guest that talks down to him in earshot of his close-knit colleagues.

Olaf Krohne

The owner of The Regina in Bad Gastein, Austria, saw opening a hotel as a chance to revive an Alpine town.

"Opening a hotel is like falling in love," says Olaf Krohne. The German businessman spent his childhood summers in Bad Gastein, a small Austrian town that was once the playground of European royalty and statesmen who were drawn to its thermal spas. Though he'd had a successful run opening restaurants and hotels in Hamburg and Copenhagen in the 1990s and early 2000s, Krohne had always dreamed of returning to the spa town to work. So when the chance arose to take over The Regina in 2009, he jumped at it: "You fall in love and then you act. We had only two months to renovate before we launched."

Changes to the 32-room hotel, which dates back to the early 20th century, included adding a cinema and reviving the sauna and spa. But a canny hotelier is always making subtle shifts, as well as bigger renovations. "You need to keep working on the quality of the project," says Krohne. That means everything from tweaking menus to refreshing furniture. Nonetheless, after their hard work Krohne and his partner Jason Houzer paused to celebrate the grand reopening by inviting everyone they knew over from Germany.

In 2017 Krohne fell in love all over again and snapped up another hotel in town. The Grüner Baum is an even more traditional Alpine lodge, with 50 rooms across several buildings. Nowadays, Krohne doesn't need to persuade friends to visit.

◀

Krohne's top tips

1. Build the right team: You need people – from housekeepers to desk staff – to believe in the idea of the hotel.

2. Don't prevaricate: Unmade decisions will pile up so don't hold off on making them.

3. Get the food right: We have experimented a lot with our menu. We settled on a mix of Mediterranean and Austrian dishes so we have something for everyone; the original owners were Italian so we honour that too.

Inés Miró-Sans

The entrepreneur had never opened a hotel before but got it right first time with Barcelona's Casa Bonay.

Barcelona's Casa Bonay (*see page 25*) is so well conceived, it's hard to believe there's no big-name group behind it and that it's actually the first hotel project by young entrepreneur Inés Miró-Sans. The ESADE Business School graduate spent three years working as a brand strategist at the Ace Hotel in New York but soon returned home to launch her own venture. The canvas for her ideas was an 1869 townhouse, on which she negotiated a 37-year lease. New York-based Studio Tack (*see page 190*) came in to uncover the building's character – mosaic floors and stained-glass windows – while adding contemporary touches that make for a unique and sophisticated space.

Local collaborations were at the heart of Miró-Sans' philosophy. Much of the furniture is by Gràcia-based AOO, the playful wallpaper and cushions are by Batabasta and light fixtures come courtesy of Santa & Cole. She also invited some of the city's brightest business owners to take over spaces on the ground floor, with an eye to attracting residents and tourists alike. There's Satan's Coffee Corner (run by local barista Marcos Bartolomé), a small bookshop by local publisher Blackie Books and the lively Libertine bar, which has become a go-to for the city's cognoscenti. To top it off, chef Estanislao Carenzo mans Southeast Asian restaurant Elephant, Crocodile, Monkey, while the rooftop Chiringuito bar hosts regular barbecues.

Miró-Sans' top tips

1. Assess the market and think about what the city is missing: Barcelona has a million tapas bars but it didn't have a single high-quality Southeast Asian restaurant.

2. Be the place to be: Think beyond the bed-for-the-night. Bring in sought-after bands and invite the whole neighbourhood.

3. Collaborate more: Barcelona is full of time-honoured establishments and young, talented entrepreneurs.

Ronald Akili

Katamama, Bali, is a showcase of Indonesian craftsmanship – and a childhood dream come true.

"In a talent show in fourth grade, I drew a building and said I wanted to be a hotelier," says Ronald Akili, co-founder and CEO of the Potato Head Family, the Indonesian group behind the Katamama hotel in Seminyak, Bali (*see pages 88 to 89*). Growing up with parents who worked in the travel industry, visiting one hotel after another, made a big impression on the young Akili. "It still amazes me. It feels like a big theatre."

With Katamama, Akili was able to create the playhouse of his dreams but the project is far more intricate than his childhood sketch. Helped by Andra Matin, one of Indonesia's leading architects, Akili has built a showcase for both Bali's craftsmanship and his love of mid-century style (known here as *Jengki*). The details show a great deal of consideration, from the red bricks inspired by Balinese temples to the terrazzo floors and indigo-dyed ikat dressing gowns.

There were many naysayers who pointed to the high costs of hand-making much of the building's construction materials and furniture, as well as to the dearth of local companies equipped to run the building project. But Akili and his partners skipped around these problems by setting up their own firm and project-management team to achieve the quality they desired. The service is equally original. Guests won't find a mini-bar in their rooms, for instance; instead, a bartender who mixes drinks in-room can be summoned at any hour.

Akili's top tips

1. Be bold: Don't be afraid to challenge the status quo and do what you believe in.

2. Be original: Don't follow trends, which I believe a lot of big hotel brands do. Don't cater to the so-called millennial or Generation Z.

3. Be unique: Create a hotel that's personalised, with character and soul.

Matthew & Emma Goodwin

From point break to weekend breaks, this couple's seafront Malibu motel is making waves.

Having grown up in Malibu and surfed throughout his childhood, Matthew Goodwin remembered The Surfrider motel with a mixture of fondness and nostalgia. Built in 1953, it was an exemplar of the mid-century, car-centric lodgings that are often romanticised today. So when he and his wife Emma heard that The Surfrider was up for sale, "it was an immediate emotional reaction," he recalls. "Of course we had to do it."

The pair teamed up with Alessandro Zampedri (a professional racing car driver and entrepreneur) in the summer of 2014 and started work. Together they began a three-year overhaul, leaving much of the original motel intact but updating key aspects, opening up the vaulted ceilings, making more of the sea views and turning it into the perfect Malibu beach house.

Neither Matthew nor Emma had any hotel experience but that did little to deter them. "Ignorance is bliss but it also brings innovation because you really don't know any better," says Emma. Matthew is a trained architect and designer while she has worked in branding, so they felt confident doing plenty of the design work themselves. "I don't know if it was smart," she admits, laughing, but it allowed them to approach all facets through the same lens and build the hotel they wanted from scratch, right down to the last detail.

▶ The Goodwins' top tips

1. Give yourself time: Do a lot of dry runs and form your team and operation early on.

2. Consistency is key: Everyone needs to tell the same story across the brand, from the staff to the PR.

3. Train well: Choose a team and teach them. We go on fields trips. We got a big bus and took our staff around Malibu so they could understand the off-the-beaten-path experience.

Jeanette Mix

Ett Hem in Stockholm was founded by a hands-on hotelier who was hankering after something real.

The story of Ett Hem (*see pages 26 to 27*) began with a phone call. "A friend rang me and said, 'You know that dream you've always had of starting your own hotel? There is a beautiful house for sale in this neighbourhood. It's perfect for you,'" says Jeanette Mix, looking back to 2006 and the start of her life as a hotelier. She looked around the former townhouse in Stockholm's Lärkstaden district and bought it with little hesitation.

Mix had long harboured that dream of opening her own place. Having worked in restaurants and hotels in her teens, and studied at the IHTTI hospitality school in Switzerland, she was steeped in the industry. But life had taken her to London and a marriage then children followed. In 2006, back in Sweden, she was ready for a new challenge: "Back then there were lots of fancy design hotels but they never felt real. When I travel, I'm looking for something different, something truer, more genuine and honest."

It took two years for Mix to find the right designer; eventually she met British designer Ilse Crawford. "She didn't present any mood boards or anything," says Mix. "Ilse just had an intellectual understanding of what I wanted." The 12-room hotel that resulted has lots of inviting spaces and subtle details. Mix wanted it to feel like "a good friend's house". It's perhaps not surprising that that's exactly what Ett Hem has become to many of her loyal guests.

Mix's top tips

1. Do your research: If you have the means, you should absolutely travel and see what others are doing and how that makes you feel.

2. Details matter: We put a thermos of chilled water by our guests' beds each night. It's a detail that sticks with people after they leave.

3. Be present: I'm there every day, pointing things out. I have amazing staff but I'm there to correct them and tell them about the guests.

Stephan Gerhard

Hamburg's 25hours Hotels is growing apace, having found the formula for properties with personality.

"We sat together for 30 minutes before we swore 'eternal loyalty' to each other in creating the most individual of hotels. At least that's how the legend goes," says Stephan Gerhard, who co-founded the Hamburg-based 25hours Hotel Company with Christoph Hoffmann, Kai Hollmann and Ardi Goldman in 2005. As founder of the Treugast Solutions Group, one of Europe's leading hospitality consultancy firms, Gerhard had the experience to help bring the idea of a smart, business-minded but playful hotel group to fruition.

"When we launched 25hours we wanted to create an international brand, not a chain," says Gerhard. "This isn't easy to do, as every single one of our properties is individually designed, but at the heart they all share recognisable DNA." Each hotel tells the story of its neighbourhood and engages with its surroundings. The 25hours Hotel Bikini Berlin, for example, overlooks the city's zoo, so rooms facing the animal enclosure have been kitted out with binoculars with which to spy on the cheeky monkeys below.

With nearly a dozen properties across Germany, Austria and Switzerland, 25hours teamed up with AccorHotels to expand further afield to France and beyond. Its sister, Bikini Island & Mountain Hotels, is also making waves with its first opening in Mallorca. Ironically, it seems there's little time to rest in the hospitality industry.

Gerhard's top tips

1. Have a vision: You need a clear idea of what specific type of hotel you want to open.

2. Gather knowledge: You need partners from the architectural and design worlds who have actual experience in the hotel industry. Creativity shouldn't fall short of functionality.

3. Hire the best: Find highly qualified staff, trained at the best schools and hotels, who have a casual yet welcoming attitude – it's not always an easy feat.

Keisuke Yui

The man behind Nine Hours was responsible for the arrival of the Japanese capsule hotel.

Images of Japanese capsule hotels often give an odd, sci-fi view of the experience – packed tubes in high-density areas that offer spaces in which to sleep or scrub up. But in 2009, Keisuke Yui rewrote the brief with his Nine Hours premises in Kyoto (*see page 63*).

Yui's father ran a capsule hotel in Akihabara, Tokyo, while Yui had a career at what was then Japan's biggest venture capital investment company. In 1999, however, his father died, leaving the hotel with ¥500m (€3.8m) of debt and only ¥10m (€75,300) in cash. The hotel was lacking in technology and design but Yui focused on the finances and by 2004 he had turned the business around. "I realised that the capsule hotel could be exported," he says. "It's so space-efficient."

Teaming up with industrial designer Fumie Shibata, he masterminded a round-the-clock urban-transit service. "We really specialise in two things – showering and sleeping – at the finest level." Yui assembled a crack team of architects and suppliers for the best bath amenities, bedding and loungewear. With minimal signage by Masaaki Hiromura, Nine Hours was born.

"The idea is to have multiple Nine Hours locations in a city so guests can use them all to drop off and collect their suitcases, shower and sleep," adds Yui. "You can explore the city in an unprecedented way. I want to take the idea to London and New York and open there."

Yui's top tips

1. Keep it simple: Avoid superficial and overly decorative design.

2. Keep it clean: Don't underestimate the importance of the basics; always keep the hotel spick and span.

3. Train your team: Invest in your staff – all services come from and through them.

Avra Jain

Past experience on Wall Street came in surprisingly handy for the founder of the Vagabond Hotel Miami.

Avra Jain's career path was a winding one. She studied engineering in Indiana before moving to New York and joining Wall Street. The trajectory from trader to hotelier isn't as odd as it might seem though. In her financial life she had to be tough – because "there were perhaps four women in a room of 150" – and comfortable taking risks. Both vital skills, she explains, in hospitality.

Jain's first forays into the world of property started in New York, where she began investing in districts such as Tribeca in the 1990s. When she left finance and moved to Miami, she continued. She identified the Biscayne Boulevard area just north of Midtown as full of potential due to its stunning mid-century Miami Modern buildings. The area wasn't desirable at the time and the motel she spotted had been shuttered for years. "Looking back, I don't think I was thinking; I was just so mesmerised by the property," she says. "In real estate if the property is really special you buy it and figure it out later."

With the help of designer friend Stephane Dupox, she refurbished the building and the Vagabond was born in 2012. Its fun, 1950s aesthetic – including revived neon signage – was an instant success. Since then, Jain has opened a hotel in Jamaica called The Cliff and refurbished a property called the Miami River Inn. Now she's eyeing a second motel on Biscayne Boulevard. Her unofficial motto: "Sometimes being naïve is a gift."

Jain's top tips

1. The space matters: Start with a great property (which probably needs a lot of work and love) and take it to the next level.

2. Think local: Be a part of the neighbourhood and community. With the help of your staff, strive to make the hotel feel homey.

3. Create a narrative: The hotel experience needs to tell a story. Revive the history of the property and start a new chapter.

Sarah Sklash & April Brown

Only after the two first-timers did up an old motel in Ontario did they realise what they'd stumbled onto.

Over the past few years, picturesque Prince Edward County, a two-hour drive east of Toronto along the shore of Lake Ontario, has become one of Canada's best food and drink-producing regions. Its wineries are among the finest in the country and its small-scale cheese-makers and vegetable farmers now supply the menus of some of Canada's best dining rooms. However, the growing number of visitors posed a problem: a lack of good places to stay.

"We both realised what a special place Prince Edward County was," says Sarah Sklash (*pictured, left*), who set up The June Motel in 2017 with business partner April Brown. "But we felt there was nowhere we really wanted to stay; it was either dingy old motels or old-school B&Bs." When an old motel popular with hobby fishermen came on the market, the pair took the plunge.

The 16 bedrooms were revamped, vintage furniture sourced and playful wallpapers pasted on the walls to create a contemporary take on the roadside motel. "We like to call ourselves moteliers," says Brown. "It's a feeling and an era that we were trying to recreate."

For these first-time hoteliers, advertising took the form of word-of-mouth publicity and images shared online. "We realised that we'd stumbled on something," says Brown, "that we'd created something that people were genuinely eager for and excited about."

Sklash and Brown's top tips:

1. Experiment: We're doing less but doing those things exceptionally well.

2. Be authentic: We weren't afraid to roll up our sleeves. We worked the reception desk a lot when we first opened.

3. Know your brand: We painted our doors pink – everyone tried to talk us out of it. We knew some people wouldn't want to stay here but you don't have to be everything to everyone.

Rogério Fasano

The Fasano São Paulo was just the beginning for this hotelier – now one of the biggest names in the industry.

One night in the early hours, Brazilian hotelier Rogério Fasano was awoken by a phone call from his staff at the Fasano São Paulo (*see page 66*), the hotel he opened in 2003. Former US president George W Bush, who was staying at the hotel, couldn't sleep. Another guest was playing an instrument on a terrace below and it had woken him. "[It was] Mr Clinton," Fasano recalls, of the late-night saxophonist, who also happened to be staying the night. "I told the staff, 'Tell Mr Bush to call Mr Clinton on the 19th floor and talk with him personally.' So they got a bottle of cognac and started talking."

Deftly solving delicate problems like these, presidential or personal, has become something of a calling card for Fasano since he entered the business and created one of the most respected hotel brands in Latin America. The Fasano family name has been a cornerstone of São Paulo's restaurant industry since the early 20th century. Fasano's ambition, once he opened his own dining room in 1982 at 20 years of age, was to transpose the name to the hotel business too. "I think I was obsessed with making it happen," he says.

There are now five Fasano hotels dotted across the continent, with more to follow. "People love to say that a hotel should feel like home," Fasano says. "But if you feel at home here, it's because I'm doing everything wrong. You should not feel at home in a hotel; you should be in a hotel."

Fasano's top tips

1. Bend the rules: Everyone said, "this is going to be a failure", but we did it and it's a huge success.

2. Stay loyal: When we open a hotel we give opportunities to those who have been with us for 30 years. I think we're growing in a very safe way.

3. Care for the details: I'm here every day. I'm in the lobby talking to clients and staff and I think that makes all the difference.

Mirjam & Tom Espinosa

Hotel V's founders may have skipped hospitality school but their Amsterdam abode passes with flying colours.

Unperturbed by being rejected from hospitality schools in the Netherlands, Mirjam and Tom Espinosa still dreamed of starting their own hotel. They met on a dance floor at Amsterdam's former nightclub The Roxy and decided that they wanted to contribute something to their city. Fast forward to the present day and Mirjam and Tom have opened three locations under the name Hotel V, in Frederiksplein and Nesplein in the central district and Fizeaustraat due east. Hotel V Fizeaustraat (*see page 40*) is housed in a former office block designed by modernist architect Piet Zanstra. Hotel V Nesplein is in the theatre district; upon entering you're welcomed by a chandelier that previously hung in a 1940s French performance space.

Hospitality is in Tom's blood. His grandmother ran a boarding house in the 1960s and his parents owned a small hotel in Amsterdam's Rivierenbuurt. Upon his mother's retirement in 1999, Tom and Mirjam left their careers in marketing and finance to transform the spot into one of Amsterdam's first and finest independent hotels. "Back then, attention paid to design was equated with high costs but we wanted to make it accessible for everyone to enjoy," says Mirjam. Over the past 20 years, Hotel V has opened three more (and sold the first) and have gone on to add two restaurants (both called The Lobby). Not bad for a pair of hospitality-school rejects.

The Espinosas' top tips

1. Do it because you love it: If you're only in it for the money, don't do it. You have to love making guests happy, otherwise this industry won't sustain you emotionally in the long run.

2. Stay up-to-date: Constantly renewing is important for long-term success.

3. Don't take half measures: Do everything with passion, soul and complete devotion.

Kamal Mouzawak & Rabih Kayrouz

The duo behind Beit Douma are peppering Lebanon with places to stay.

It felt like a natural step for fashion designer Rabih Kayrouz and food campaigner Kamal Mouzawak (*pictured*) to open a guesthouse in the Lebanese mountain village of Douma. "We didn't start it as a business. It was more a desire to build a home and share it," says Kayrouz, who launched his eponymous womenswear label in 1997. "After hosting friends for more than 10 years, we decided to open a home in a professional capacity."

After a long search, the pair settled on a 19th-century stone house 1,100 metres up in the Batroun Mountains. In just three months, the duo renovated and then opened Beit Douma. "It was about replicating our home and our way of life," says Mouzawak, a key player in Beirut's food scene with market Souk el Tayeb and farm-to-table restaurant Tawlet.

By early 2018, the duo's joint business, Beit, consisted of four guesthouses across the country. But they learned to extend the lead-up to opening, spending more time on developing the personality of each property. Every inch is carefully conceived, without ever feeling contrived. You'll never see a fancily made bed, logos on the towels or a kettle and sachet of instant coffee in your room. "Do you have that stuff in your own home?" asks Mouzawak. "The answer is 'no'. We want our *beits* to remind you of your grandmother's house."

Mouzawak and Kayrouz's top tips

1. Know what you're in for: Just because people like cooking it doesn't mean they should open a restaurant. The same applies to opening a B&B. You have to have a lot of perseverance.

2. Design is important: Style to both your taste and to allow the property to feel in harmony with the surroundings.

3. Generosity is key: Like and know how to host and show generosity to your guests.

Alessandro Catenacci

The impresario behind the Nobis Hospitality Group used Stockholm as a springboard for expansion.

"You can teach a monkey to make a reservation on the internet but you can't teach a person how to take care of people – and this is what it's all about," says Alessandro Catenacci, with good humour. "That's why we often employ people who have never worked in the industry before."

"Sandro", as he's known, is as comfortable with the world of restaurants as any other and for years didn't imagine he'd be involved in hotels. Having learned about hospitality from his chef-father (with whom he opened his first restaurant), he went on to import restaurant machinery from Italy to Sweden. It was during this time that he first considered opening a hotel but still some while before he committed. "This was 1982," he says. "My first hotel came in 2000."

Today his properties include Miss Clara Hotel, Nobis Hotel and Hotel Skeppsholmen in Stockholm, as well as a second Nobis that opened in Copenhagen in 2017 (*see page 31*). He also plans to open two hotels in Palma and another in Stockholm.

"When the internet came, work in the hotel industry totally changed: it opened up the world. It would have been impossible for me to do what I do 25 or 30 years ago. We now have the opportunity to reach out to guests and our guests in turn have the opportunity to find what suits them," he says. "For us the major challenge is just to deliver what we do every day."

Catenacci's top tips

1. Be keen: I still say that we're very enthusiastic amateurs. But enthusiasm is a strength.

2. Don't let it go to your head: Be humble and take your work seriously.

3. Don't out-price your punters: You'll be excluding a lot of people. I want to create a kind of club.

Sharan Pasricha

The founder of London's Ennismore and owner of The Hoxton talks about creating a hotel for the community.

"I've always been a very curious traveller and have loved visiting interesting cities and neighbourhoods," says Sharan Pasricha, founder of hospitality developer Ennismore. "I've been a closet hotelier for most of my life; it combines my passions for eating, drinking and sleeping." In 2012 the company took over The Hoxton in Shoreditch and turned it into an international brand. It has since expanded with openings in Paris (*see page 67*), Amsterdam and the US.

"When we came across The Hoxton there was something exciting about the way it stood out in a crowded marketplace. We kept the name but changed many things," says Pasricha, who spent a year working in the back office to learn about the hospitality business. "Hotels haven't innovated at the same pace as other industries," he adds. "I wanted to bring people from other industries to challenge the status quo. So we assembled a team with backgrounds from fashion to design to help build the brand."

It was important for The Hoxton to embrace the neighbourhood and be a place for visitors and residents alike. The lobby was turned into a lounge and meeting place, a cultural calendar was put in place and The Apartment was designed as an events space. "We like what Airbnb has done in terms of disrupting the industry," says Pasricha. "In a way we're more akin to Airbnb than a traditional hotel because The Hoxton is about seeing the city through a local lens."

Pasricha's top tips

1. Tell a story: You need a purpose to distinguish yourself from the other places out there.

2. Don't be trendy: The words "on trend" and "cool" are banned from our office. Trends fade. For us it's about comfort. We want to be a great place to eat, drink and sleep.

3. Be neighbourly: Success is not always defined by occupancy but more by how we engage with locals and how much the community engages in our spaces and at our events.

Ian Schrager

How New York's legendary club owner went on to become New York's legendary hotelier.

A New York accent in New York is rare these days, being the global city that it is with a constant hum of arrivals and departures. But the Brooklyn comes tumbling out of Ian Schrager's mouth almost before he starts to talk. Back in the 1970s, when the city was teetering on the edge of bankruptcy and dealing with a wealth of social ills, it was Schrager and his business partner Steve Rubell who brought glamour, fun and celebrity to what would probably become the most famous nightclub in the world, the short-lived but legendary Studio 54.

After dabbling in another nightclub called Palladium, Schrager and Rubell found a buyer for Studio 54. Part of the deal was done in promissory notes but when the buyer ended up not being able to pay they accepted his interests in a hotel instead. From there, Schrager hasn't looked back. His first hotel, Morgans Hotel, was in his hometown. It was "subversive and broke the status quo", just like the nightclubs he'd been behind.

Schrager's idea was to think about design, mood and food in ways that hadn't been combined before and, for many, this model was the archetype of the modern hotel. Schrager has gone on to work on nearly 50 hotels, including a larger-scale project with Marriott called Edition and his own Public brand. There are few signs he's getting bored. "I still have things I want to say and do," he says, with that unmistakable Brooklyn twang.

Schrager's top tips

1. Service is key: If you can make people feel comfortable and welcome then everything else follows.

2. It's all about an idea: Think of the direction you want to go in and the ethos of the hotel – and stay true to it.

3. Luxury has changed: It's now for everyone. That's an important idea: hoteliers taking luxury and democratising it.

Sigurlaug Sverrisdóttir

The Ion Adventure Hotel, Iceland, may be in the middle of nowhere but it's become a desirable destination.

Opening a hotel was far from Sigurlaug Sverrisdóttir's mind when she was living in Switzerland and travelling the world as a flight attendant. Having left her native Iceland after the financial crisis, she was lured back in 2011 by the thought of buying a summer house for her family. Instead of a small cottage, she ended up touring the former staff quarters of a geothermal plant – a disused building close to the springs that still provide most of Reykjavík's hot-water supply. The austere concrete structure was no good for a second home but it occurred to her that it could make for a stunning hotel.

"A lot of people thought we were crazy. Why open a hotel in the middle of nowhere?" says Sverrisdóttir. "But we went for it anyway." She, her husband and an investor focused on how many rooms they would need to make the hotel profitable. The figure they landed on was 44, which called for an extension of the original structure. To safeguard the building from earthquakes, the architects placed it on stilts, giving it an even more breathtaking and otherworldly form.

Sverrisdóttir opened a second hotel in 2017 near the centre of Reykjavík to take advantage of Iceland's booming tourist numbers. Both locations rely heavily on Icelandic design and produce. "Business-wise it's important to have a concept," says Sverrisdóttir. "People are looking for experiences. It's like a theatre."

Sverrisdóttir's top tips

1. Ignorance is bliss: If I'd known everything opening a hotel would entail, I might not have started. You have to take a chance, though, and follow your own ideas.

2. Bigger is better: Try not to go below 50 rooms. It's very costly to build a hotel in the middle of nowhere.

3. Trust your instincts: Building our bar was the best decision we made, even if it was very expensive. It's the "wow" factor of the building.

1. École hôtelière de Lausanne

Lausanne, Switzerland

"Man-buns are not accepted," says a poster in the hallway next to a full-length mirror that reads, "You never get a second chance to make a first impression." "Just this morning I had to send a girl home because she wasn't dressed appropriately," says Christophe Laurent, the so-called values ambassador at the oldest hotel school in the world, as he tucks a red card back into his pressed suit pocket like a forceful football referee. "People may criticise, or say that our dress code is boring and old-fashioned, but we are preparing our students for the best."

The strict dress code is only a taste of the professionalism that's ingrained in the students at École hôtelière de Lausanne (EHL). EHL has been an outpost of Swiss hospitality since 1893, when Jacques Tschumi opened the school to cater to Switzerland's newly blossoming tourism industry.

The first classes were taught at Hôtel d'Angleterre on the banks of Lake Geneva. Since 1975, the campus has been located among rolling hills in Le Chalet-à-Gobet, a few kilometres north of Lausanne proper. When MONOCLE visits it's only the third day of term and already students in tall toques are busy folding delicate pastries, setting tables at the school's restaurant and serving coffees at the M Bar, the beating heart of the campus. One such cappuccino is carefully placed in front of Michel Rochat, EHL's CEO, as he talks.

"I never planned on becoming CEO," says Rochat, sporting a pale-pink tie, as he takes a seat in the lobby. "I was a member of the board and we had a discussion about the future of the institution. I was the only one to explain that expansion was the way to go. The others had a pretty Swiss attitude: they said, 'the best chocolate comes in small boxes.' I said, 'no, you have to go out, tear down the walls and expand.'" That attitude got him the job. "We teach students to be open-minded, to think out of the box. You have to be open to bring people together and our facilities reflect what we teach," he says, as he scans the spacious hall with close attention.

With the hospitality market growing by 5 per cent a year, it's natural that EHL, which has some 2,800 students from 119 countries, is expanding too. And not only in Lausanne; a satellite school

in Asia is in the works, as are further online courses. "I want to be part of the next development of disruption in higher education," says Rochat. "My dream is to have no more exams."

No more exams – that would also be a wish fulfilled for Scott Risk, who is in his final year at EHL. As always, he's dressed in a tailored suit with a pocket square and polished dress shoes. As part of his bachelor's degree in hospitality management he has interned at Claridge's in London and is about to take on his final challenge – the Student Business Project, where students become junior consultants, liaising with clients and partners ranging from LVMH to the Metro Group.

"Initially I wanted to go into medicine. Helping people, that was what interested me," he says. "Eventually I decided to study hospitality as I would rather help people on a more personal level." About half of the students remain in the traditional hospitality sector after graduation. Risk isn't yet sure whether he'll be one of them but he's certain of one thing: "Every city in the world is home to a hotel managed by EHL alumni so we have an unparalleled network."

The beauty of the bilingual French and English bachelor's programme is that it prepares students for a career in almost any sector that values customer experience. More than 95 per cent of graduates find themselves employed within six months of leaving school.

Looking around EHL's classrooms, including the Peter Michael wine-tasting lab and the Berceau des Sens restaurant, it's clear that students here are taught from the ground up. They start out chopping onions and by the end of their studies they're conversing in at least four languages and have the understanding to manage and establish the hotels of the future.
ehl.edu

School in numbers

Founded: 1893

Number of students: 2,800

Length and cost of bachelor programme: Course takes four years and costs about CHF160,000 (more than €135,000); discounts are available for Swiss nationals. Further courses include a masterclass in culinary arts, an executive MBA, the master of science in hospitality business and an executive MBA in hospitality

Graduates who secure a job within six months: 95 per cent

Alumni network: 25,000 alumni in 120 countries

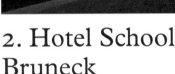

2. Hotel School Bruneck

Bruneck, Italy

The sight of the simple multiplication problem (7 × 3) scrawled on a whiteboard normally wouldn't faze a 15-year-old but the pupils in Sabine Putz's class are on edge during their morning exercise. Putz is one of the instructors at Hotel School Bruneck in Italy's South Tyrol and the figures on the board refer to the seven tables of three she's asking her class to set for a three-course menu.

Her pupils pick out the correct cutlery to match the menu, checking that the utensils align with the bottom rim of each plate and sit an inch from the table's edge. Dressed in dark trousers and white shirts, with the boys in ties, students move with an air not unlike waiters at a top London restaurant. "From day one we want them to be accustomed to the real world of hospitality," says Putz. "Wearing a uniform should be second nature."

Funded by the government of South Tyrol, teaching facilities are five-star. The classroom restaurant has Hans J Wegner-designed chairs, teaching kitchens have top-of-the-line convection ovens and professors conducting language courses use interactive touchscreen displays in place of chalkboards. Instructors are veterans, many having worked in high-end restaurants and on front desks from Singapore to New York. "Tourism is the backbone of our economy, so we need to prepare the next generation as best we can," says school co-ordinator Marlene Kranebitter.

Enrolment is made up almost entirely of students from the surrounding Puster Valley; many hail from families running hotels, restaurants or farmhouse B&Bs. Unlike most hotel schools in Italy, pupils don't specialise in one discipline. Studies take up to five years and graduates leave with the equivalent of a high-school diploma. Pupils are expected to work three summers, interning in hotels. In the first summer they wait tables, in the second they cook and in the third they man the reception desk.

"We want well-rounded trainees who can troubleshoot any situation," says instructor Andrea Bovo. "Many end up taking over the family business." In Bovo's class, students from the primarily German-speaking region polish their Italian, while French and English are also on the curriculum. Though many are still under

legal drinking age, there are bartending workshops and sommelier courses. "We may not be able to drink but we need to get the basics right," says a 16-year-old student.

In the pristine kitchens overseen by chef Konrad Gartner, the adolescents knead dough, grate cheese and dice vegetables. For today's menu, Gartner has them making Tyrolean *knödel* (dumplings) with beetroot followed by tiramisu and a mocha gelato in a sweet pesto sauce. "We expose them to traditional cuisine as well as Mediterranean and international food," says Gartner. "Hollandaise sauce, sushi: they learn a bit of everything because travellers coming to this region expect to eat well."
landeshotelfachschule-bruneck.jimdo.com

School in numbers

Founded: 2013

Number of students: About 525

Budget: Authorities spent €26m to erect the five-storey school building and adjacent dormitory, which also has a cafeteria; €2.6m of that was spent on furnishings, including Carl Hansen & Søn and Thonet furniture

Annual food budget of school kitchen: €175,000

3. The Japan Hotel School

Tokyo

At the Japan Hotel School in Tokyo, students are learning to take an order, proffer a menu, lean in at just the right angle and pour a glass of wine. With their bow ties, white shirts and black waistcoats, they look the part. It's a lively class with plenty of missteps and a fair few giggles. The stumbling block for most is successfully opening a bottle of wine graciously with a waiter's corkscrew.

Not all of them manage. But the instructor Shinji Ueno, a graduate of the school, guides the students and corrects their mistakes with good humour. This classroom has been decorated to suggest a smart restaurant; another has a reception desk. But the pièce de résistance is a hotel room complete with bathroom and amenities. "We show this to high-school students who are deciding on their career path," says Tsutomu Ishizuka (*pictured, above centre*), the school's president. "This room seals the deal."

Founded by the Prince hotel chain in 1971, the nation's only dedicated hotel training school became known as the Japan Hotel School in 1976. At this time, it was put under the auspices of the Ministry of Transportation, just as the government decided it was time to develop Japan's hotel industry. Since 2009 the school has been overseen by the city authorities. Today, with the government determined to attract 40 million visitors a year, trained hotel workers are more in demand than ever.

At ¥1.6m (€12,100) a year for tuition, the school isn't cheap, but it has such strong connections to the hotel industry that most students secure a job before graduation, almost all in Japan. There are classes on a range of subjects, from languages to French wine and cutlery placement. Students study for two years but six months of that is spent doing paid internships at some of the top hotels in Tokyo. "Of course we already have a culture of Japanese *omotenashi* [hospitality]," says Mansaku Nakayama, who manages the education programme. "But that only takes you so far. It's important to do the fieldwork to get a more international perspective."

According to school president Ishizuka, hotel management education at a senior level is lacking

in Japan, where people have traditionally learned on the job. And that isn't necessarily a bad thing. "I've travelled to more than 40 countries to look at hotels around the world and the level of Japanese service is very high. Japanese hotel staff really care," says Ishizuka. "We have requests from universities in Asia to go and teach them 'the Japanese way' but you cannot teach these things in a short time. You have to do it."

At the end of their course students sit a series of proficiency tests and emerge ready to start careers. "I was always interested in hospitality," says Ryoji Kato, a 20-year-old graduate from Kanagawa. "I want to aim for the very top and for me that's the Imperial Hotel, Tokyo." *jhs.ac.jp*

School in numbers

Founded: 1971

Number of students: 845 (520 on the main hotel course; the rest are shared between the bridal course and the English-language course)

Length and price of the course: Two years; ¥1.6m (€12,100) a year

Number of graduates who leave with a job: 100 per cent

合った場合も、知らん顔をするのでは

お辞儀の仕方

4. Cornell School of Hotel Administration

Ithaca, USA

Four hours northwest of New York, amid the natural gorges of Ithaca, you'll find the US's finest hotel school. One of Cornell University's seven colleges, the School of Hotel Administration (SHA) has been the gold standard for hospitality since 1922. The school guides students through every facet of how to run a stellar hospitality firm.

"We're training tomorrow's industry leaders," says Hotel School dean Kate Walsh (*pictured*). That's hard to deny with alumni including Drew Nieporent (the man behind New York's Myriad Restaurant Group) and Harris Rosen (CEO of the eponymous resort company). "We view ourselves as the ecosystem of the hospitality industry because our graduates really are at senior leadership roles throughout the industry. They're part of what we call our 'secret sauce'."

Alumni are always a presence at SHA and its 960 undergraduate students are invited to weekly lectures held by former students, who are flown in to share their own experiences and pitfalls – and, of course, to help with post-graduation jobs.

Students must complete 800 hours in the industry before graduating, with some working at the Statler, the school's own on-site, 153-room hotel. "I don't know of any other 20-year-old who can say they've managed a hotel," says student and hotel manager Noella Moon.

One thing you hear often from "hotelies", as the students call themselves, is how the college is focused on all aspects of hospitality. "These courses may be focused on one industry but there are always transferable skills," says senior Kayti Stanley. "I know that no matter where I am in the world, there is always a 'hotelie' nearby."
sha.cornell.edu

School in numbers

Founded: 1922

Number of students: 960 undergraduates

Length and price of the bachelor's programme: The course takes four years and costs about $220,000

Number of graduates who leave with a job: 85 per cent upon graduation and 96 per cent within six months of graduation

Learning on the job

Hotel schools aren't the only route into the business and neither is going it alone.

Training schemes remain a popular and rigorous introduction through which many of the industry's movers and shakers have moved and shaken. The world's largest hotel groups know how lucrative such schemes can be and many offer prestigious programmes for graduates.

The Voyage scheme, for one, is a 12 to 18-month leadership development programme led by the Marriott Group, which runs some 6,500 properties across 127 countries. The course lets applicants work across various departments – from housekeeping to bartending – at one of the brand's many properties, including the Ritz-Carlton, Edition and W Hotels. Similar schemes are available at Mandarin Oriental and Hyatt. Each offers an opportunity for graduates to get a foot in the door at an international hotel brand.

While the big players require applicants to have a bachelor's degree, small to mid-sized hotels offer more flexibility. One of them is the Hotel Bachmair Weissach (*see page 120*), an independent hotel in the Tegernsee Valley just outside Munich. As a veteran in the business, its owner and CEO Korbinian Kohler shares his insights about on-the-job learning and what it takes to make it in the hospitality industry.

Q&A
Korbinian Kohler, CEO of the Bachmair Weissach, Tegernsee, Germany

Q: Is it necessary to attend a hotel school or can you learn on the job just as well?
KK: The dual curriculum is the best of both worlds. By combining a traditional training scheme with an academic course, you can earn a bachelor's degree while gaining the practical experience that's so important in the hospitality industry. For businesses, these graduates are particularly attractive because they are academically and professionally further along than those who would join a company straight out of school.

But traditional apprenticeships are still important in the hotel sector, especially in F&B. Our industry is very hands-on.

Q: How many apprenticeships does the Bachmair Weissach offer?
KK: We fluctuate between 30 and 40 trainees. Apprenticeships have always played a role at our establishment but it was only about five years ago that we decided to address the subject in a way that's new and different.

Q: What sets the apprenticeship programme apart?
KK: All trainees receive an in-house month-long introductory course where they get to know the establishment and the Tegernsee Valley, and are taught etiquette and basic hospitality and service skills. After one month an apprentice at the Bachmair Weissach is, we feel, at the same level as a trainee who's spent a year pitching in elsewhere. Once a year we take all our apprentices on a trip abroad. One year we visited Vienna, the year before we toured the top hotels in London. We also reward good grades with financial bonuses. Those who score top marks receive an extra €3,500 a year.

Q: Is it a good time to be in the industry?
KK: First, the career prospects are better than ever before. If you're really engaged and have a strong theoretical as well as practical education you'll go far. Second, the industry is currently reinventing itself. New hotel concepts are cropping up everywhere, helped along by the personalisation that digitalisation allows. The hotel business will continue to grow.

Q: What do you look for in applicants?
KK: A high school diploma is ideal but it's not a hard and fast rule. We value a person for their personality and drive, attentiveness and curiosity.

Q: What should you take into consideration before going into the hospitality industry?
KK: A career in the hotel business demands endurance. You need to be passionate about what you do. It's a tough and stressful business, with long working hours, but if you like being part of a team and enjoy making others happy there's nothing more beautiful in the world.
bachmair-weissach.com

Part 3:

Here to stay

3.

Why good hotels will stand the test of time

Despite app-based apartment sharing, we at MONOCLE wholeheartedly believe that hotels still have the capacity to transport guests, transform neighbourhoods and thrive. Here we dispense a few home truths from writers and respondents on subjects from staging an affair to rethinking the motel. Plus what the sunlounger saw.

We also meet a few colourful characters whose lives have unfolded in these storied buildings, from an octogenarian pool attendant in France to the scion of one of Hong Kong's biggest and best groups. We tell a few tales of where hotels have provided the stage for everything from revolutions and wars to literary movements, and tour three hotels that have survived admirably and undimmed despite a few setbacks.

Plus we sound a cautionary call to arms against renovating (and ruining) great hotels for the sake of novelty. Sometimes survival in a tough market is about sticking to your guns and doing things differently instead of following the pack and folding under the pressure.

I.
How to design a hotel

by *William Brian Smith*

Designers are often quizzed for secrets: easy dos and don'ts. My answer is usually disappointing. "It depends," I'll utter with a shrug. Magazines, newspapers and blogs announce trends with buzzwords or hastily written headlines: "Three ways to use baby pink"; "Seven must-haves to make a space feel organic". I typically dismiss such trends as empty but occasionally these catchphrases can help demystify or democratise design. I've been given a little hope by the increased use of one word: "authentic". Unlike prescriptive trends advocating a particular pink or labelling a tumbledown hotel "shabby chic", authenticity encourages us to pick our brains, not just a colour.

In the early 1900s, the Russian actor Konstantin Stanislavski had the idea to introduce reality into theatre, a technique that later evolved into method acting. He noticed that audiences weren't connecting with theatre because the acting felt hokey. Schools were training actors to mimic emotions rather than feel them. Sad? Frown. Angry? Shake a fist.

Stanislavski implored actors to dream up detailed narratives about their character's life and to ask themselves why the character is doing what they're doing. Armed with a deeper understanding of their character, actors began realistically capturing subtlety and better portraying the authenticity of the role. This philosophy always chimed with my understanding of design. It also prompted a question: how can details from thoughtfully constructed stories convincingly connect guests to the life of a hotel? There are, it turns out, lots of ways to do it but for now I'll share two.

The hotels we create at Studio Tack use signals in the form of art, objects or signage, which elaborate on and tell the hotel's story. They should reinforce the design story but never retell it. If you're designing a hotel in Brooklyn, avoid art and signage that repeats the borough's name or murals of its famous bridge: they'll feel lazy. Even the least observant guests already know where they are before they step into your lobby.

Instead, try subtler prompts to tell the city's story: a pop-up magazine kiosk with the best of the city's print; a florist flogging locally grown blooms; a coffee shop from a nearby roaster-done-good. These experiences relate directly to a positive story about entrepreneurship and the city beyond the hotel's door. In effect, we create vignettes of miniature cities within our hotels, hinting at what's best about the city as a whole: abundance of choice, accessibility and possibility.

Secondly I'd suggest that designers and hoteliers consider touch points: doorknobs, switches, taps and curtains. Anything guests can grip should send a message, feel sturdy and be forged from the best materials your budget will stretch to. The goal is for the guest literally (and figuratively) to connect with the design. Individually, these details are minor, simple upgrades but, when applied throughout, they make a big difference.

Think about the light switch as the first line of the room's story: a wobbly, cheap one is the equivalent of a spelling mistake in the first sentence. The knurled knob of an engineered dimmer tells a guest you've got the grammar right and they'll be ready to hear more of your story. Curtains in flax linen and bronze drawer handles wrapped in vegetable-tanned leather show commitment to the narrative's details.

Next time you're at a hotel, ask yourself what story it's telling, whether you're thinking about it or not, whether it's authentic or otherwise. The walls are talking. The important question is, do you believe them?

About the writer: *William Brian Smith is a partner at interior-design firm Studio Tack.*

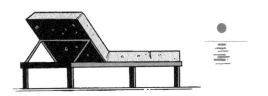

2.
A day in the life of a sunlounger

by *Saul Taylor*

Not all sunloungers are created equal. Some of us come pre-formed in bright white plastic and leave fleshy grooves in pink calves; some of us have faded wooden slats and sit sad and idle as the seasons batter our dignity. Then there are those of us born into the Kettal family in the little Catalan town of Bellvei. We are destined for greater things and grace the well-kept lawns and decks of the Mediterranean's more elegant hotels.

05.30: Daybreak. We can be found pointing pool-ward in a chevron formation, awoken by that rare species of early bird, the power swimmer, who drops his towel at our feet, dives into the still expanse to embark upon 30 heart-starting laps, then leaves without a trace before breakfast. By now, crisp white towels have miraculously appeared on our nether regions while the bar service is announced by quiet clinks behind closed shutters.

08.00: The day's sun-seekers arrive, brushing croissant flakes from their mouths in the rush to bag the best spot. We brace ourselves for impact – please, not the German with the ample arse and chronic skin condition again! The water, still chilly from the night before, elicits sharp breaths and we're soaked as guests shriek with cries of joy in anticipation of the day ahead.

08.30: Folded towels are shaken open and someone creaks my neck awkwardly at 45 degrees while unceremoniously tumbling books, magazines and newspapers onto me. Clothes come off, suntan lotion is slopped on and the first refreshments are ordered in one hurried summer gesture.

10.30: The familiar moan of a young couple who've over-imbibed the previous evening rings a little too loudly across the calm. They plonk themselves heavily onto two of my poor compadres, adopting the foetal position to avoid the glare of the sun. Everyone else makes their first manoeuvre of the day, lifting us aloft and positioning our frames directly into the path of the solar arc.

13.00: Lunch menus are distributed and entire families draped in damp towels huddle around small tables filled with club sandwiches while we groan under the weight of their backsides. Stuffed and satisfied, some seek the solace of a siesta in their room while others stay with us to doze in the light of the overhanging pines, only to be awoken by the cries and flirtatious splashing of the young couple (they've shaken off their hangover with a long drink or two).

16.30: A sudden change in the afternoon light, from squint-inducing white to warm yellow, heralds cocktail hour. The deep-tanned bar staff in navy polos and starched white shorts dart effortlessly from lounger to lounger with goblets of fizzing gin and tumblers of ruddy aperitivi. When the sun disappears behind the main building and the warming effects of the alcohol begin to subside, there's a sad exodus of guests who bundle up their things and desert us for the balmy after-sun of their rooms.

01.15: The young couple comes creeping down for a spot of forbidden skinny-dipping and we're left with the realisation that, much like loungers, not all men are created equal.

About the writer: *Saul Taylor isn't a sunlounger. Instead, he's a contributing editor at Monocle.*

3.
The rules of the ryokan

by *Fiona Wilson*

A night in a proper Japanese ryokan (inn) is unlike any other hotel experience – and all the better for it. It's worth remembering that ryokan are the product of centuries of tradition; asking for services you'd find at a generic hotel would miss the point entirely. Here are a few tips to ensure you make the most of this unique experience.

1. Check-in is unlikely to be earlier than 15.00 so don't turn up in the morning. And don't hang around when it comes to departure time; most guests leave soon after breakfast.

2. On arrival you'll be expected to remove your shoes as soon as you cross the threshold; the ryokan is a private space and relaxation begins by saying sayonara to your shoes and switching to slippers. Spiked heels and muddy boots would also wreck the tatami mats that cover the floor. You'll be greeted by the manager, known as an *okami* – usually a no-nonsense woman in a kimono who is also likely to be a member of the family that owns the place. A room attendant (*nakai-san*) will show you to your room.

3. It's obvious to those who know but often startling to newcomers: your room will be empty apart from a low table and a couple of legless chairs. Don't bother looking for the beds, they're folded up in cupboards behind the sliding doors.

4. Don't look for the ensuite bathroom either – while your room is likely to have a lavatory (with a heated seat), private bathrooms don't feature in traditional ryokan; instead, you'll bathe in a shared bath. If you're lucky enough to be staying somewhere mountainous this could also involve a soak in a mineral-rich outdoor hot spring bath, known as a *rotenburo*.

5. Unless you're planning to head out of the inn (and Japanese guests wouldn't – they're here to relax), change into ryokan garb: a starched full-length cotton *yukata* robe, which will probably be folded in a basket in your room. If it's cold, there will be an extra jacket to wear on top; this is acceptable wear throughout the ryokan, including at mealtimes.

6. Bathing in Japan can be a baffling experience for novices. The rules, however, are simple. On no account wear swimming costumes or trunks in a Japanese bath, indoor or out; before you enter the steamy bathroom, remove your *yukata* and put it in the basket that will be laid out in an anteroom (you can always use the postage stamp-sized towel supplied to maintain your modesty). Head to the row of thigh-high showers at the side of the bath and sit on one of the low stools – you don't go near a Japanese bath until you've showered and rinsed thoroughly. And the shower isn't supposed to be a quick spritz either; get stuck in with the soap and shampoo that will be next to the shower. Only then should you go to the water. The bath is for relaxation, not washing.

7. After a bath, you'll go for what's likely to be an early dinner, which will be served on the table back in your room. Dinner is included in the cost, which can explain the spectacular prices of top ryokan. Depending on the quality of the inn, it will be a long affair, involving many courses served in succession. Don't expect to turn up at 21.00 and ask for

dinner; ryokan run like clockwork and 19.30 would be late for a meal.

8. Once dinner is over, retreat for another bath while the beds are made up. When you re-enter your room it will be transformed – lights low and futon mattresses laid out, with fluffy quilts and rice-filled pillows. Don't be alarmed by the prospect of sleeping on the floor. A combination of the hot *onsen* water, the saké served at dinner and the comfortable set-up leads to most guests having the best night's sleep they can remember.

9. In the morning, breakfast may be served in a public room. For Japanese guests, it will comprise grilled fish, *natto* (fermented soy), sharp *umeboshi* (pickled plums) and rice. The western option will likely be white toast with an egg, salad and a cup of coffee; don't make requests for granola and soy milk.

10. Remember that prices quoted are generally per person, not per room. Also, don't book for a whole week, particularly in a city. For most Japanese, one night at a ryokan does the trick.

About the writer: *Fiona Wilson is a ryokan regular and Monocle's Tokyo bureau chief.*

4.
How to stage an affair

by *Robert Bound*

Slip in the key card and feel the release. What is it about hotels? I see you in the bar and I come over, sit next to you and say, "Hi". I wouldn't normally but I do. And you say it, too, right back, after a beat. No, two. I make a play of guessing what you might like to drink; narrow my eyes and purse my lips like a smile but it isn't a smile, not yet, rather a suggestion that one might come. You bite your lip, look away and read aloud the label on a bottle behind the bar and say, "Yes, two". And let's not play games. You're under low lamplight in a hotel bar at 21.00 pretending to have a late dinner but we both know you're not here for the food.

What is it about hotels? Managers and maître d's know. They've noticed that woman on a week-long business trip – whose husband sent flowers to the hotel on their anniversary – drop her key into the breast pocket of a man who's just added a night to his stay. Perhaps the man thought she'd say no. Or perhaps he knew she'd say yes but would still rather do the sleeping part on his own. And, probably, so would she. And you?

When you wake up with someone for the first time and know it's the last, you stretch, smile, kiss them and leave. Back in your own room, you gaze at the bathroom mirror and smile through the steam, maybe sing in the shower. No need for a swim this morning; your back aches and you're happy. You just hope the bite marks fade on the plane. The receptionist twinkles: "We hope your stay was a happy one, sir." She knows. It had been late when she brought up the silver tray with the ice bucket, vodka, limes and glasses. Yes, two.

What is it about hotels? Are you alone in feeling, as you sit in these rooms, that tonight may be the last night on Earth? In feeling you'd be a fool, before the world stops spinning – say, tomorrow at 10.00 – not to go for a drink at the bar with a folded newspaper and an open disposition? I bet it's not just you who feels that, who knows that if hotels are theatre and romance then nights like these, stolen out of a script unwritten, are like little operas. The stories are improbable, the acting regretful but the best parts, those arias that swirl from nowhere, are deep in you somewhere. You'll smile again in plenty more bathroom mirrors. Stay another night? No, two.

About the writer: *Robert Bound is a paragon of fidelity and Culture editor at Monocle.*

5.
The housemaid's tale

by *Kimberly Bradley*

In his essay "Shipping Out", penned on a Caribbean cruise, the late writer David Foster Wallace captures something of the oddity of having someone look after you without ever meeting them. He develops a "searing crush" on an elusive cabin stewardess called Petra and touchingly tries to fathom how she keeps his cabin so pristine. His obsession deepens as he pops out for short periods, darts around corners and waits, fruitlessly, for Petra to appear in plain sight. He muses on his invisible benefactor as "a figure of magical and abiding charm, and well worth a postcard all her own".

My own Petra moment came at the Mandarin Oriental in New York. Every time I left my room – even for half an hour – something small would be adjusted in my absence: toiletries tweaked, bed turned down, a delicate blossom placed on the pillow. How did he or she know I wasn't there? I channelled Wallace and began bluffing, leaving the room for shorter intervals and moving the little bed-rug a few inches out of place. Sure enough, on my return, the rug had been returned to its intended position. Like Wallace, I never did catch anyone in the act of fixing it but it did make me wonder about these mysterious visitors who so painstakingly perfected my stay.

Years later, I had the pleasure of talking to a lady called Claudia, the head of housekeeping at a starry ski hotel in Vorarlberg, Austria. A known haunt for royals and celebrities, it's also where I finally learned how the best housekeepers transform a shambolic room into a chamber literally fit for a king.

"We watch for when people leave but mostly we listen," said Claudia. "You can hear when the door falls shut." In her hotel, the housekeepers hover in a small, secret office on each floor, waiting for guests to scuttle off and springing into action when they're safely out of sight. Claudia and her staff clean 50 rooms every day, all day.

Some of their work is anticipation. Regulars leave feedback about how they want their rooms and their predilections are stored on a database. "Two regular guests have customised mattresses," said Claudia. "Some want four pillows, some want seven and some want a feather bed."

A few cunning (or perhaps immeasurably bored) guests, like Wallace, have tried to trick Claudia and her team. "Some leave, say, a coin in a strange place, to see what happens to it," she said. "I used to be a nurse in surgery, so I'm extremely conscious of cleanliness, even sterility. I can see everything. So I always find things like this. I check every single room before I approve it and every room in the building must be approved every day."

The inspection involves looking under beds and toilets, examining everything from the sewing kit to the remote control. Tiny items are cleaned individually with cotton swabs. Cleaning supplies are kept as natural as possible (bleach? Heaven forbid), even if every once in a while there's a bigger spill requiring more stringent measures. Crucially, said Claudia, keeping things clean is about speed: a guest returning to the room mid-sweep, she insists, is awkward for everyone (unless for you, like Wallace, this is the ultimate victory).

What does Claudia like most about her work? "I like going home at night and knowing we've done a good job. I like it when the room looks beautiful, smells good and people are happy." Whether or not we ever meet our elusive housekeepers, staying in a clean, fragrant and cared-for room is a mark of the most enduring luxury. It's a simple sentiment and a rather sweet one – something to mull over any time you pluck a chocolate from your pillow or plunge under the clean covers of an immaculately made bed.

About the writer: *Kimberly Bradley is a tidy hotel guest and Monocle's Vienna correspondent.*

6.
Hotels and high drama

by *Luke Barr*

My first job when I moved to New York was at the Royalton, the Ian Schrager (*see page 174*) hotel on 44th Street, designed by Philippe Starck. I'd never heard of Schrager or Starck or the Royalton – I was a kid, I knew nothing. But when I walked into the lobby in 1994, I felt all the mysterious glamour of New York concentrated in a single room. It was like walking onto a film set.

Long, narrow, dark-blue carpet ran from the front doors back to the restaurant. It was lit with spotlights, like a fashion-show runway. All eyes were on you, both because of the lighting and because of the architecture, which set that walkway a few steps above the rest of the lobby, so guests would glance up to see who was making an entrance. Music played (Massive Attack or Sade) and odd, horn-shaped lights protruded from a mahogany wall like something out of a David Lynch film. Then there were the guests, impossibly beautiful and glamorous: Karl Lagerfeld surrounded by a menagerie of models and hangers-on; Tina Brown and Anna Wintour at their usual banquet tables; Tupac sinking a drink.

Working there, I could see backstage and understand how it all worked. We pored over the VIP list at the start of every shift, listing everyone of note and any special requests or warnings. There were frequent adjustments to the lighting and music, depending on the time of day. I remember the care, bordering on obsession, given to the seating arrangements in the restaurant, crowned by the brilliant cooking of an ambitious chef. It was an ultra-competent but never obsequious service we knew to provide.

A new genre of hotel and hotel lobby was being invented that harnessed the power of design to create a seductive fantasy. The Royalton was by no means New York's fanciest or most expensive hotel but it was the white-hot centre of social chic.

I thought about the Royalton recently, as I worked on my book, *Ritz & Escoffier: The Hotelier, the Chef, and the Rise of the Leisure Class*, which tells the story of the London Savoy and the Paris Ritz in the 1890s. Just like the Royalton 100 years later, the Savoy and Ritz redefined luxury and the cosmopolitanism at the end of the century.

Hotelier César Ritz and chef Auguste Escoffier set up the concept of hotel and restaurant as a theatre of food for anyone with money to foot the bill. The resulting openness, welcoming a never-before-seen mix of people from all parts of society, was a sign of the times, yes, but also an agent of change. The Savoy in 1890 was the first restaurant in London where respectable women came to entertain, where raffish US industrialists ate alongside princes, bohemian artists, writers, actors and opera stars.

César Ritz was intent on creating an abiding atmosphere of aristocratic wealth and glamour but with an unfussy look. He hated wallpaper, knick-knacks and anything that could gather dust. He loved flowers and put them everywhere. Every suite had a private bathroom, then unheard of in Europe. An orchestra played on weekend nights. Obsessed with lighting, he spent hours testing lampshades to find the perfect and most flattering apricot-peach hue and he meticulously kept track of all his guests' preferences: who needed a bottle of water on his bedside table and who required what kind of pillow.

As at the Royalton years later, Ritz ensured his lobbies were spaces of high drama – places to see and be seen in. At the Carlton hotel in London, he asked the builder to make an expensive late change by installing a flight of marble steps between the palm court and the restaurant, "so that ladies entering the dining room or leaving it may do so dramatically". Like Schrager and Starck, Ritz was thinking like a director and never forgetting that the hotel lobby was his set.

About the writer: *Luke Barr is a US-based author.*

7.
Fully booked – hotels in literature

by *Chloë Ashby*

When I asked Ian McEwan why he chose a hotel as a backdrop for his 2007 novel *On Chesil Beach*, he told me, "Hotels – whether they are gorgeous or grim – are a kind of blank slate on which the novelist finds a form of freedom. Isolated from the clutter, demands and familiarity of home, the guests, as characters in a novel, enact the drama of existence between sea and sky."

In *On Chesil Beach*, that drama is a single disastrous sex scene. The novel opens with newlyweds Edward and Florence arriving at a Georgian inn on the pebbly Dorset coast in the summer of 1962. He's raring to go, she's racked with nerves. They sit down to a dour and tasteless dinner – "this was not a good moment in the history of English cuisine" – before retreating to a tidy bedroom to consummate their fledgling marriage. "The bed squeaked mournfully when they moved, a reminder of other honeymoon couples who had passed through, all surely more adept than they were."

Hotels make for attractive literary backdrops because they present the opportunity for chance encounters, overheard conversations and, as in McEwan's novel, intimate and awkward interactions. As a guest settles into bed she might hear the creaking of a door, a service trolley rattling along the corridor – or, if she's an Agatha Christie character, the clatter of a bloodied knife falling on a stone floor. *Evil Under the Sun* is about a murder in a secluded hotel in south Devon. Who dunnit? The retired officer, the former teacher, the fashionable dressmaker? Christie gives us an eclectic cast in uncomfortably close quarters.

For Ali Smith, a hotel is "a gift of concise hierarchical social structure" with "people who can afford to stay there, people who can't and a workforce keeping the machine running". Her first novel, *Hotel World*, is set in The Global Hotel, a plush pad in a gritty northern English town. It tells the story of five very different

women from very different backgrounds, including melancholic receptionist Lise and Else, a homeless woman permanently parked outside the hotel's revolving front doors. Chapter one opens with the ghost of chambermaid Sara Wilby gliding through the sky: she narrates post-mortem, having plunged to her death in a silver-coloured dumbwaiter shaft. "Nobody could say I didn't have a classy passage out; the rooms very newly and tastefully furnished with good hard expensive beds and corniced high ceilings."

Herman Melville, too, brings opposites together in *Moby Dick*. Ishmael spends a night in the run-down Spouter-Inn in the whaling port of New Bedford, Massachusetts. With no free rooms, the landlord invites the good Christian to share a bed with the pagan harpooner Queequeg. After judging that the alternative, a wooden bench in the hotel bar, is a tad uncomfortable, Ishmael agrees and learns there's more to this "savage" than his shaved head and garish tattoos.

Naturally, not all hotels in literature are good advertisements for the industry – in fact, Stephen King's *The Shining* almost screams, "Don't check in!". Writer Jack Torrance takes an off-season caretaking gig at the secluded Overlook Hotel

in the Colorado Rockies, hoping to put pen to paper and resist reaching for a drink. You know the story: he and his family get snowed in, his psychic son Danny sees the hotel's ghastly past and Jack goes mad. The novel was inspired by King's own visit to The Stanley Hotel in Colorado (and his recovery from alcoholism).

John Irving's *The Hotel New Hampshire* is full of equally chaotic events but, on the whole, funnier and less frightening – featuring a bear called State O'Maine, a girl in a bear suit called Susie and a stuffed dog called Sorrow. It tells the story of the eccentric Berry family, who run a succession of three hotels, all called Hotel New Hampshire. The first is actually in New Hampshire, the second is in Vienna and the third is in Maine. Win Berry, meanwhile, is a dreamer whose "imagination was his own hotel".

McEwan ranks Thomas Mann's *Death in Venice* and *The Magic Mountain* as the greatest hotel novels. In the former, a love story of sorts plays out against the glistening backdrop of the Lido's Grand Hôtel des Bains – frequented by Hollywood darlings until it was shuttered in 2010. The latter is set in a tuberculosis sanatorium in the Swiss Alps – a semi-hotel for semi-invalids?

Hotels appeal to writers because they offer a blank canvas on which to project dreams, desires, fantasies and failings – and I suspect they appeal to guests for the same reason. When you check into a hotel, at least on holiday, you leave your worries at the door. A room is ready and waiting, perhaps like Edward's and Florence's with a four-poster bed "pure white and stretched startlingly smooth, as though by no human hand". Whether you're a novelist or a guest, the room is yours, a clean slate to make of it what you will.

About the writer: *Fittingly, bookworm Chloë Ashby is associate editor of Monocle's Books team.*

8.
Raising the bar
by *Dan Poole*

Hotel bars have so much to recommend them that it would be impossible to do the topic justice in the space afforded here. It would take a whole book, in fact – I offered to write it but the editor said something about sitting down quietly and getting on with my day job.

Anyway, it helps that if you are in a hotel bar you're probably on holiday. I wouldn't mind betting that there's sound science to prove that the combination of alcohol and annual leave produces enough oxytocin to border on the orgasmic. Imagine your state of heightened arousal when, sat at a bar having ordered something amber-coloured on ice, the bartender utters those immortal words: "Shall I charge this to your room?" Yes, my good man, you shall. Because then it will feel like I am receiving this drink for free. Reality may bite come check-out time but who cares? I'm pleasantly inebriated, that bowl of nibbles has just been refilled and soon I'll have a bath in the middle of the day *because I can.*

Another reason to love hotel bars: they stay open late. Once I was in a hotel with friends in the English county of Kent; I forget its name but that's probably because it had a security guard who doubled as a 24-hour barman. Every time we required more drinks we'd wave at this fine gentleman; he'd sigh, get up from behind reception and replenish us. The later it got, the grumpier he got, and the more muscular and menacing he looked. But who doesn't like a whiff of danger with their pint?

There have been other highlights. The Royal Harbour Hotel in Ramsgate has a lounge and library that features books (of all things), board games, a record player, a roaring fire when required and views over England's south coast. Tying all these elements together? A delightful little honesty bar. Further afield, at the Hotel Palácio do Governador in Lisbon, my wife and I were presented with a complimentary glass of port in its Occasus Bar, which we enjoyed on the terrace. Original? Not particularly. Enjoyable nonetheless? Abso-bloody-lutely.

The wonder of the hotel bar is that it feels familiar yet exclusive; you should be as relaxed as if you're at home but looked after enough to feel special. Any hotel without a bar should not be trusted; it's akin to a scuba-diving outfit without an oxygen tank. So check in and make a beeline for the person in bow tie and waistcoat. Drop by often enough for them to know your usual and by check-out you'll have achieved the final stage of enlightenment.

About the writer: *Dan Poole loves a whiff of danger with his pint and is chief sub-editor at Monocle.*

9.
Ode to the concierge

by *Melkon Charchoglyan*

As technology runs amok and marketeers seek new ways to cut costs, we're in danger of losing the concierge. Some may scoff at the loss, imagining a smartphone knows a city better than a local. But armed with little black books of contacts and reassuring smiles, concierges are more than speedy bookers of taxis – they're people who look out for you.

My first debt of gratitude to a concierge came as a seven-year-old on a family trip to Rome. After dinner at the foot of the Borghese Gardens, we hopped into a cab to our hotel. But once in the lobby my mother realised her handbag, complete with wallets and passports, was still in the taxi. She sank into the sofa in shock and gathered her thoughts. Suddenly Aldo, the sprightly sexagenarian concierge was standing over us, my mother's bag in hand; he'd hopped on his scooter and hared after the taxi. "I recognised the car as you pulled up," he said. "Those drivers all meet in Piazza Sonnino at this time of night." That, to me, is the role of the concierge. To help, sure. To rescue, perhaps. But also to surprise.

A survey of my colleagues showed I wasn't alone in my appreciation of these guardian angels. Our Vienna correspondent, staying at the Paramount in New York in the aftermath of 9/11, was grateful for daily transport when the city was in a gridlock. "I wouldn't have made it through that harrowing time without Clayton," she says of her concierge. Meanwhile, when our advertising manager pulled up at a hotel in London's Mayfair, a year after his last and only other stay, he was chuffed that the concierge, Paul, opened the door and remembered his name.

The best concierges go out of their way to look after you. As our Culture editor learned, they'll often solve a problem before you know you have one. One night, he was approached at Seoul's Grand Hyatt by a concierge and housekeeper. The latter suspected she had added a rip to his shirt, which he'd tossed in the laundry that morning. "No, no, it was like that before," our editor insisted. But the concierge would hear nothing of the sort and handed over a bespoke replacement, made that day by the in-house tailor. "I still have it and, yes, it's my favourite," he says. Did he return to the Grand Hyatt next time he was in Seoul? You bet your best shirt he did.

About the writer: *Melkon Charchoglyan takes good care of his belongings and is a writer on Monocle's Books team.*

10.
Coming of age in a hotel

by *Hugo Macdonald*

My parents were dealt a strange hand early in their marriage. My father's father died suddenly and they moved to the Isle of Skye to look after my grandmother, inheriting a large amount of debt and a 17th-century hunting lodge. Spurred on to clear the former, the pair spent a year turning the latter into a hotel. They were barely in their twenties and couldn't have imagined how it would shape the course of the rest of their lives. Mum did all the interiors and cooking, Dad managed the staff and business, and together they were hosts.

Growing up in a remote hotel on a Hebridean island off the west coast of Scotland – at the time only connected to the mainland by a small car-ferry – was weird and wonderful. The original building had 11 bedrooms, a dining room and two drawing rooms, and our family home was a small extension connected to the hotel by doors on the first and ground floors. Yet, despite these private-public thresholds, our lives were utterly intertwined with the goings on in the hotel. We were all staff and the staff were all family.

In the 1980s, during my childhood, it was an intrepid guest who holidayed on Skye. It was the perfect foil to the potential loneliness that extreme rural isolation might bring, to be surrounded by an endless cast of eccentric characters. My horizons, and those of my three older sisters, were broadened; our overactive imaginations were constantly fed by the lives and stories of guests. Because it felt like we were at the end of the world, people would come to stay to escape from their lives and, due to the intimate scale of the hotel and its location, there

wasn't much room for anonymity. At times it felt like the hotel was a residential therapy facility and we were the carers.

Strange dramas consumed us. There was the lady whose dog died slowly and loudly, and the guest whose husband died quietly during the night. There was the man who walked up the mountain at sunset never to return, and another man who did the same but was found alive by the mountain-rescue team hours later (he claimed that he'd been overcome by a strangely magnetic sensation that he had to keep walking). There was corridor creeping and partner swapping. Mum found two strangers "locked in a carnal embrace" in the drawing room one night, long after everyone else had gone to bed. Our hotel gave people permission to behave strangely and gave us the opportunity to observe human life with all of its idiosyncrasies.

As soon as we were deemed responsible enough, my sisters and I were allowed to work in the hotel, which despite a more formal education was the greatest learning experience of my life. Working in a small hotel, you don't just learn how to change bedding in seconds or peel 50 potatoes in 30 minutes, you also learn to quickly read people from small signals. You detect personality types from cleaning bedrooms and serving breakfasts, plotting daily excursions on a map and topping up someone's whisky after dinner. The same people who think it's fine not to flush the toilet often struggle to look you in the eye as you pour their coffee.

My parents ran our hotel instinctively as an extension of our home, creating a feeling of hospitality that was relaxed, comfortable and fun. Nothing was more rewarding than seeing people arrive frosty then visibly melt after a day or two. Once, Dad famously asked a guest who was angry and rude to pack their bags and leave because they threatened to destroy the experience for everyone else. Despite cringing with embarrassment at the time, I look back and admire his reasoning that this was our home and he would not tolerate rudeness under our roof, whether someone was paying or not. This was long before TripAdvisor.

I do believe that the warmth and personality of my parents meant guests miraculously forgave situations that might have finished them off in today's regulated, risk-averse climate of trial by social media. We were at the mercy of the elements, in wilderness territory. Our water supply, which came from a deep river pool higher up the mountain behind the lodge, would freeze during prolonged or heavy frosts. Dad would disappear up the mountain in the dark and defrost the pipes with a blowtorch. When storms blew in, the electricity would go out and Mum would visit every guest with a supply of candles and matches, as well as Thermos flasks of tea made on our gas Aga. One winter, the little bridge that connected us to the rest of the world washed away and the army had to come to rebuild it. This was part and parcel of the adventure and, so long as things were restored relatively quickly, it only added to the experience. The log fires would always be roaring and the bar was always open.

It was peculiar to grow up in such a remote setting yet to be so heavily involved in many people's lives – but that's precisely what made the experience special. We were brought up to understand the importance of basic hospitality – that it is engendered not through a checklist of amenities but through a feeling of deep care. I have vivid memories of Mum rushing outside to welcome guests in from the wind and rain with promises of fresh cake and a wee dram of whisky by the fire.

Much of the hotel industry today has lost sight of the true meaning of hospitality, replacing it with blander aspirations of convenience and consistency. Remote check-ins and automated check-outs don't inspire a genuine feeling of welcome. Happy memories are made from human contact.

About the writer: *Hugo Macdonald is a writer, journalist and author of 'How to Live in the City' (Pan Macmillan).*

II.
Why I love a good motel

by *Jayson Seidman*

We Americans used to be mobile. With a system of endless highways at our beck and call and a healthy – some would argue unhealthy – car culture, motels boomed from the 1950s onwards, offering cheap stopovers for travelling salesmen and discreet rendezvous spots (not to mention, if Hollywood is to be believed, the odd messy shoot-out).

By the time I was a kid in the 1990s, the motel's heyday had passed. My family, however, still stayed in them on holiday. I remember the neat, woody interiors; while people lounged by the pool, I would stand on the wraparound mezzanine, peering down at the comings and goings of guests: some families like mine, some travelling salesmen, some leading furtive affairs. It's a nostalgic image: the neon sign, suspended from a banner and flashing "vacancy".

The motel had a simple, low-lying, linear and ever-so-modern premise. Guest rooms were located along the first floor, facing an inner courtyard; there might be a pool, maybe

a café or diner for passing trade and guests to hunker down in. The comparative cheapness of these one or two-storey structures allowed for fast construction and led to a substantial spike in building. By the mid-1960s, their popularity began to wane as demand for greater luxury increased and the notion of the motel became altogether seedier and dingier. With rising real-estate costs and the desire to build vertically and ever more vertiginously, the motel was forgotten, deemed inefficient and eventually undesirable.

But one thing has been ignored in the rush for newer and taller hotels with more and more rooms: the guest experience isn't always elevated the further you get from the ground. Actually, the higher you go, the more secluded you feel. Historically, motels were about simplifying the guest experience. The horizontal structure and open, often playful, architecture lent itself to a more communal atmosphere, chance encounters, the ability to watch others as they schlepped in and out. Motels create a relaxed backdrop for overnighters and locals to rub shoulders and even clink glasses. Unlike congested downtown hotels, motels also have the advantage of location: room for a pool, perhaps, but also quick access to the countryside and forests, beaches or rolling plains.

Sadly, however, motels have barely survived and few do justice to the sunny optimism that spawned them. Many have been abandoned, some torn down in favour of shinier chain-run stopovers. But in the demolition of such relics we lose a lot. The motel tells a story of the US, of the open road and frontiersmanship. It's why I'm an advocate for renovation and restoration. When I see a motel in the middle of Bushwick, Brooklyn or on California's Highway 1, I don't see a sad story or an outmoded space, I see possibility: to restore them to their former glory and provide personable hospitality to people travelling either on or off the beaten path. It's the reason I chose to restore a previously ill-fated 1950s motel in New Orleans, Louisiana.

I called it The Drifter (*see page 23*), a name dreamed up as an image of both my travels and what I believe to be a growing population of free-spirited explorers. It's a space that was created to bring people together. That said, restoring motels isn't about making them what they were but rather what they need to be in order to work today. I discarded the car park in favour of a sizeable pool surrounded by palm trees. Without the parking area, The Drifter gains peace and quiet: it's a serene space where guests and locals can escape the chaos of New Orleans surrounded by nostalgic, mid-century architecture. But more than just a hotel, The Drifter riffs on New Orleans' design history, while adding footfall to a formerly quiet neighbourhood.

Hotels touting exclusivity are a thing of the past. Today it's about creating something smaller, more intimate and with a more communal feel. Should any of you in the hospitality industry roll up to a comely motel that's still standing and that has an owner who is inclined to sell (seldom the case), I urge you to resuscitate it. Failing that, do feel free to let me know about it.

About the writer: *Motel-minded Jayson Seidman is a New Orleans-based hotelier.*

12.
Alpine hotels

by *Jessica Carmi*

Alpine hospitality – of that fireside, fresh-aired sort – has had some distinct ups and downs over the past few years. When skiing became popular at the beginning of the 20th century, most Alpine hotels were small family-run holdings that were ill-equipped to cater for the influx of international guests. From the end of the Second World War until the 1970s, flights became cheaper and the mass market for winter sports boomed. The small mountainside chalets transformed into mazes of megahotels: many with the same Alpine decor, most without the charm that lured people in the first place.

Today, however, a new generation of travellers is bypassing the pre-packaged experiences of Alpine Europe in favour of the independents. One such authentic affair is the Taxhof, an *almhotel* (meaning it's in a mountain meadow) made from farms not far from Austria's Hohe Tauern mountains. The buildings sit on a piece of land that's been in the Unterberger family since 1687; the daughters prepare breakfast and their father Matthias takes care of the animals. As of 2016, new suites were on offer in a grove of 500-year-old maples.

Other hotels – such as the Almhof Schneider in Lech, an exclusive but homely hamlet in the Austrian province of Vorarlberg – combine stately service with family history. The Almhof story began in 1451, when the Schneiders came to the Arlberg region with many other Walser (a Swiss clan from the Valais region that colonised Arlberg). "I don't see this as a hotel," says Hannelore Schneider, the matriarch of Almhof Schneider. "It's a big household." One look at the contented guests and you'll see her statement rings true. Her son Gerold and his wife Katia are architects who updated the hotel's interior, adding a smart spa for apres-ski indulgence in 2017.

Other properties, such as the Piz Linard hotel in Lavin (*see page 99*) – a town of 200 people in Switzerland's Lower Engadine Valley – are newer ventures. In 2007, hotelier Hans Schmid quit his job as cultural director of the town of Sankt Gallen to run the place with his family.

"People want to be closer to nature and go back to simple, honest things," says the Taxhof's Berta Unterberger. Here's hoping such family-owned stopovers remain popular. It's these hotels – not the glitzy chalets and megahotels – that made the Alps favourable to visit in the first place and to which people will continue to return.

About the writer: *Jessica Carmi is a US-born writer and high-altitude-hotel enthusiast based in Mitteleuropa.*

13.
Keeping it in the family

by *James Chambers*

Every Sunday, The Peninsula's Cantonese restaurant Spring Moon serves dim sum to Hong Kongers. This iconic hotel on the Kowloon side of the harbour has a special place in the social fabric of the city regardless of which famous heads and heads of state are resting in the 300-odd rooms upstairs. But the Peninsula (*see page 77*) is a family hotel in more ways than one.

Founded in 1928 by Lawrence and Horace Kadoorie, Mizrahi Jewish brothers born in Hong Kong to immigrant parents, it is to this day majority-owned by the same family. Sir Michael Kadoorie, current chairman of The Peninsula's holding company, has fond memories of growing up in the hotel as a child in the 1950s and is grooming his children to take over the business.

Few pre-war hotels have remained under the stewardship of the same family for so long and grown into internationally renowned brands. The modern Peninsula is part of a global hospitality chain, with locations from Beijing to Beverly Hills.

The first mention of the Hong Kong hotel in the company archive is a 1924 entry in a large ledger. It is entered under land assets with a book value of HK$385,000 (€39,600). Today, its value has surpassed HK$12bn (€1.2bn). It is little surprise that such a place is headquartered in Hong Kong, where family-owned property companies dominate the business landscape.

However, family ownership doesn't always endure. The original Hilton opened in Dallas at the same time as the original Peninsula. The 14-storey building, also a horseshoe shape, lasted little more than a decade under Conrad Hilton's ownership before being sold and renamed.

Hilton profited from the Texas oil boom, suffered during the depression, then prospered as the first international hotel chain that catered to the US's postwar leisure market. Today there are more than 500 Hiltons operating in more than 85 countries but Hilton's son Barron sold the final family stake in 2007 to a private equity group.

The Marriotts and the Pritzkers – owners of Hyatt Hotels Corporation – are two other great US hotel families that followed in Hilton's footsteps. Both got their start in hotels in 1957 and almost 60 years later the two companies grappled over the Starwood stable of brands, which includes the St Regis and W Hotels. Marriott won, spending $13.6bn in 2016 to become the world's largest hotel operator.

The JW Marriott brand stands as a legacy to the founder John Willard Marriott Sr, who died in 1985. But not every founder of a global hotel chain is immortalised in neon lights. Two are still actively involved in the business and chose not to commercialise: Isadore Sharp of Four Seasons and Robert Kuok of Shangri-La.

Sharp began in his father's Toronto construction firm while Kuok was a major commodities trader. Launched within a decade of each other, the Four Seasons and Shangri-La have grown into five-star hotel groups with more than 100 properties apiece. But in that time the two founders have seen their shareholdings reverse. Sharp's stake has been reduced to 5 per cent as billionaire Bill Gates and Saudi prince Alwaleed bin Talal have come on board. Kuok started with a 10 per cent stake before taking control and passing management to his children.

The Malaysian businessman, now in Hong Kong, has talked about the family business continuing. Shangri-La's most recent brand, the Kerry, opened its first Hong Kong hotel in 2017 on the Kowloon harbour. But it will take several generations – ideally under the steady stewardship of a family with the long term in mind – for it to become a hospitality landmark like the Peninsula, just 2km along the water.

About the writer: *James Chambers loves Spring Moon and is Monocle's Hong Kong bureau chief.*

14.
In praise of pop-ups

by *Gregor Wöltje*

Take a look around your city and you'll spy temporary cafés, temporary cinemas and temporary shops – few spaces are truly permanent. Even those establishments that have been around for a long time may suddenly host the prefix "pop-up". And why not? Although there's plenty to be said for continuity in cities, these pop-ups make the most of gaps between rents in which spaces, parks and corners might otherwise sit empty.

Pop-ups aren't new. They started when artists were looking for temporary studios or exhibition spaces (Andy Warhol's Factory in New York springs to mind) but today they're home to a plethora of marketing campaigns for everything from ateliers to kitchens. It stands to reason that an empty space can be put to better use, even if only temporarily.

Now for a confession: I enjoy sleeping in unusual places. When I was a child I moved my bed into my wardrobe, I slept outside under a construction of deckchairs and I always, perhaps unusually, dreamed of overnighting in a vault. In 2017 I came fairly close to fulfilling that dream when we opened a two-year, pop-up hotel in a one-time bank building in Munich. The building was stuck in limbo, caught up in a court dispute, so I thought, "Why not make use of it while we can?"

When embarking on the concept of the temporary Lovelace hotel, our research revealed few short-term spaces from which to draw inspiration or ideas. Those that did exist were mostly mobile structures and our idea was more in keeping with a grand hotel than a "glamping" experience. We remodelled the top three floors of the listed building into 30 guest rooms but also left scope for spaces that could be used for gigs and exhibitions, or simply in which to sink a drink. We included a coffee shop, a rooftop bar and spaces for live music, exhibitions, temporary shops, workspaces, film screenings and more.

We quickly learned why there were so few intrepid pop-up hoteliers before us: the amount of work and money that needs to be invested seemed unreasonably high and the short shelf-life meant there was only a finite amount of time to recoup it. It was a risk but a worthwhile one.

So what does it take to turn a bank into a happening hotel for a fleeting 18-month stint? Here's what I learned.

1. **Bring your own money:** Banks don't like to finance pop-up projects, plus you will be more thrifty with your own funds.

2. **Be time-conscious:** It's more important to get the place up and running so that you can test and refine it using real people than it is to plan to the finest detail before launch.

3. **Stay away from built-in fixtures:** Flexible furniture allows flexible use. Our hotel rooms can be used as makeshift bars, concert venues and showrooms.

4. **Write your own story:** Just being a pop-up doesn't get the job done. What makes your place unique? Invite the locals and turn it into a place for fun. Make room for events and culture and invest in a regular programme.

5. **Think of it like a song:** The hotel brings the basic melody, the rhythm. The guests join in, improvising with the staff and the locals, until one day it's all over. All the encores are done, the lights go up and the show moves to the next venue.

About the writer: *Gregor Wöltje is a Munich-based entrepreneur and co-founder of the Lovelace.*

15.
How to stay independent

by *María Ulecia*

■■■■■■■■■■

When I was first contacted by a big booking site, I was running a small hotel in a former 18th-century Portuguese convent. It said it would help me fill the place for a 20 per cent commission on each booking. My answer was "no". Instead, I invested 20 per cent of my income into creating my own website and booking system, as well as a small press kit that I sent to my favourite magazines and newspapers. The following year we were reviewed by some of the most influential travel and design publications in the world.

In July 2006 I opened Micasaenlisboa (*see page 45*), a one-bedroom guesthouse in Lisbon. As I was fully booked that December I travelled and conducted some research. I sampled some B&Bs and a few chains too. I alternated between booking with the owner directly and tour operators. When dealing with middlemen, I realised, I never knew what sort of hotel I'd be stepping into.

When I returned to Lisbon I wanted to ensure that my hotel would stay real and independent. "I'll draft the concept from scratch and create a unique place where I'd want to go on holiday," I vowed. I launched a simple, self-written site with no way of booking other than through me. Soon there was a small article in *El País*, praising the breakfast. My little guesthouse went from having one bedroom to four bedrooms before I knew it.

Over the years I've had to wrestle with plenty more booking platforms – Airbnb is not a new form of adversary for independent hotels. What it has done, however, is make the world think that it's new and unique – as if it reinvented the B&B. And it's ballooned since. What began in 2008 as a lean start-up trumpeting fairness and the sharing economy has become a financial behemoth, with less time for the guest and host.

It can be difficult to stay independent but it is possible – and a positive thing to do. Collaborating with small booking platforms is inevitable – my rule is I only accept sites that feature fewer than 15 places in the city and that I'd consider using myself. After a long refurbishment and another enlargement, Micasaenlisboa is a nine-room independent guesthouse. Call by if you'd like to see what a thriving independent hotel looks like.

About the writer: *María Ulecia is the founder and owner of Micasaenlisboa, Lisbon's prettiest hotel and best breakfast.*

16.
A war reporter's guide to hotels

by *Lyse Doucet*

■■■■■■■■■■

"How long will you be staying?" I stood in the cold gloom of the cavernous lobby and pondered my reply to the Afghan hotel clerk in a sombre black suit. "Would it be six days or six weeks?" I asked myself. I simply did not know.

The clock behind me was similarly stuck for an answer. Its metal hands had stopped, frozen in time in the dark depths of a Kabul winter in the last days of the Cold War. I hadn't expected to end up at Kabul's Intercontinental Hotel on Christmas Eve in 1988, a date that happens to be my birthday. But when a rare visa was issued by the communist government, I rushed to the Afghan capital as Soviet troops started their pull-out after a decade-long disastrous engagement.

Other journalists did the same. And, as so often in war zones, the rhythms of hotel life were written into this moment of history-making headlines around the world.

Actually, there were two hotels of note. The Intercontinental was perched on a hill to the north. The Kabul hotel, a dull Soviet-era block, sat in the very heart of a capital gripped by fear of rockets fired by western-backed *mujahideen* rebels in the snow-capped slopes of the famed Hindu Kush. Word spread that the Intercontinental, with its superior telex and telephone services, should be the destination of choice for deadline-obsessed hacks. It wasn't exactly the suite-life though. Kabul's first so-called luxury hotel, opened in 1969, lost its connection to the famed Intercontinental chain when Soviet troops invaded a decade later.

Nonetheless, the camaraderie was wonderful. Journalists came and went; I stayed on. The world's best snappers left me copies of their photographs to hang in my room. New correspondents showed up at my door, in the hope of gleaning some useful tips. They also wanted to glimpse the Afghan carpets brightening up my quarters – on loan from discerning Afghan merchants who, in keeping with tradition, urged me to take them to my new home until I made up my mind.

My "home away from home" had a charm of its own. Farid, who headed room service, cheerily served me chicken kebab, usually with Afghan spinach, almost every day. When the hotel manager took chicken off the menu as market prices soared, Farid threatened to resign. (Chicken kebabs remained firmly on the menu.)

Nasser, who worked the hotel's telephone exchange, knew that my daily call to London was the most important service of all. So cut off was Kabul that there were, curiously, only two international lines: one through Moscow and one through Glasgow. The operators at the Glasgow Exchange became my dear friends. The service went both ways. They connected me to the BBC every day without fail and routed calls from frustrated journalists without visas trying to reach Kabul through me.

The winter of Soviet withdrawal turned into the spring of rocket salvos and the summer of major battles on several front lines. By then, the hotel was almost empty, except for *The New York Times* correspondent John Burns and myself. We decided to make an expedition to neighbouring Pakistan, a base for *mujahideen* fighters, to see

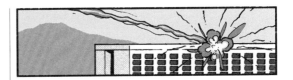

the war from the other side. Coincidentally or not, it was the only week that the hotel, the highest point in the capital, was hit by a rocket. By the time I returned to Kabul, I found that agents from Khad, the feared Afghan intelligence services, had moved into my fourth-floor room. With a profound apology from the staff, I was moved into another. In the end, I stayed for 10 months. To this day, when I walk into hotel rooms with worn carpets and wooden furniture that's had its day, I'm brought back to the feel of my room. It's the feeling of history.

The Safir hotel in the Syrian city of Homs, one of my latest outposts, has felt much the same over the past seven years. Time and again, I've returned to a place whose darkened lobby offered a front-row seat on a worsening war. The UN's blue-helmeted peacekeepers came and went, so did spooks in black, and aid workers have taken rooms on long lease.

As I sat sipping Syria's delicious flower tea on my last visit, news came that my cherished Kabul home was under attack. The Intercontinental, with a lobby now sparkling with glittering chandeliers, was under ferocious assault by suicide bombers; frightened guests were trapped inside.

The news took me back to what seems like Afghanistan's forever war. Most of all I remembered 1992, when the *mujahideen* finally stormed into the city, bringing down a government that lost its ally when the Soviet Union collapsed. Not long after, I had stood on the hotel terrace in the warm Kabul sun. Sharif, the manager, beamed with pride as he showed me samples of new crockery on order, as well as new uniforms for the staff. He was brimming with ideas for what he dared to believe would be a new beginning.

The next day a rocket slammed into the fabled Intercontinental. Sharif – the man at the front desk who first welcomed me into a hotel that quickly became my home – was killed instantly.

About the writer: *Canadian journalist Lyse Doucet is the BBC's chief international correspondent.*

Nikolaj Tamakloe

General manager — Hotel Sanders, Copenhagen — *The GM who sailed through jobs serving coffee before getting the top posting*

The title of "general manager" may merge two vague terms but few who've worked in a hospitality setting would doubt the importance of the role. They're the eyes, ears and often the light touch of an operation.

Born and raised just north of Copenhagen, Nikolaj Tamakloe began his career in hospitality as a barista after high school. "By coincidence, I became the manager of the coffee shop and six months later I was in charge of 80 staff," he says. "I rose very quickly and that's rewarded my passion for the industry."

After graduation from hospitality school in Oxford, UK, and a management trainee programme, he moved back to Copenhagen and worked on a few restaurant and hotel openings before joining shipping giant Maersk. "The firm bought a manor house north of Copenhagen," he says. "It was a small country club for its top management for meetings and training sessions." It wasn't long before Alexander Kølpin, owner of the then soon-to-open Hotel Sanders (*see page 38*), learned of Tamakloe's reputation and got in touch.

A good GM must possess a wide and varied skill set, from staff training to finances, but most of all they must be "people people".

Tamakloe says his role relies on an excellent rapport with his staff – the way he communicates the Sanders message to his charges eventually filters down to his customers. "When making coffee, we want people to see beautiful movements. You keep your surface clean and make it a habit to create these flowing movements when you're pouring milk into the container. If you get into these rhythms even making a cup of coffee can be beautiful," he says.

Owner Kølpin is a former dancer at the Royal Ballet and sees customer experience as akin to a dramatic production. "Alexander wants to create a play that never closes," says Tamakloe. "I feel that with beautiful costumes, a certain Sanders scent and comfortable chairs to sit in, guests have a chance to forget place and time."

Tamakloe believes that service is about creating unique moments. "Sometimes we pack a picnic basket for guests and say, 'Instead of eating at the restaurants or with the tourists, go and sit down by the harbour with your feet in the water. Here are some cups and a bottle of wine,'" he says. "This is the kind of service that makes a hotel."

Yukiko Koike

Manager of housekeeping office — Imperial Hotel, Tokyo — *The hotel housekeeper who has her art down to a tea*

Dressed in her plum-coloured kimono, Yukiko Koike is perfectly poised and understated; she has the uncanny ability to anticipate guests' needs before they actually materialise. Koike entered the Imperial Hotel, Tokyo (*see pages 64 to 65*) in 1961 at the age of 18 – and she's never left. Over the past half-century, she has been responsible for countless guests returning to this Japanese mainstay.

Today Koike still works five days a week, leading the 16 staff on the premier Imperial floor. She has a personal, concierge-like capacity, welcoming guests at the reception, unpacking their luggage, making tea and standing by for requests until she sees them off. She also remembers their preferences, from how they like their coffee to the temperature to keep their room.

It all started when she was in the fifth grade. She saw the Imperial on television when Marilyn Monroe was staying on her honeymoon. "I decided that I was going to work here," she says. "It was such a beautiful world." After high school, her dream came true when she joined the hotel's housekeeping department. "I wanted to work in a fancier section such as the restaurant," she

says, recalling how she didn't take to being told to clean the rooms. "On my third day, I wanted to quit." But Koike stayed and now she spends most of her waking hours within the establishment, save for a two-hour daily commute from her hometown of Saitama.

"It was extraordinary, majestic," she says of the now-demolished Frank Lloyd Wright building from 1923. When she started, most guests stayed for a while. There were dancers from the Ginza cabaret, Mikado, who spent a month, while some foreign guests stayed for years. Big-name politicians favoured her service, as did film stars such as John Wayne and French heartthrob Alain Delon.

Koike maintains that she's part of the hotel staff but also unofficially plays the role of friend, sister, daughter and mother. Many of her guests talk to her about their personal life. "I write back to everyone," she says, holding a pile of letters she's received.

Five decades on, Koike stays true to the lesson she learned during her first days. "Housekeeping isn't the grandest role but the bedroom is where guests can unwind and relax the most." Any plan to retire? "I still have a yearning for this place." Not yet, it seems.

Adrian Zecha

Hotelier — Can Tho, Vietnam — *The serial hotel founder and hospitality mogul on his indefatigable energy for the business*

Adrian Zecha is a busy man. Since entering the hospitality industry in 1973, the former journalist has been involved in the development of more than 120 hotels – many small in scale and located on remote islands in Indonesia or far-flung parts of Bhutan.

Best known for co-founding Aman Resorts in 1988, Zecha is back at it again with the fledgling Azerai brand. Indeed, he cut the ribbon on the first of this new brand of hotel in 2017 at the tender age of 83 and plans to open two or three a year for the foreseeable future.

"I don't follow trends. If I did, why would I have done Aman?" asks Zecha, who is no longer part of the company and still in legal proceedings over it. "When I entered the hospitality business, the mantra was that you can't make money with a new hotel unless you have 500 rooms. We proved that wrong."

AZ, as the boss is known, only spends one week a month at his home in Singapore. The rest of the time he's on the road or in the air, visiting potential sites and checking in on existing developments.

"Right from the beginning these opportunities have come to me, so I'm very lucky," he says, his voice raising in pitch with excitement as he discusses his hotel deals past and present. Zecha's current web of hospitality interests include being chairman of General Hotel Management (the owner of Chedi hotels) and a new Chinese hotel brand called Ahn Luh.

"Asia will always be about the rule of relationships rather than the rule of law," he says, even though his personal approach to deal-making is proving itself just as effective in Europe and the US. He's currently creating a new hotel brand for a Chinese investor in the US.

Listening to Zecha speak about his frenetic dealmaking is an adventure in itself. He claims, nevertheless, to get most satisfaction from opening hotels and he bristles at any suggestion that hospitality is his hobby (it's "serious business", he insists).

He claims boldly that every hotel he has opened has turned a healthy profit and he expects this to continue as the opportunities to make money increase. "There are still so many beautiful places around the world to discover," he says.

Sonia Cheng

CEO — Rosewood Hotel Group, Hong Kong — *The hotelier who's not afraid to take on online, app-based competitors*

Who wants to own a hotel in the age of flat-shares and online competition? Sonia Cheng, for one. And as luck would have it she's the CEO of Hong Kong's Rosewood Hotel Group, which manages more than 11,000 rooms in 22 countries.

The group has enjoyed steady growth – a heartening headline that shows the roof is far from caving in on the hotel industry. But Cheng isn't resting on her laurels. She has opened eight Rosewoods (with one due to open in her hometown of Hong Kong) and launched a brand called KHOS for business travellers in 2018. "Our guests want more than a place in which to sleep," she says. "Be it Hôtel de Crillon [Paris] or Rosewood Phuket, we put great effort into bringing a sense of place to each hotel, as much as picking which painting to hang on the wall."

Flying to each location to check on development keeps the CEO in the air much of the time but she admits to also getting plenty of inspiration when travelling to locations without a Rosewood presence. "For me the hotel business is all about entrepreneurship and creativity," says Cheng. "It's a people business." With no formal education in hospitality,

the Harvard maths and economics graduate has always placed great importance on learning on the job. And in this sense she started young. She grew up in a globe-trotting family that started its first hotel in 1976 under the New World brand, a conglomerate that spans from property development to the world's largest jewellery chain.

After a spell in finance, Cheng joined the hotel business in 2006; five years later she took over the top job. That same year, the business added the Rosewood brand to its portfolio, establishing its first Asian property in Beijing in 2014.

Opening an outpost in the Chinese capital was a career milestone for Cheng, although she remains humble as the group eyes a sizeable push across Asia. "We target unexpected locations alongside key gateway cities such as Tokyo, Seoul and Shanghai." She also plans to open Hong Kong's first Rosewood on the site of the former New World Centre in Kowloon, where her late grandfather started out in hospitality almost 40 years ago. Overlooking Victoria Harbour, the building will have 413 rooms and 183 residences, a set-up that would make the best-looking flat-share blush.

Ivica 'Max' Krizmanic

General manager — Hotel Esplanade, Zagreb — *The man who carved a glittering career out of a fleeting summer job*

His father was a doorman at Zagreb's original grand hotel. Now Ivica "Max" Krizmanic has years under his belt as general manager at the Esplanade. "It was like a fairy tale to me," he says, of the first time he set foot in the Esplanade. "I was three years old and my father brought me to the hotel. It was completely different in the communist era; the marble floor in the lobby was carpeted back then. But the Esplanade was always something special. It wasn't just the decor but the spirit."

Krizmanic's career at the grand hotel adjacent to Zagreb's main railway station might never have begun if the Esplanade had not been short of staff in 1992, during Croatia's war of independence.

He was studying for a degree in mechanical engineering when a summer job as a doorman came up and, in extremis, the hotel waived its usual restrictions on employing relatives of staff. He was supposed to stay for a month; he never returned to university.

In the 26 years that have followed, Krizmanic has filled some of the roles his father did during his own three decades at the Esplanade – bellboy, doorman and concierge – as well as operating the switchboard and working at the front office. Along the way, he inherited his father's nickname, "Max". In 2012, perhaps realising that no one knew the hotel better, the owners asked him to take up the mantle of general manager.

"I have never applied for any position in the hotel. I was just appointed," says Krizmanic. "Even when I was a doorman, I was trying to be the best. The hotel is my big love. If I didn't work at the Esplanade, I would not work in hospitality. At the Esplanade I feel like a boy all the time."

Now the boy who saw the Esplanade as a fairy tale come to life is the man piloting the hotel towards its centenary. He prefers to hire staff who have never worked in other hotels – "we try to get people to rise with us" – and believes that top-class service allows an employee's personality to shine through.

On becoming a father, Krizmanic called his son Ennio Max, in honour of both musical maestro (and Esplanade guest) Morricone and his own father. Following in the family tradition, junior is already a regular at the hotel, prompting staff to quip that the search for the next general manager is over.

Tara Bernerd

Interior architect — London — *The designer who hoteliers the world over call for an inside job*

London-based interior architect Tara Bernerd's design work is a lush and lively counterpoint to the stuffy and staid world that some older hotels have slipped into over the years. "I think hotels are watching out for app-based competitors and, if they aren't, they really should be. People associate Airbnb with guests who can't afford to stay in a hotel but you know there are rentals for £1,500, even up to £3,000 a night. It's as much as a suite from a luxury hotel brand. So the hotels should be watching," she says, as we sit in the Bernerd-designed finery of the Il Pampero restaurant at London's Hari hotel. "Location still really matters," she adds with a smile.

Bernerd's eponymous design firm runs projects from Los Angeles to London and New York to Osaka. Her Belgravia-based team has grown on Bernerd's successful residential projects (plus the odd yacht) and commissions from the likes of Thompson Hotels, Belmont and Sixty, The Hari Group and the terracotta grandeur of the 2018-opened Principal hotel in London's Russell Square. "I have always loved hotels, even as a little girl," she muses. "I remember everything I ever saw. I was fascinated by the interiors.

When I grew up, I opened my business on the back of my work with YOO [the design firm founded by John Hitchcox and Philippe Starck]. The criteria there was to bring design into property developments. I think in a way we were all on a crusade. In a sense, from doing a restaurant to someone's living room to hundreds of apartments, if you put that all together, you've got a hotel."

Bernerd has made up for lost time and seen plenty of changes as her clients' briefs have moved away from glitz and towards creating less formal spaces. "Marble and gold used to be a go-to in some of the older hotels. As a civilization, we don't want it so much anymore but there are countries and cultures that still do. Hotels today are in some way homes, or should be," she says.

Despite Bernerd's readiness to embrace change, she regards technology as a sticking point. "I think things such as efficiency should be improved: from lighting to USB chargers in the wall. We like instant gratification technology-wise and we need to be up to the minute," she says. "What we don't really need, however, is a half-hour explanation from a concierge or a robot to show you around."

Ociric Beato

Lift operator — The Carlyle, New York — *The guy who'll be there for all your ups and downs*

"We are definitely a dying breed," says Ociric Beato as he slides the doors of the 1930s lift shut and presses the button to the 17th floor of the Carlyle Hotel on Manhattan's Upper East Side. OC, as he's better known (and what you'll see if you glance at his gleaming name badge), is referring to his own, white-gloved profession: manually operating the lifts for guests in what is a rapidly dwindling art form. He's one of 12 operators at the New York institution, which is renowned for its old-world charm. It's a job that he has held for more than a decade, after seven years serving in different roles behind the scenes at the hotel.

The Carlyle is a family affair for Beato. He came to the hotel as a young man, joining his father who was working in the hotel's kitchen (and recently retired after 35 years there). He started with stints in room service and banqueting before finding his niche and climbing the ranks; he's now next in line for the coveted bellman position. "A lot of people say 'You're just pushing a button', but it takes personality and charisma," he says.

Guests' interaction may be brief with Beato (the length of a 15-second ride between floors, perhaps) but he makes sure they leave feeling attended to. For those wanting to chat, he might manage to mention the news, ask how their stay is going or comment on the chance of rain.

He keeps two simple rules for his work: "Try not to speak about anything personal or political. And whatever happens in the elevator stays in the elevator." His conversations in the lift are often riddled with jokes. "It has its ups and downs – that's George Clooney's favourite line," he says of one of the Carlyle's well-known guests, who likes to joke around with Beato on regular visits.

He's never able to keep count of his journeys up from the lobby but he knows which is his busiest shift. It's the night of the Met Gala in May, when guests cram into the lifts – he can fit 12, give or take – in beautiful gowns and tuxedos.

While it can get a little claustrophobic, Beato admits he hardly feels like he's working. There's too much to take in for that. "So many people come into this elevator," he says. "We've had everyone from presidents and dignitaries to actresses and actors. You name 'em, they've been here."

Laura Lahoud

Hotelier — Al Bustan, Beit Mery — *The third-generation matriarch whose family is steeped in hospitality and bequeathed her one of Lebanon's loveliest hotels*

A dark-grey Range Rover bypasses a static row of Beirut-bound motorists and glides deftly in the opposite direction. In its back-seat is Laura Lahoud, the third-generation hotelier behind hilltop hideaway Al Bustan. Her driver Gaby steers the car off the main road to zip up the twisting back lanes towards the mountain resort town of Beit Mery.

During the half-hour journey Lahoud emails board members, phones suppliers and checks progress on plans for the hotel's annual performing-arts festival. "No day resembles the other," says Lahoud, who takes care of all the tasks of running the hotel, from welcoming guests to fixing fresh flowers.

In 1962, Lahoud's grandfather Emile Bustani drafted plans for a guesthouse for friends and colleagues. But in 1963, with the hotel partly built, he died in a plane crash.

"My grandmother wanted to honour his dream," says Lahoud of Laura Bustani, who opened Al Bustan in 1967. "As a child my mother used to take me to the hotel for lunch on Sundays. There was always some-thing exciting happening." The family-run business boomed in the late 1960s and early 1970s. But in 1975, the Lebanese war started.

For 20 years Lahoud and her mother, who had served a year as a member of parliament after the death of her father, sought safety in London. At the war's end in 1993, Lahoud's mother Myrna Bustani returned to renovate and run the hotel.

"At first, I organised art fairs in the hotel. I was always interested in the work from the beginning and I gradually became more involved over the years." Under the guidance of her mother, Lahoud has begun assisting with the management of the hotel. "Sometimes you have to do things yourself in order to achieve what you want," she says.

Lahoud climbs out of the Range Rover and passes beneath the vast pines to enter the striking mid-century building. Up here the air is cooler, the pace a beat slower. The white-and-carmine balconies, the wood-panelled phone booths and the concierges' teal jackets all hark back to Al Bustan's 1960s charm.

Lahoud feels a weight of responsibility to her matriarchal forebears; her mother lives in a room upstairs. "She's still very present and involved. Whenever there is a major decision to make, I always check with her first," she says. "And I hope she agrees."

Pierre Gruneberg

Swimming instructor — Grand-Hôtel du Cap-Ferrat, Saint-Jean-Cap-Ferrat —
The man who taught the stars to swim

When Pierre Gruneberg first stepped onto the poolside at the Grand-Hôtel du Cap-Ferrat's Club Dauphin he was just 19 years old. That was in 1950. Since then, the handsome, tanned and white-haired swimming instructor has been on the job every season from June to September (his winters are spent teaching skiing in Courchevel).

Gruneberg used to start at 09.00 but arrives at the pool at 10.30 or 11.00 these days, often after an hour-long swim in the sea. ("I prefer swimming in the sea," he confesses.) After this daily routine, he spends his days around the Club Dauphin's pool, where he gives lessons, says "hello" to the clients and does some in-person public relations work until his shift finishes at 19.00 sharp.

His 67 years working by the pool at the legendary hotel on the French Riviera have turned Gruneberg into a local star. He has thousands of stories to tell and has met the great and the good, from Charlie Chaplin to Pablo Picasso and Jean Cocteau. "They were all my clients and most of them became my friends. In 2017 two of my clients passed away on the same day. They were the famous French singer Johnny Hallyday and the academic Jean d'Ormesson, who I taught to ski in Courchevel."

The secret to swimming, he says, is breathing correctly. "I'm originally a physiotherapist. My method is to teach my clients to breathe into a salad bowl. I fill it with water and I ask them to exhale, make bubbles, hold their breath or open their eyes in this salad bowl. This aquatic breathing technique gives them confidence – I've cured some hydrophobic clients after just two or three hours."

This is how he taught politicians Edgar Faure and Hubert Védrine, as well as fashion designer Domenico Dolce (of Dolce & Gabbana), how to swim. "Ralph Lauren wasn't a great swimmer," he says. "I took him to the sea and observed his breathing in depth. I totally changed his breathing and he *became* a great swimmer."

When we address the possible subject of retirement, Gruneberg seems, for the first time, reluctant to talk. "I hate this word. It's a situation that I refuse to imagine as long as I've got the physical capacities to do my job. I swim every day, four months a year, and ski four months a year, and I'm in very good shape. I'm a very happy man."

Johnny Chung

Bartender — Peninsula, Hong Kong — *The cocktail-maker who's been shaking it for more than half a century*

"Guests love drinking and chatting around familiar faces," says Johnny Chung. Indeed, to say that Chung is a familiar face would be something of an understatement given that the bartender at the Peninsula's first outpost in Hong Kong also happens to be the hotel's longest-serving staff member. Since 1957, Chung has lived his life in this grand old hotel. He started at 15 when his father died, taking over his job as a messenger boy. He moved to the bar after four years. "Back then, hotel business was all about personal connections," says the septuagenarian, who has been living and working here ever since.

More than six decades of being in the same workplace is a testament to Chung's devotion. There have been many enticing offers along the way, especially during the city's hotel boom in the 1980s and 1990s, but none could lure him away. "The family atmosphere here is genuine and that's what keeps the staff turnover low and has kept me here for a long time."

The outbreak of the Sars epidemic in 2003 showed just how much the Peninsula values retaining its staff – even during a moment of crisis like that, when guest numbers plummeted. "Our management reduced costs in other areas rather than cutting the headcount," says Chung. "The people-oriented approach isn't just an HR slogan," he adds, recalling the difficult times in the industry when many of his friends working for other hotels were laid off due to the unprecedentedly low check-in rate.

Chung also has his fair share of memories. "It was eye-opening for me as a little boy, meeting some of the most famous people in the world," he says. He fondly remembers encounters with Hollywood stars, including William Holden and Roger Moore, as well as the former US secretary of state George Shultz and former Philippines president Ferdinand Marcos.

Memorising for decades what guests like is the secret of Chung's enduring popularity. "The fundamental skill set of this job – besides stirring and shaking – is remembering people's names and their preferences." While his razor-sharp memory is already a pull for some guests, not to mention the pristine white suit and slicked-back hair, there's also something else in the mix. "At the end of the day, a smile is always the best ingredient."

Hotel Metropol Moscow, *Russia*

Old hotels often have juicier stories to tell than new ones. We tour three grandes dames that are poignant symbols of both continuity and change, starting in Moscow.

History hangs heavy in the Russian capital and few places are touched as deeply by the past as Room 2217 of the Hotel Metropol Moscow, a corner suite with views out across Revolution Square and the Bolshoi Theatre. Once a premier room in Tsarist Moscow's most opulent hotel, in 1917 it became a bunker for imperialist soldiers who fired on the advancing Red Army from its windows. The Metropol was the last line of defence between the Soviets and the Kremlin. After pocking its masonry with bullet holes, shrapnel and artillery fire, the victorious Bolsheviks moved in and nationalised the hotel. Back in Room 2217, as the proletarian revolution raged in the streets below, party chairman Yakov Sverdlov locked the door on a group of secretaries. When they emerged, they had drafted Soviet Russia's first constitution.

"Each and every door hides a different story," says Ekaterina Egorova, one of the Metropol's three in-house historians. "The entire history of 20th-century Russia is in some way connected to the hotel. A lot of fates were decided here," she adds, padding down a wide, carpet-lined corridor. In recent decades, modern rivals in steel and glass have risen to cater for tourists and Russia's newly minted rich. The Park Hyatt and the Ritz-Carlton may have more swagger but, for guests at the 350-key Metropol, the hairline cracks in the marble floors are a small price to pay for strolling to breakfast along corridors in which history was forged.

Built in 1905 in the art nouveau style by a team of architects that included the UK's William Walcot, the Metropol was a focal point of social life in Tsarist Moscow, its glass-domed dining hall filled with the city's elite. Even after renouncing his aristocratic status, an elderly Leo Tolstoy couldn't resist a spot of lunch here in frugal peasant garb. In the centre of the hall sits a large marble fountain, where diners could once choose a fish swimming in the lower pond to be caught, cooked and served (the practice stopped in 1986). In the post-revolution years, Lenin and Trotsky delivered fiery speeches from the stage.

Little about the building has changed. Today original stained-glass windows surround the lift shaft and gilded stuccos line corridors. The hotel's façade has a majolica frieze by Mikhail Vrubel depicting Princess Lointaine from a play by French dramatist Edmond Rostand. "The original owners were not trying to save money," says Egorova.

After it was converted from a bureaucratic HQ back into a hotel in 1931, the fame of the average guest didn't diminish (though those with offices were reluctant to leave, with the last negotiating a late checkout of 1964). George Bernard Shaw lived here in the 1930s and was fond of the *shchi*, a traditional Russian cabbage soup. Meanwhile, opera singer Fyodor Shalyapin would relax after performances at the Bolshoi Theatre and entertain followers in the hotel bar, which now bears his name.

During the Second World War it was the base for foreign correspondents sent to cover the eastern front. Japanese reporters used to march into dinner singing the "Kimigayo", the national anthem, to mark Pacific victories against the US army, all to the chagrin of the US press corps. Staff had to employ their finest dinner-time diplomacy to prevent the restaurant from turning into a front of its own. After the war, it was one of a handful of hotels accessible to foreign citizens (complete with listening devices), where each floor manager was rumoured to be employed by the KGB.

Today's clientele are just as international. "I come here because it takes me back to a century I enjoy," says a guest, who's from Rome, while French, US and Russian businessmen chatter around him. The barman Artur pours Moscow Mules in traditional copper mugs and (if you're lucky) ice-cold vodka in pre-revolution glasses. In the underground kitchens that cater the hotel's restaurant Savva, chef Andrey Shmakov, a graduate of Noma and the grandson of a Red Army general, is plating reindeer, cherry borsch and kvass-glazed eel.

But a hotel can't live off history alone. Bought in 2012 by Alexander Klyachin, the Metropol is renovating 70 rooms. Delicate work. When the hotel was updated in the 1980s, workers peeled off eight layers of paint to reach the original walls. "When the new designs for the renovation arrived, we all said, 'How awful!'," says general manager Dominique Nicolas Godat. "It could have been Dubai or Tokyo. You want to know you're in Moscow." Progress, it seems, is inevitable but one wonders if Lenin would have viewed the Nespresso machines as a bourgeois excess or fuel for the people.

Hotel New Grand, *Yokohama, Japan*

Rebuilt from the rubble of an earthquake and tastefully renovated over the years, the Hotel New Grand is a symbol of renewal for this Japanese port town.

The busy port of Yokohama has had a grand hotel since 1873 but the original was destroyed in the Great Kanto Earthquake of 1923. The city and its residents, though, were determined to establish another hotel in its place. "People thought it would be a symbol of hope," says hotel staffer Momoko Nakajima. The town's mayor Chuichi Ariyoshi led the effort to raise the ¥1.2m (€9,080) needed to get the Hotel New Grand off the ground. The architect, Jin Watanabe (who went on to design the Tokyo National Museum in 1938), built a five-storey concrete building with a melange of influences from Asia and Europe. The first general manager and head chef were flown in from Paris and 3,000 people attended the ribbon cutting in 1927.

The hotel's rooms have since been renovated but the original lobby, staircase and banqueting rooms remain blissfully frozen in time. Italianate tiles line the staircase and Japanese Oya stone-and-mahogany pillars stand in the lobby. There are generously sized sink-in chairs, built by Yokohama Furniture to accommodate larger western guests, and a frieze of embroidered kimono fabric above the elevator by fêted Kyoto maker Jinbei Kawashima II.

The Rainbow Ballroom, where the opening ceremony was held, still has thick wooden doors and delicate *shikkui* plasterwork cornicing on the ceiling. The Phoenix Room, the scene of the reception party, is also intact, with its high ceilings and intricate lanterns that riff on Japanese designs with a distinctly European feel. Fitting grandeur for the guests who have graced the hotel's halls since opening. Charlie Chaplin stayed here, as did general Douglas MacArthur, who oversaw the Allied occupation of Japan after the war. The general set up his first office in Room 315, which has been known as MacArthur's Suite ever since (and still has his desk, chair and portrait). Prince Akihito, now the Japanese emperor, stopped for lunch in 1958 on the way to his summerhouse in Hayama.

The city owns the land and the building while the hotel's chairman, Shinzo Hara, looks after the business side of things. "We're fortunate to have the full support of the city," says the general manager Koichiro Aoki. An 18-storey hotel tower with 193 rooms – all with harbour views – was added in 1991 and, in 2016, the Shimizu Corporation (the antecedent of which had built the original 1927 structure) reinforced the old structure to strengthen it against future earthquakes and prevent damage to the delicate decorations.

The hotel still attracts a trickle of architecture buffs from all over, while the locals come for the *yoshoku*: Japanese-style western cuisine. Swiss-born Saly Weil, the New Grand's first head chef, was personally credited with creating some of the classic *yoshoku* staples enjoyed around Japan today. The current head chef, Shigeru Usagami, is continuing the tradition (he joined the hotel as a kitchen hand in 1973 and never left).

The hotel celebrated its 90th anniversary in 2017. Aoki, who spent three decades at the Imperial Hotel, Tokyo (*see pages 64 to 65*), knows he has to be on his toes in these competitive times. "It's not enough just to have history in this business," says Aoki. "We need to safeguard the hotel's heritage while also updating facilities and services to keep us in good shape for the next 150 years."

Hotel Antumalal, *Pucón, Chile*

Nestled in a nature reserve and packed with original 1950s details, the Antumalal is as pristinely preserved as the surrounding landscape.

Some time in the 1940s, the then president of Chile, Gabriel González Videla, sat down for tea and berry cake at a small waterfront café on the shore of Lake Villarrica. Like many visitors, he was spending his vacation in Chile's Lake District, an increasingly popular spot 725km south of the capital, Santiago. As he marvelled at the views across the lake and over patches of rainforest, the café's owner approached him. Guillermo Pollak, a Czechoslovakian immigrant, had a dream of expanding his business to include an on-site hotel and wanted to see if Videla could help him get a loan for his project.

Ambitious? Yes. But if you don't ask you don't get. In 1947, with the backing of the head of state, Pollak began work on the Antumalal. He commissioned architect Jorge Elton, a graduate from the Universidad Católica in Santiago, who had designed the lakeside café that previously stood on the site. The young Elton was one in a new generation of Chilean architects, spurred by a rising demand for residential and recreational properties that sought to provide resorts and spaces on a par with those in Europe or North America for the country's growing middle class.

Like the masters of modern architecture (such as Le Corbusier, Frank Lloyd Wright and Richard Neutra), Elton and his contemporaries understood their discipline as a search for beauty in form as in function. The approach resonated with Elton's patron Pollak, a lover of photography, and his wife Catalina, an avid gardener. "My father Guillermo and Jorge would spend their weekends walking through the grounds and discussing plans for the hotel and its park," says Pollak's daughter Ana Verónica, Antumalal's current owner. "Over years of close collaboration they became good friends, brought together by their sensitivity for nature and passion for what they did."

Scenic though it was, Pollak's plot of land – spread across a steep, tree-covered slope with irregular, rocky terrain – complicated the development. "There were three rules," says architect Miguel Eyquem, who supported Elton on the project. "All trees are sacred. This was the first. The second was, since wood burns, only concrete is to be used on the façade. The third was that other elements of the terrain are equally untouchable."

After hand-drawing a topographic plan, Elton and Pollak found that there was only one possible setting that would allow the structure to blend with its surroundings: the hotel was to be placed on a platform and embedded in a rugged slope.

Hotel Antumalal opened in 1950. The name (meaning "Corral of the Sun" in the indigenous language Mapudungun) alludes to the unobstructed sunset vistas that twinkle off Lake Villarrica. Perching on concrete slabs that extend over the edges of a cliff, Antumalal appears to float above the lake. It consists of two wings that form an L-shape, one a single-storey with nine guest rooms, the other a two-storey with common areas, a suspended terrace and four rooms (plus two family suites) upstairs. At the meeting point between both units lies an airy living room, the main feature of which is a stone-paved wall that hugs the form of one of the garden's oldest lingue trees.

In almost 70 years, Antumalal has maintained all the established flora. "Elton's creation is a delicate machine from which to contemplate the landscape," says Fernando Pérez Oyarzun, head of architectural and urban studies at the Universidad Católica. "Everything was designed to obtain an interior quality that is rooted in the building's relationship with the exterior." Guests access Antumalal by a shaded path that winds through bellflower meadows. In homage to Lloyd Wright, Elton incorporated a waterfall that still trickles beneath the living-room end of the concrete platform. The bedrooms and four chalets bring elements from the natural world to the interior: the individual fireplaces nod to the active Villarrica volcano that rises behind the hotel. Everything is an ode to the land and culture of the Unesco-protected reserve in which the hotel sits, from the floor lamps and bedside tables made from fallen trees to the sheepskin mats made by the Mapuche community.

All furnishings were designed by Elton and Pollak, including an Antumalal variation of the butterfly chair with its leather seats and iron frame, and a dining room clad in araucaria wood to contrast with the concrete exterior. Updates include a pool house, carved into the rock in the 1960s, as well as a bamboo roof to cover the terrace. Although the guest rooms now have flat-screen TVs, they're no competition for the main highlight: the view.

235

Hotel Okura, *Tokyo*

Hotels often tell the story of their city, architecture and a moment in time.
That's why the destruction of the Hotel Okura can teach us all a lesson.

Travel magazines and newspaper column inches (and books like the one you're holding) regularly focus on hotels by talking about new openings. They use the same few words: a "boutique" property, a "design" hotel touted as "redefining luxury" or some other such trite cliché. In almost all instances, these new hotels aren't redefining luxury at all – and in a depressing way many of these aren't the businesses that will last.

Often, older hotels just tell better stories and speak of more interesting times, an era before the ubiquity of exposed-brick walls, poured concrete floors and fit-outs that look the same from Tokyo to Toronto. As marketeers attempt to cater to the mythical, phone-gazing cohort of "millennials" (or worse, the meaningless epithet "digital natives"), we're all in danger of losing out as hotel experiences become increasingly samey.

Hoteliers should think twice before changing what they already have. They must hesitate before turning their modernist gems, fin-de-siècle finery or alpine almshouses into gleaming, glass-covered towers. They should resist turning their small or mid-sized holdings into gargantuan ones with worse service, too-bright LED lights and fiddly iPads that purport to control the room (what's wrong with a simple light switch or dimmer?).

It's this trigger-happy and unsentimental desire to renovate that underpins one of the toughest-to-take examples of development for its own sake that we've seen in recent years. Rumours had been swirling for months and then it came in May 2014, the news all lovers of modern Japanese architecture had feared: the redevelopment of the 1962-built Hotel Okura in Tokyo. The word "iconic" is overused but this hotel fully deserves the label. In September 2015 the best bits of the hotel were torn down by its owners to make way for a 38-storey glass tower. It was an irreparable loss and worth pondering closely.

Located in Toranomon, the Okura was an extraordinary testament to a key moment in Japanese design. It was built two years ahead of the Tokyo Olympics in 1964, with an annex added in 1973, by a gifted group including architects Yoshiro Taniguchi and Hideo Kosaka, the folk artist Shiko Munakata and the potter Kenkichi Tomimoto.

Until the end, visitors could walk into the main building of the Hotel Okura and drink in the atmosphere of the 1960s. The lobby was a perfect combination of wood, paper screens and pendant lights. Tomimoto's vast mural dominated one wall. The signage was simple and concise. The lobby attendants wore their kimonos with unselfconscious ease. Even the displays of foliage, courtesy of an *ikebana* (traditional flower arranging) school, were an understated affirmation of the life the hotel seemed to embody.

If you were designing a hotel today you might not think to include a tea ceremony room or a *Go* salon for players of Japan's version of chess – but the Okura had both. It also had staff in tuxedos and bow ties, a Japanese garden and a bar where they've been making highballs since they were fashionable the first time around.

Redeveloping the Okura makes sense in economic terms and the vested interests of construction and property are sometimes too powerful to resist. The new 550-room hotel reopens in 2019 and no doubt there will be talk of "Japanese aesthetics" and *omotenashi* (hospitality) – both of which the old hotel already had in spades.

We're not worried about apartment-sharing apps eclipsing hotels (at least not the good ones) but the hotels that will thrive will be the ones telling the best stories. Sometimes a steady hand, a long view and the courage to celebrate difference instead of seeking sameness will set the best hotels apart from the rest of them.

1. —— The hotel as sanctuary

During the Second World War, London's hotels were places of refuge for politicians, spies and royalty who temporarily lived their eccentric lives among the gilded corridors.

The grand hotel exists to protect its patrons from the world beyond its doors. In peacetime, that performance is measured in the softness of the pillows, the quietness of the rooms and the plausibility of the staff's expressions of delight. During the Second World War, other indicators were more important: the thickness of the walls, the absence of horseflesh in the stockpot and the band's willingness to play on through the bombardment.

Between 1939 and 1945, London's hotel guests learned the rules of wartime hospitality: careful calculations about comfort, convenience and the likelihood of being killed. Claridge's was constructed before the era of steel or concrete and offered a room at the top for a mere 35 shillings (still a few hundred pounds in today's money). But it was a space that put little between the patrons and the parachute mines.

At least they were risking death in elevated company. On Brook Street, King George of Greece signed the register as "Mr Brown" and fooled nobody; King Haakon of Norway grazed a smorgasbord set up in a former billiard room and Queen Wilhelmina of the Netherlands descended the grand staircase in a flannel dressing gown. In 1945, Winston Churchill took the unusual step of declaring Suite 212 Yugoslav territory for one night only, allowing Crown Prince Alexander to be born in his ancestral homeland.

The Savoy – another building formed of frail Victorian brick – bolstered its public spaces with scaffolding painted in the colours of the Union Jack and encouraged its guests to hope for the best. The lower floor housed ranks of camp beds separated by satin partitions and patrolled by a uniformed snore warden. Behind a curtained recess slept the Duke and Duchess of Kent.

This indulgence did not go unpunished. On 14 September 1940, a phalanx of East End communists marched into the hotel to protest against the government's refusal to let the public take refuge on the London Underground. As the air-raid sirens had already sounded, the management was obliged to admit them to the shelter. The demonstrators ordered bread and butter, and persuaded the waiting staff to limit the charge to twopence a head – the same price listed on the menu of a Lyons Corner House. The incident produced disquiet in Churchill's War Cabinet but it achieved its aim. A week later London Transport opened Aldwych Station to those seeking refuge from the bombing, an underground berth far safer than the Savoy could offer.

The Ritz was made of stronger stuff: steel beams of New York skyscraper standard, which was reassuring (if nobody mentioned that they were made in Germany). The safest spot, the Lower Bar, became a favourite meeting place for employees of nearby MI5 – and another of London's clandestine communities. One notoriously camp patron, Kim de la Taste Tickell (doomed to be known by his school nickname "Testicle"), carried a respirator box that contained nothing but the Max Factor he used to top up the tan he'd acquired in North Africa.

Safest of all, however, was the Dorchester: 50,000 tonnes of concrete supported by 1,600km of steel rods. In the basement ballroom, Lew Stone and his band became so insouciant about air raids that they incorporated them into their act, transforming the sound of a six-stick incendiary into the first bars of the Anvil Chorus from *Il Trovatore*. The Dorchester, wrote the Canadian diplomat Charles Ritchie, was "a luxury liner on which the remnants of London society have embarked in the midst of a storm … a fortress propped up with money bags".

The conduct of some of the clientele, however, demonstrated that the power of privilege had its limits. The foreign secretary, Lord Edward Halifax, set up a bedroom in the Dorchester's subterranean Turkish bath. An observant Anglo-Catholic, he furnished it with a crucifix and small altar. (He also furnished it with his mistress, Alexandra "Baba" Metcalfe, who was conducting a parallel romance with Dino Grandi, Mussolini's representative in London.) This was, however, the most dangerous spot in the building: it lay beneath the drive in front of the main entrance. If a bomb had fallen here, his chances of survival would have been as slight as those booked into a cheap room under the rafters.

About the writer
Matthew Sweet presents the BBC radio programmes *Free Thinking, Sound of Cinema* and *The Philosopher's Arms*. His books include *The West End Front* and *Operation Chaos: The Vietnam Deserters Who Fought the CIA, the Brainwashers and Themselves.*

Pictured:
Top: air-raid shelter in the grounds of the Savoy Hotel in 1940. Above: gas-mask drill fails to interfere with dinner service at the Grosvenor House Hotel, 1940

2. —— The hotel as political plaything

Cuba's hotels have seen it all, from the heady days of Hemingway to Castro's nationalisation and the arrival of international chains.

Cuba is a country cloaked in legend. For some, the allure of that legend lies in a deep nostalgia for a Cuba before Fidel Castro, when US "guys and dolls" jetted down to Havana for weekends of gambling and other unmentionable fun. For others, Cuba's mythic appeal lies in the proud defiance of its revolution and the "glory days" of the early 1960s, when Castro thumbed his nose at Uncle Sam, resisted a US-backed exile invasion at the Bay of Pigs and brought the world to the brink of nuclear armageddon during the tense 13 days of the Cuban Missile Crisis. Another thing Castro did – despite playing host to an international hospitality convention in Havana in late 1959 – was nationalise the entire tourism industry within two years.

Ernest Hemingway is a staple of Cuban folklore. One story is that the expat author, who lived in Cuba on and off during the 1930s before settling in 1939, diligently put pen to paper each morning. He worked from a room that he rented for $1.50 a night in Hotel Ambos Mundos but he often had trouble when his drinking buddies came knocking. As a solution, he secretly rented a second room under an assumed name at the nearby Hotel Sevilla. This secret was so well kept that today Sevilla makes no mention of its link to Hemingway, unlike Ambos Mundos, which stands as a museum to the master.

Hemingway always called it quits at noon with a daiquiri at El Floridita. He then strolled (or stumbled) back through Havana's colonial core, ending the day with a mojito or two at La Bodeguita del Medio. Of course, he wasn't the first to stumble through those cobblestone streets. The same rum-induced swagger was surely common among the sailors, soldiers, rogues and revolutionaries who blew into the port city for their months-long layovers.

These visitors fuelled the country's economy and gave birth to industries, chief among them hospitality. As such, Havana is home to scores of other legendary hotels. The now refurbished rooms and defunct casino (but still lively cabarets) of the Hotel Nacional hosted many a mid-century US luminary: Gary Cooper in the 1930s, Rita Hayworth in the 1940s and Frank Sinatra in the 1950s. This is to say nothing of mobsters such as Lucky Luciano, who were often behind the scenes and on the take. At the same time, the African-American chanteuse Josephine Baker was turned away in 1950 because

there was "no room at the inn" during peak season. Others denied entry included crooner Nat King Cole and boxer Joe Louis. But Baker had the last laugh when she was invited by the Castro government to return in the 1960s, by which time the hotel was "under new management" (to put it mildly).

The Hilton family got into the Cuban hospitality act a tad late, by completing the Havana Hilton on the eve of what turned out to be a socialist revolution. As a sign of things to come, Castro and his bearded entourage commandeered the top floors as their makeshift HQ in the first months of 1959. The government eventually "nationalised" the Hilton (along with all the island's other hotels), rechristening it, without irony, Hotel Havana Libre.

There followed a 30-year hiatus, during which international hotels were either shuttered, turned into schools and clinics or enlisted to show socialist solidarity to delegates and dignitaries visiting from the Soviet bloc. Then Cuba's pre-revolutionary tradition of capitalist hospitality was renewed in the early 1990s to bring in cash following the collapse of the USSR and the evaporation of Soviet trade.

Now, another 30 years or so on, Cuba is home to some 380 hotels. More than 80 have four or five stars and are managed by or run as joint ventures with international hospitality chains, including the European groups Meliá and Kempinski. These big corporate fish compete with more than 28,000 *casas particulares* (private homes), which have been granted licences to rent rooms to tourists over the past 20 years.

Ask today's tourists why they're travelling to the forbidden island and the most common refrain is, "I want to see it before it changes." But one of the few constants in Cuba over the past half-century is change – not change of the system the revolution put into place but incremental changes within the system itself. And perhaps nowhere else has this change been more drastic than in the island's variously grand and down-at-heel hotels.

About the writer
Ted Henken is an associate professor of sociology and Latin American studies at Baruch College, City University of New York. Since 1997 he has travelled to Cuba more than 30 times to conduct research and lead student groups or educational tours.

Pictured:
Fidel Castro and his son, Fidelito, in a room at the Havana Hilton in 1959

3. —— The hotel as embassy

The Nile Hilton and Shepheard's Hotel in Cairo have both been host to a long list of war generals, heads of state and empire-builders.

"If you want to see the world," wrote Mohammed Al-Tabei, the godfather of Egyptian journalism, "all you have to do is sit on the terrace at Shepheard's Hotel." From Napoleon to Egyptian president Gamal Abdel Nasser, wars and political volatility have shaped the fortunes of Cairo's hotels. The legacy of empire, entrepreneurship and espionage is embodied in the stories of two such landmark properties: the Victorian-era Shepheard's Hotel (for its brash British colonialism and ultimate destruction) and the mid-century Nile Hilton (for the rising influence of the US in the Near East).

The former was a 340-room stop-in that served as the Second World War HQ of the British command in the region. The site was originally a Mamluk palace (commandeered by Napoleon Bonaparte in 1798). When Napoleon left Cairo, he bequeathed it to Jean-Baptiste Kléber, an unlucky stay-behind commander, for the final phase of the disastrous occupation of Egypt by French forces.

By 1849 the building was being used as a school but the Khedive Abbas, who maintained the Ottoman Empire's then nominal hold on Egypt, thought the real estate would be better served by a swish hotel. He then gave the property to his hunting buddy Samuel Shepheard.

Early on, Shepheard's catered to intrepid travellers, including Mark Twain. Major-General Charles Gordon checked in before meeting his demise in Khartoum, as did British troops deployed from India to serve on the Crimean front – an unpleasant experience for the owner, who chased deadbeat officers to Sebastopol in order to settle their hotel bills.

Located between the medieval Islamic city and the Haussmann-style boulevards west of Al Azhar, Shepheard's skirted oriental bazaars, the beaux arts Cairo Opera House and the red-light district. The hieroglyphic-clad columns in the Pharaonic-style lobby and the Arab Lounge show how the hotel was constructed as "an idea of Egypt: envisioned, created, modified and controlled by the West", says Tarek Ibrahim, a scholar of architectural history. "It provided not only rooms but also an experience."

That experience was problematic – and often racist – to many Egyptians and Arabs. Some visitors complained that en-suite service bell buttons were labelled "native". This prejudice is immortalised by the Long Bar scene in the 1962 classic *Lawrence of Arabia*. "This is a bar for British officers," exclaims the bartender as the dusty-robed hero enters with a Bedouin companion. "That's all right, we're not particular," retorts Peter O'Toole as Lawrence.

The hotel served again as HQ for Britain's Middle East command-centre as Rommel and Montgomery faced off at the 1942 Battle of El Alamein. The top brass of the allied North Africa campaign lodged at Shepheard's alongside play-wright Noël Coward. All enjoyed cocktails mixed at the fabled Long Bar by Joe Scialom, who created a concoction called the Suffering Bastard.

In 1952, British forces shot dead 50 Egyptian policemen in the Suez Canal city of Ismailia. Anti-colonial sentiments stirred. Rioters raided Barclays Bank and killed Englishmen at the exclusive Turf Club. But it was the destruction of Shepheard's that underscored the end of British colonial Cairo: the 111-year-old hotel burned to cinders in 20 minutes.

While the state-owned Egyptian Hotels Ltd built a new Shepheard's half a mile away from the original in 1957, by 1958 it faced competition from the Nile Hilton, built on the Qasr Al-Nil barracks of the departed British army. "The glory of the place was the bar on the mezzanine overlooking the Nile," says Dr Terry Waltz, former director of the American Research Center in Egypt.

Arab heads of state met at the Nile Hilton to put an end to the Black September clashes in 1970 between supporters of Jordan's King Hussein and Palestinian leader Yasser Arafat. Nasser died of a heart attack within hours of the summit – yet nobody blamed the hotel's famous cheeseburgers.

The Hilton's mid-century modern structure still flanks the river and Tahrir Square though a 2015 remodel and rebranding as a Ritz-Carlton has resulted in an interior more evocative of a big-box fit-out exported from Dallas or Dubai. Today a petrol station stands at the site of the original Shepheard's Hotel, a fittingly incendiary legacy for Egypt's most controversial hotel.

About the writer
Jacob Wirtschafter is a freelance journalist covering Egypt and the Middle East for publications such as *USA Today*, *The Washington Times* and *The National Times of Abu Dhabi*. His downtown Cairo flat is in equal walking distance to the former Shepheard's Hotel and the still-open Nile Hilton.

Pictured:
Top: (Left to right) Libyan leader Muammar Gaddafi, PLO chief Yasser Arafat, Egyptian president Gamal Abdel
Nasser and King Hussein of Jordan at the Nile Hilton in 1970. Above: Joe Scialom at Shepheard's Hotel, 1942

4. —— The hotel as artist's studio

F Scott Fitzgerald immortalised it and generations of artists and Hollywood actors have checked in. The Hotel du Cap-Eden-Roc is the epitome of Côte d'Azur cool.

That the Côte d'Azur is a playground for the rich and famous is an established fact, proved each summer by photographs of Hollywood's elite traipsing around sun-drenched Riviera towns and lolling on the decks of flashy yachts moored off its shores. But no destination has played such a significant role in making it so as the Hotel du Cap-Eden-Roc, the magnificent Napoleon III-style palace on a private point between Juan-les-Pins and Antibes. This cream-coloured hotel was a creative haven before the notion was fashionable.

Though the Du Cap has been painstakingly preserved – an alleged €52.6m, seven-year-long restoration starting in 2007 that added modern amenities is referred to as "the most expensive renovation that you can hardly see" – it was already remarkably ahead of the curve when it was built in 1870. It was a clever antecedent to the glitzy retreat that the Côte d'Azur would become. Created as a writers' retreat by Auguste de Villemessant, the founder of French newspaper *Le Figaro*, the grand edifice was something of a white elephant: a gorgeous oasis off the au-courant grid that greeted only a few guests. Nineteen years later, under the ownership of Italian hotelier Antoine Sella, it officially became a hotel, accommodating guests during the winter months (Victorian fashion declared that the Mediterranean summer climate was detrimental to one's health).

In the 1920s the hotel began its reign as a sanctuary for artists, welcoming guests such as George Bernard Shaw and French writer Anatole France. American patrons Gerald and Sara Murphy set up camp at the Du Cap in 1923, bringing their exclusive coterie of pals including Gertrude Stein, Ezra Pound and Jean Cocteau along for the ride, and in turn officially shifting it into a summer destination. F Scott Fitzgerald and Ernest Hemingway, heroes of the Lost Generation, ensconced themselves here in the 1930s, with Fitzgerald memorialising the hotel as Hôtel des Étrangers in his iconic final novel *Tender is the Night*. His ingénue protagonist Rosemary Hoyt seeks solace from her new turn as a celebrity and falls in love with the enigmatic Nicole and Dick Diver (based on Sara and Gerald Murphy) on the little beach that they "invented" where the hotel's lawns meet the sea.

It was in the same decade that Eden-Roc Pavilion, the glamorous beach club and complex carved into the rocks just above the water, was expanded to accommodate new generations of artistes, including Marc Chagall, who painted the beach cabanas. From the 1920s through to the 1960s, the Du Cap cemented itself as a creative oasis without comparison. It played host to the sultry French actress Suzanne Georgette Charpentier, known as "Annabella", and her Hollywood heartthrob husband Tyrone Power. The Duke and Duchess of Windsor checked in, as did Pablo Picasso (who even agreed to hand-draw the new restaurant menus) and his Russian ballerina wife, Olga, who danced in Diaghilev's troupe.

The Du Cap didn't begin to accept credit cards until 2012. Entrepreneur and film-maker Charles P Finch, who grew up spending summers there with his thespian parents, the actors Peter Finch and Yolande Turner, says that for the right sort of person "exceptions were made, paintings were swapped". He recalls watching as bronzed beauties stretched out on poolside mattresses and basked in the sun, anointing themselves with fragrant Mediterranean olive oil from little bowls of the stuff placed there for exactly that purpose. "I remember it for its sensuality," he says.

Finch remembers the Hotel du Cap-Eden-Roc – today the jewel in the crown of the Oetker collection, which includes Le Bristol Paris and Courchevel in the French Alps – as a "family retreat" where the lucky broods would reconvene each summer, laughing and luxuriating. "By the 1970s the hotel had been taken over by the super-rich," he says. "Brigitte Bardot, David Niven, Italian magnate Gianni Agnelli, my father, they all came for lunch off their boats or for a night or two but they didn't stay for long because they had their own houses." Today the Hotel du Cap-Eden-Roc plays host to the star-studded AMFAR benefit each year and our modern-day celebrities continue to frolic in its salons and on its manicured paths. "This said, the era of moving in for a long stay or season has passed."

About the writer
Tarajia Morrell is a freelance journalist whose food, wine and travel writing appears in *WSJ Magazine*, *Food & Wine*, *Condé Nast Traveler* and others. She's also a partner at Metta, a sustainability-focused restaurant in Brooklyn, New York.

Pictured:
Top: Eden-Roc pool carved into the cliff below the pavilion, 1948. Above: view of Eden-Roc Pavilion
from a yacht, 1948

5. —— The hotel as front line

In times of conflict, hotels can be a safe haven where war correspondents find a semblance of normality that allows them to keep working (and drink too much whiskey).

During the siege of Sarajevo, which ran from 1992 to 1995, room 435 of the Holiday Inn was my home. Life there consisted of zigzagging your way to the front door to avoid the hillside snipers who were taking aim at your knees, eating cardboard-flavoured food from humanitarian aid ration packs, writing by candlelight and drinking too much whiskey. It was wartime, which was miserable, but I was strangely happy.

Built in 1984 for the Winter Olympics in Sarajevo, the Holiday Inn wasn't a good-looking hotel. From the outside it was a mass of bright–yellow, Lego-like bricks. Inside it resembled a dorm in a third-rate university, with a stained purple carpet and dull plywood furniture. Nonetheless, even during the shelling, maids made up our beds and folded our sleeping bags on top. Along with the hotel restaurant's bow-tied waiters, they were a grim testament to the country's resilience.

When reporting in a war zone, your hotel becomes a strange haven, an essential sanctuary, an information depot. It may not have much water or electricity but it's a safe place where you can drop off your pack, remove your boots and flak jacket and tap away at your computer.

One of the most luxurious war hotels remains the American Colony Hotel in east Jerusalem. At the height of the first intifada ("uprising") in the late 1980s and early 1990s, the management was so in tune with what journalists needed that it installed an AP wire machine in the lobby. That way, reporters could continue to gather in the lemon-scented courtyard of the former pasha's palace and keep track of the West Bank clashes between Palestinian youth and Israeli security. At night they slept in well-kept rooms with Persian rugs laid out on beautiful dark hardwood floors and with antique furniture aplenty.

The al-Rashid Hotel in Baghdad was another hotel I called home while we waited for the US invasion that finally came in April 2003. During the Saddam Hussein days it was an oasis, with an admittedly slimy pool, a winding garden where I used to jog and a restaurant that served fresh juice in the morning – watermelon, pomegranate or grapefruit. I left several bags of winter clothing in my room when I had to flee in a hurry – and never retrieved them. Today the hotel is part of the fortified Green Zone, behind barbed wire, walls and checkpoints.

I remember sipping cold beers in the garden of the American Colony Hotel during the first and second Palestinian intifadas, checking into the Fairview in Nairobi between assignments in Somalia and Rwanda and bedding down in Hotel Ivoire during the coup d'état in Abidjan. I can still taste the salty caviar and vodka served in the restaurant at the extravagant Esplanade in Zagreb, where I stood under a hot shower for the first time in six weeks after my stint in Sarajevo.

In Damascus, I stayed in surreal luxury. The Dama Rose, where UN monitors were also staying, hosted bacchanalian Thursday afternoon pool parties, even while the acrid smoke was curling into the sky from dropping bombs in the distant suburbs. Then there was the Caravelle in Saigon and the Gandamack Lodge in Kabul. The list goes on and on.

When conflict ends, some war hotels assume second lives as places of leisure. In truth, journalists can't afford to stay in the American Colony Hotel anymore but diplomats and UN officials can. Today the Fairview in Nairobi is the first stop-off for tourists before they pile into trucks and head out on safari in the Maasai Mara. These hotels are testaments to survival, physical memories of what their cities have undergone. The Holiday Inn in Sarajevo still stands, despite the snipers and bombings, only now it has a new name: Hotel Holiday. Two decades after the war ended, a group of us gathered there for a reunion and strangely it was the same – albeit a tad cleaner, with running water.

I write this from an old colonial hotel in Sri Lanka, a country that endured a 30-year civil war that tore it apart. Here, high in the hills where tea is harvested, it's quiet; you can hear the birds and nothing else, let alone the dropping of bombs. Wars eventually end and, if they're lucky, the buildings that provided refuges for some remain.

About the writer
Janine di Giovanni is the Edward R Murrow fellow at the Council on Foreign Relations in New York. She has written for *The New York Times* and *The Paris Review*, among other publications, and is the author of *The Morning They Came for Us: Dispatches from Syria*.

Pictured:
UN Peacekeeping Forces patrol outside the Holiday Inn, Sarajevo during Yugoslavia's Civil War

6. —— The hotel as museum

The characters who polished shoes, poured wine and plumped pillows were a fascinating subject for one French artist, whose portraits are a window into 1920s Parisian society.

France's leisure industry flourished in the wake of the First World War, thanks to a period of economic prosperity. Hotels were a ubiquitous part of modern life and so was the workforce behind them. In the 1920s the number of international visitors to Paris doubled and checking into the grand hotels among the names we're all familiar with – Chagall, Dalí, Hemingway – was a curious young artist called Chaïm Soutine. Uninterested in the moneyed guests, he mingled instead with the legion of liveried staff attending to them. The 30-plus portraits he created of these overlooked characters provide a snapshot of early 20th-century society.

The popularity of Paris's grand hotels brought with it a new social mix, throwing guests together with up to 400 employees in one building. The distinctive uniforms, the colour of which determined whether a wearer stood out or blended in, identified who was who. The subdued black dress and murky apron of Soutine's chambermaids meant they attracted little attention as they performed their duties. Meanwhile, the two-tone jackets, starched white shirts and snappy bow ties of his wily hotel managers made them instantly recognisable as they swaggered through the brightly lit lobby.

A penniless Jewish painter from the Baltic region of the Russian Empire, Soutine arrived in Paris in 1913 and settled in a grotty commune called La Ruche in Montparnasse. Ten years later, he got his big break: the US collector Albert C Barnes spotted his contorted portrait "The Pastry Cook" and swiftly purchased more than 50 of the artist's canvases. With his newfound commercial success, and a hefty paycheck, Soutine was now able to frequent the luxurious piles on the bourgeois Left Bank.

It's impossible not to associate his fleshy faces – a riot of butcher reds, festering yellows and bruised pinks – with the recently ended war. Though French commerce was booming, emotionally the country was still in recovery. Soutine had previously produced a series of paintings of a rotting cow carcass (briefly his rather pungent roommate at La Ruche) and the uniform of his bellboys, pockmarked with bullet-like golden buttons, is the same blood red.

The livery worn by the staff was historically inspired, a nod to the aristocratic households after which Paris's grand hotels were modelled. It was also a sign that many sought stability in the arms of tradition after the uncertainty of war. The hotels clad their employees in old-time uniforms and, in turn, Soutine painted them in poses associated with traditional portraits of great men. His "Head Waiter", a self-assured maître d', parks himself like an enthroned king, legs spread, hands on hips. Working in one of Paris's plushest hotels was something to be proud of – and doesn't he know it.

The oversized uniforms of Soutine's more youthful staff hint at the changes taking place at the time: are they part of a rapidly expanding workforce or boys doing men's work after their fathers fell in the war? Many appear adolescent and awkward, as if we're catching them mid-first-week. The "Pastry Cook of Cagnes" clasps his childlike hands in front of his milky-white jacket, the bunched chest and rolled-up sleeves of which suggest it was a hand-me-down. The expressionistic brushstrokes evoke the frantic atmosphere of a fast-paced hotel kitchen. No wonder he's nervous about spilling things.

The hotel staff may be painted against dark backdrops, divorced from their places of work, but they nonetheless welcome us as guests. The dapper "Bellboy" stands to attention, ready and waiting to carry our luggage, while the always-handy "Valet" perches on the edge of a chair, listening out for our call with his comically big ears.

The characters behind the classical façades of the fanciest Parisian hotels were surrounded by the high life yet separate from it. And though he painted their portraits, Soutine in a way neglected them too: he kept them anonymous. As well as reflecting both the hotel boom and the anxiety surrounding French identity in the early 20th century, championing modernity while clinging to tradition, his frank and mysterious portraits reveal the inner workings of society. They also reinforce the idea that Paris's grand hotels were microcosms of society in their own right. Just think: if mingling with the iPad-clutching hotel staff of today, what would his portraits suggest about the current state of affairs?

About the writer
Chloë Ashby is associate editor of the MONOCLE Books team. A graduate of the Courtauld Institute of Art, she has written about culture for *The Guardian*, the *New York Observer* and *The Daily Beast*. While working on this book, she couldn't resist squeezing in an essay about Soutine.

Pictured:
Top left: 'Room Service Waiter' (1927), self-confident (and slightly snarling?). Top right: 'The Little Pastry Cook' (1922-23), seated like a royal and sporting a floppy white crown. Above: 'The Valet' (1927-28), taking five – typical!

7. —— The hotel as monument

Demolished in 2014, the colossal Hotel Praha in Prague was a work of experimental architecture and a monument to the communist era that some would sooner forget.

On a bright day in April 2014, Arnost Navrátil, one of the only surviving architects of the legendary communist-era Hotel Praha, stood outside the gates of the Prague property and snapped images as it was being razed to the ground. Framed by blue skies and high clouds, a gaping hole was flanked by the spindly remains of both the central and third towers. "I felt sick and had to leave immediately," says Navrátil. "I couldn't understand it then and I don't today."

Constructed between 1975 and 1981 in the residential Hanspaulka neighbourhood, this nine-storey fortress was created for the Communist party of Czechoslovakia to hobnob with foreign guests. From its heyday until 1989, the hotel welcomed and entertained visitors such as Libya's Muammar Gaddafi, Zimbabwe's Robert Mugabe and Palestine's Yasser Arafat.

It was back in 1971 that architects Navrátil, Jaroslav Paroubek, Jan Sedlacek and Ludek Todl – later joined by Radek Cerny – submitted the winning proposal for an architectural competition calling for a government hotel and congress centre. Although the congress element didn't make it past the drawing board, the hotel's exceptional shape did. "Hotel Praha was an experiment in liquid architecture," says Navrátil, referring to the south façade, which merged with the sloped Petschkova Garden in a terraced wave resembling the hull of a cruise ship.

Clad in suspended concrete panels, the edifice was crowned with ceramic tiles created by sculptor Stepán Kotrba. Inside, leading Czechoslovakian artists contributed works: there was an abstract glass frieze by Stanislav Libensky and Jaroslava Brychtová and a stained-glass wall by Benjamín Hejlek. "The hotel was a Gesamtkunstwerk [ideal work of art]," says Navrátil, "with an overall unity of architecture, interior design, furniture and art."

The loss of objects from this Gesamtkunstwerk went on to play a major role in the hotel's eventual demise, following a complicated and controversial string of owners. So too did its gargantuan size. But the Hotel Praha didn't go down without a fight from those who believed it was worth saving.

Following the fall of the Communist regime in 1989, the hotel was nationalised between 1990 and 2002. "An idyllic period," says sculptor Pavel Karous, who, together with art historian Milena Bartlová and conservationist Ladislav Zikmund-Lender, submitted an initiative to the Ministry of Culture to register the building as a state-protected monument. Despite its prosperity, not to mention a local fan base, the hotel was sold in 2002. The buyer was a company with little apparent hotel-operating experience and the hotel suffered. "Privatisation was the beginning of the end for Hotel Praha," says Karous.

That end came in 2013, after the hotel was bought by investment firm PPF Group. Founded in 1991 by Petr Kellner, the Czech Republic's wealthiest citizen, the group eventually admitted it would demolish the hotel. "PPF Group acquired Hotel Praha in a state of complete disrepair," says the group's spokeswoman Zuzana Migdalová. "The bulk of the valuable interior decoration had been carried off or destroyed and the building was simply oversized. Maintaining it or running it as an operational hotel was therefore clearly uneconomical."

The removal of those interior elements was cited by the Ministry as a reason for its rejection of Karous's initiative. Karous suspects that it was common knowledge that damage to the interior would reduce the chances of the hotel being registered as a state-protected monument.

With the support of artists, theorists, architects and the public, a petition was created and protests held in a last effort to save the hotel. But in 2014 Hotel Praha, an eyesore to some and an artwork to others, was permanently removed from the landscape. Today all that remains is a private park behind a gate.

"The architecture of Hotel Praha was exceptional. Sculpture-like buildings almost didn't exist at that time in central Europe," says Karous. "It had an intriguing history that described the transformation of Czech society from real socialism to real capitalism." Scars and all, you can't deny the past. But, apparently, you can erase it.

About the writer
Joann Plockova is a Prague-based journalist writing mainly about design, architecture and travel. A regular contributor to MONOCLE, she also counts *The New York Times* and the *Financial Times* among her credits. Originally from the US, she has called Prague home since 2007.

Pictured:
Meeting room in the Hotel Praha, which in its heyday hosted heads of state and Communist leaders, adorned by the work of glass artist Pavel Hlava

8. —— The hotel as investment

Hotels in Tokyo, like most of the city's architecture, are built, demolished and rebuilt at dizzying speed. Sometimes it's the people who run them that stay the same.

If you came to Tokyo 20 years ago, the city's skyline would have looked quite different. There was no Roppongi Hills, no soaring Tokyo Skytree (the tallest structure in Japan). There was no Shiodome – the cluster of high-rises that now crowd the waterfront area close to Ginza – and Mitsubishi had yet to re-imagine the area around Tokyo Station as the forest of towering blocks it is today.

The hotel scene was different too, coming to the end of an era that had begun nearly 40 years before. The Park Hyatt had opened in 1994 but the crowd of international luxury hotels now present in Tokyo had yet to arrive. Big Japanese hotels dominated and were still in their original digs. Almost all dated back to the early 1960s, an optimistic moment when Japan was shedding the gloom of war and racing towards economic insuperability. The list included legendary Tokyo hotel names: the Capitol Hotel Tokyu, the Hotel New Otani and the Palace Hotel. For anyone who loved unadulterated 1960s architecture, Tokyo was tops.

Two decades ago, the Capitol – which opened in 1963 as the Tokyo Hilton, Japan's first foreign-owned hotel – wasn't so different from when the Beatles stayed there in 1966. Prime minister Shinzo Abe and his leonine predecessor Junichiro Koizumi were both still regulars at Muragi, a barbershop that had been in the hotel since it opened. The Palace was similarly vintage, its French restaurant Crown still a favourite with the city's power brokers. When it was built in 1961, on the site of Hotel Teito, which was founded in 1947 by occupying Allied Forces, the Palace was the most contemporary hotel of its time and went on to win an award from the Architectural Industry Association.

How different the view is today. The Capitol was demolished in 2007 (tears were shed) and rebuilt in a modern Japanese style by the architect Kengo Kuma, designer of Japan's new National Stadium. The Palace closed in 2009 and was rebuilt at a cost of ¥90bn (€678m) before reopening in 2012. Only the New Otani is still in place, although its main building from 1964 has been re-glazed and doesn't look as it did when it appeared as the HQ of the fictional Osato Chemicals and Engineering company in the 1967 James Bond classic *You Only Live Twice*.

If some lament the loss of these buildings, others see it as no more than part of the endless cycle of renewal that has shaped modern Tokyo. No hotel illustrates this more clearly than the Imperial Hotel, Tokyo (*see pages 64 to 65*), an institution whose history is intertwined with the city's recent past.

Japan's first western-style hotel, the Imperial opened in a grand building in 1890, a symbol of the country's eagerness to open to the world after years of isolation. Its second incarnation was designed by Frank Lloyd Wright and opened on 1 September 1923, the same day as the Great Kanto Earthquake. The hotel survived (while much around it was destroyed) and housed homeless embassies and news bureaux. It hosted the crew and passengers of the Graf Zeppelin airship on its first round-the-world voyage in 1929 and its chefs fed athletes at the 1964 Tokyo Olympics. It had the first hotel shopping arcade, the first hotel wedding and the first hotel laundry service in Japan.

But even Lloyd Wright's building was demolished and replaced by a modern tower in 1970. The old lobby, with its volcanic Oya stone blocks, is preserved in an architecture park near Nagoya. The 1970s tower was joined by another in the 1980s. Rebuilding is now on the cards again and yet, no matter what building it's in, the Imperial still exudes its rich heritage.

Unlike their western counterparts, Japanese hotel managers rarely rove the globe like foreign diplomats; they stay put and so does the army of workers that keeps a hotel running smoothly. The Imperial has two members of staff who worked in the Lloyd Wright building. At more recently rebuilt hotels such as the Palace, many of the old staff returned and with them came a sense of continuity with the past; the general manager at the Palace has been there for more than three decades. In a city that has been repeatedly destroyed and rebuilt, there is sometimes painfully little sentimentality about old buildings but the one consolation is the possibility that history can reside not only in the architecture but in the people who inhabit it.

About the writer
Fiona Wilson is MONOCLE's Asia bureau chief and has lived in Tokyo for many years. Never having a car in the city means she has walked its length and breadth – and seen the demolition of some great modernist hotels. Her love of the city remains undimmed.

Pictured:
The Hotel New Otani opened in 1964 as part of a drive to accommodate visitors to the Tokyo Olympics that same year. This picture shows the Garden Tower, which was added in 1974

9. —— The hotel as hideout

The anonymity that hotels offer has made them attractive to countless sketchy characters over the years – and the backdrop for many a mafia shooting.

At the Stockyards Hotel in Fort Worth and the Alcalde Hotel in Gonzales, you can stay in the same rooms occupied by Bonnie Parker and Clyde Barrow at different stages of the Texas leg of their bloody crime spree of the early 1930s. It is, when you think about it, a curious selling point. Bonnie and Clyde were thoroughly bad people who stole a lot of money, terrorised a great many entirely blameless folk and committed murders running into double figures, including those of several police officers. Yet the prospect that we are occupying the same space – regarding the same views – as criminals on the lam taps into one of the most profound appeals of staying in hotels: that as far as the building, its staff and other occupants are concerned, we could be anyone.

The anonymity offered by hotels – at least, the anonymity offered by hotels back when checking in under the name "Smith" and paying cash wasn't likely to raise more questions than it discouraged – means that many such establishments have served as backdrops to infamous moments in the history of crime. What's interesting is which ones become a selling point for the establishment in question.

The Cecil Hotel in Los Angeles, for instance, has quite a history – it's sort of a Hotel California that you can (if you're unlucky) leave without checking out, an establishment infamous for violence, suicides and general weirdness. Richard "Night Stalker" Ramirez, the serial killer who stalked Los Angeles and San Francisco in the mid-1980s, stayed at the Cecil between murders. A few years later, the same hotel was chosen, possibly not coincidentally, by Austrian maniac Jack Unterweger. He had earned considerable acclaim for his prison writings, composed while serving a sentence for an earlier murder back home, and had parlayed his literary fame into a magazine assignment to write about crime in Los Angeles – the statistics of which he contributed to by killing three more people.

The Cecil was reported in 2017 as undergoing renovation as an upscale boutique inn: it seems unlikely that it will offer a Ramirez Room or an Unterweger Suite in the way that some hotels flaunt the patronage of scarcely less dreadful criminals. Another hotel reticent about shady aspects of its history is New York's Park Central, where Arnold Rothstein, the mobster who (may have) fixed the 1919 World Series, was shot and fatally injured in 1928, and where Gambino family boss Albert Anastasia was gunned down in the barbershop in 1957. Several US hotels have served as the backdrop for actual or attempted assassinations: Robert F Kennedy at the Ambassador in Los Angeles, Ronald Reagan outside the Hilton in Washington, Gerald Ford as he left the St Francis in San Francisco – a hotel also associated with the disgrace and downfall of 1920s silent film star Roscoe "Fatty" Arbuckle. And one – the Watergate in Washington – had a crime named after it and the last syllable of its name thereafter enter the language as a suffix denoting scandal.

Perhaps it's just a question of sufficient time elapsing. The website of the plush Biltmore hotel in Miami cheerfully acknowledges the tenancy of Al Capone – although it glosses over the fact that, while he conducted his gangster organisation from the sumptuous Everglades Suite, Capone may have played a role in the murder, on the premises, of hit man Thomas "Fatty" Walsh, whose ghost is said to haunt the elevator still. Hotel Congress in Tucson is able to shroud its criminal association in inadvertent virtue: bank robber John Dillinger was captured in 1934 after he and his gang were flushed out by a fire alarm (the Congress celebrates, around the anniversary, every third weekend of January by staging themed "Dillinger Days").

All questions of taste are rendered helpfully redundant when the hotel in question no longer exists. Ann Jones' Glenrowan Inn, in the tiny Victorian town of the same name, entered Australian mythology in 1880 when it was the site of the last stand of Ned Kelly and his gang, clad in homemade suits of armour, shooting it out with a legion of police. The hotel burned to the ground during the siege. It says much about Kelly's prominence in Australian folklore that the lot where it once stood is regarded as a tourist attraction.

About the writer
Andrew Mueller is a contributing editor at MONOCLE. He's written three books and performs in country band The Blazing Zoos. His favourite hotel is the Hermitage in Nashville, mostly because he once walked into the lobby with a guitar and patrons made gratifyingly errant assumptions.

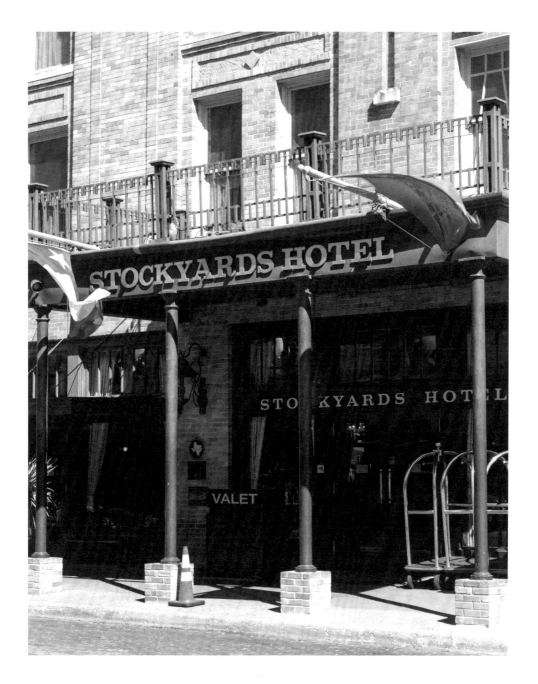

Pictured:
The Stockyards Hotel in Fort Worth, where the Bonnie & Clyde Suite is still decorated with Bonnie Parker's pistol

Building blocks

No matter its incarnation – from roadside inns to boutique boltholes via plush 'palaces of the public' – the hotel has always been a barometer of society and a space that's reflected both public and private realms.

It started with the inn: that pit-stop for weary passengers to find food, a brew and a bed. In the days before combustion-powered travel, networks of taverns, staging posts, Persian caravanserais and Japanese ryokan lined the world's thoroughfares. Lodgings were usually run by families and could be rough billets. Customers couldn't expect much in the way of service and often had to share a bed with a stranger.

It wasn't until late in the 18th century that purpose-built digs evolved. "The hotel was very much a visionary project," says Andrew Sandoval-Strausz, an associate professor of history at the Pennsylvania State University, who has written a book on early hotels. "It was part of the imagination of some well-to-do merchants and entrepreneurs right after the creation of the American Republic's first constitution in 1787. They thought, 'We need to have a new kind of public house for the age of the Republic.'"

These men built "palaces of the public" using an architectural language borrowed from Versailles and other grand European estates. The ambitious structures sprang from a proud and urgent desire to advance the US's reputation. The City Hotel in New York (1794) had 137 rooms and the Boston Exchange Coffee House hotel (1809) boasted a glass dome atop a 30-metre-high atrium. "They were intended to welcome not just merchants but ambassadors and trade delegations," says Sandoval-Strausz. "They wanted to send out a message that the US was just as impressive as any European nation. It was ready to welcome guests."

It didn't matter that most of these early hotels failed. The very concept of the commercial hotel – with its dining hall and long corridors of private rooms – was born. As steamer ships and railroads revolutionised mobility, hotels were built to meet their passengers. They became a reason to travel, rather than just a place to lay your head while in transit.

The hotel has never been just a business. It's a social phenomenon. It has occupied a unique status, on the thresholds of the public and private and occupying a space between commercial and political. It tells the story of the industrial revolution, colonial reach, of globalisation. "Hotels are a symptom, a barometer of society," says Caroline Field Levander, whose book *Hotel Life* explores the cultural role of the hotel. "They are a grey space, an intersection between the intensely public and the intensely private."

By the end of the 19th century "grand hotels" had sprouted all over the world, from Scarborough and Sydney to Shanghai and Baden-Baden, where César Ritz had one of his first ventures. Hotel architects such as Colonel Pfyffer von Altishofen (the man behind the Grand Hotel National in Lucerne) and Édouard Niermans (who built the Hôtel du Palais in Biarritz) were harbingers of modernity. In a sign of the times, even real palaces were turned over to paying guests. In 1873, the Palais Württemberg in Vienna became the Hotel Imperial.

Grand hotels became national monuments, signs that a city, town or region had "made it". Establishments such as the Pera Palace (*see page 29*) in what is now Istanbul resembled royal residences in ornamentation but had the density of a New York apartment block and nifty technology in the form of Swiss-built lifts.

Top: the ornate ceiling of the ballroom at the Pera Palace Hotel, Istanbul. Bottom: Pera Palace was the work of the French-Turkish architect Alexander Vallaury, who used neoclassical, art nouveau and oriental styles

The Grand Hotel
National in Lucerne
was built by Colonel
Maximilian-Alphons
Pfyffer von Altishofen.
With César Ritz as
manager, it redefined
luxury hospitality

Hotel Negresco on Nice's Promenade des Anglais was the star of the Baie des Anges when it opened in 1912 but soon became a hospital for recovering soldiers

The cosmic Druzhba Sanatorium in Yalta, Ukraine, was designed by Igor Vasilevsky and completed in 1986

While splendid, these grand projects were naive in the face of the great political shifts that were to come. They would become hosts to the tumults of the 20th century. It's no coincidence that Cairo's Continental-Savoy Hotel was the venue of Egypt's declaration of independence from Britain in 1922. It was one of the most impressive buildings in town and the favourite spot of King Farouk. Or that the 1930s-era King David Hotel in Jerusalem became the focus of Zionist militants in the 1940s.

Hotels tell stories of ambition, fortune and failure. Take the lavish art nouveau Negresco on Nice's Promenade des Anglais. Opened in 1912 by a Romanian-born former butler, it briefly dazzled high society with its pink domed roof, Baccarat chandeliers and pneumatic tube system that distributed letters to each guest room. Yet only a few years later it was commandeered as a hospital during the First World War. (It was later used as an administrative centre by the Nazis.) Henri Negresco died without seeing his hotel break even.

Postwar hostelry entered a different era altogether. In the mid-1950s, Morris Lapidus's vast Fontainebleau resort in Miami Beach began to define the concept of the resort. These were enclaves of luxury-fuelled catering and the size of small towns. Architects built up, creating towers to increase density. In the 1960s, Brazilian Oscar Niemeyer conceived a cylindrical edifice for the Hotel Nacional, which towered over the beach in Rio de Janeiro's São Conrado neighbourhood. There were also architectural experiments. In the USSR concrete resorts were designed as "social condensers". The spaceship-like Druzhba Sanatorium in Yalta, designed by Igor Vasilevsky, featured rooms that wrapped around a cinema, a dance hall and a salt-water swimming pool.

Meanwhile, figures such as Conrad Hilton began to build hotels beyond his home market in the US. He described it as an effort to counter Communism, to show host countries "the fruits of the free world". The industrialised chain hotel was born and, much like with the Fordism that dominated industry, individuality faded. Staff would follow manuals for everything from answering the phone to cleaning the bathroom. "When I say that the company's prosperity rests on such things as our 66-steps-to-clean-a-room manual, I'm not exaggerating," says JW Marriott Jr in his 1997 autobiography.

267

Left: conceived in the 1960s and completed in 1972, the 33-storey Hotel Nacional overlooks the beach from Rio de Janeiro's São Conrado neighbourhood. Its gardens were designed by landscape-planner Roberto Burle Marx. Above: Morris Lapidus's vast Fontainebleau resort in Miami Beach had 1,200 rooms and a gold-pillared lobby

The hotel's third act is still in play. Hoteliers today have begun to eschew the identikit goals of the 20th century with a focus on "boutique". The sameness that once was a benchmark of reassuring quality became a problem for chains as guests began to seek out "authenticity" in every travel experience. Brands have responded by offering smaller and more characterful stays and, as many customers desert the hotel altogether in favour of apartment rentals they find online, many hoteliers are seeking to make their properties feel more like a home.

But the hotel has always been a place of fantasy. Guests want to check in and feel like they are anywhere other than home. They want to delight in shampoo miniatures and fluffy bathrobes and be dazzled by the shining floors in the lobby. They want to feel that they are the only guest the hotel really values, there to be cosseted, cared for and loved.

There is something about the contrast of public spectacle, personal service and manufactured privacy that makes the hotel unique. As in the 1932 film *Grand Hotel*, starring Greta Garbo and John Barrymore, the lobby should be a chaotic ecosystem that hums with intrigue.

Hotels should provide an instant fix of drama, an opportunity for reinvention and anonymity, or simply a seat at the bar to observe all of the above. They also shouldn't forget their role as the "grey space" between the public and private spheres and as barometers of the times in which we live.

Part 4:

Eating and drinking

Where to dig in and drink up

From the best hotel bars to eating recommendations around the globe, we offer a little hard-won advice on which hotels are worth making a beeline for when you've worked up an appetite or need to slake your thirst.

Food and drink has become an important revenue stream as well as an exciting opportunity for hoteliers to tempt guests, even if they're not staying the night. We venerate those getting the mix of fresh food and a sharp drinks list right. Hint: it's usually those with generous portions, unflappable service and food that errs on the side of being honest and interesting rather than fussy and fancy.

Hotel restaurants
274—285

Leave room for our rundown of hotel dining rooms worth spending an evening in, even if you don't intend to stay the night. Featuring a restaurant nestled in an old-school Viennese grande dame, breakfast on a Swedish island and traditional fare on the patio in Mexico City.

Hotel bars
286—293

Hotel bars have always held an intriguing allure. The anonymity? Perhaps. The proportion of people in town for such a short time and the chance of a subtle tryst? Maybe. The drinks? Of course. Our pick of the bunch includes a Frankfurt favourite, a Miami mainstay and a St Moritz stopover to savour. Cin-cin.

Eating inn
Hotel restaurants

We're sticklers for a square meal: hearty, honest, minus the fuss and foam, and in a smart setting. And as competition in the industry stiffens, restaurants attached to hotels are luring in punters.

Yes, there's still room in our roundup for the independent pension that's serviced family bashes for generations but what about the Hong Kong buffet that's perpetually stocked? And the ideal Harbour-view pub lunch in Sydney or terrace for breakfast in Merano? Read on for our list of spots in which to refuel, catch up with a contact and kick back with old friends.

And should you over-indulge and need a lie-down, you won't have far to go. Let us show you to your table.

Mandarin Oriental, Hong Kong
Old-school supper

Hong Kong Island's oldest five-star hotel has plenty of decorated restaurants. For a taste of the city without scrimping on the haute cuisine head to Cantonese restaurant Man Wah on the 25th floor, which has been steaming classics since 1968. The views are stunning and few menus deliver more of what this city does best per mouthful.

If you want a dollop of the city's colonial past sample the fish and chips at The Chinnery or set sail for the Clipper Lounge if you think buffets are best. Wash it all down with drinks at Captain's Bar – an institution that mixes it up until late.

5 Connaught Road
+852 (0)2522 0111
mandarinoriental.com

Soho House Berlin, Berlin
Haus rules

This 1920s Bauhaus building, designed by Georg
Bauer and Siegfried Friedlander, has been both
a department store and the headquarters of the
Communist party's Central Committee. Since
2010, it's been home to Soho House, with 65
rooms and 24 apartments, a gym, a rooftop pool,
the art deco-style Club Bar and two restaurants,
which serve US and Aegean dishes respectively.

The Venetian restaurant Cecconi's, with its
open-plan kitchen, is open to non-members and
serves seafood specialities and handmade pasta.
The weekend brunches are an understandable hit.
1 Torstrasse
+49 (0)30 405 0440
sohohouseberlin.com

Bauer Venezia, Venice
Sea change

Among Venice's grand palazzos, the fascist-era
modern façade of the Bauer's Campo San Moisè
entrance stands out. The 18th-century building
first opened as a hotel in the 1880s but in the
1940s a new modern wing was built (the side
facing the Grand Canal still boasts a Byzantine-
gothic exterior). Inside is a sleek marble lobby
and sumptuous staircase, while outside there are
canalside tables at which to enjoy a drink.

Guests have access to Settimo Cielo (Seventh
Heaven), the highest terrace in Venice, where
breakfast is served against a breathtaking backdrop.
1459 Campiello San Moise
+39 041 520 7022
bauervenezia.com

Hotel Portixol, Palma, Mallorca
Beside the seaside

The Portixol is located in a marina a short walk from the centre of Palma, where a spot of lunch is accompanied by the Balearic breeze. Johanna and Mikael Landström bought the 1950s-era hotel in 1997 and revitalised the sea-facing edifice.

Shaded by white parasols, the poolside tables are populated by a mix of tourists and island residents sipping on Spanish wine and feasting on fresh seafood. After ordering the signature cocktail (strawberries and cava), afternoon will soon slip into evening and it won't be long before you're eyeing the dinner menu.

27 Carrer Sirena
+34 (0)971 27 1800
portixol.com

Grand Hyatt Erawan, Bangkok
Spoilt for choice

Grand Hyatt Erawan's eight restaurants (and one bar) mean you could sit at a different spot for every meal during a short stay.

The *khao phad kai dao* (fried chicken rice) of The Dining Room is a particularly toothsome breakfast after a red-eye, while the Erawan Tea Room's spicy Thai papaya salad, satays and curries on round teak tables are memorable spreads. There are also weekend champagne brunches at Tables Grill, which serves mouthwatering meat and seafood, besides an Italian restaurant, wine bar, a bakery and more.

494 Rajdamri Road
+66 (0)2 254 1234
bangkok.grand.hyatt.com

ArtHotel Blaue Gans, Salzburg
Have a gander

The "blue goose" is in Salzburg's art and museum district, just opposite the Festival Hall. The hotel has 32 rooms and three suites (we recommend the two-floor Suite Maisonette), plus two restaurants.

The Gewölbe Restaurant, which has been going since 1350, has a traditional feel with its hand-painted murals and wooden panels but the menu is far from old-fashioned. From Wiener Schnitzel to duck-liver parfait, each dish has been given a twist and is seasoned with herbs from the garden. The more informal Brasserie-Bar serves simple yet hearty food along with good music.

41-43 Getreidegasse
+43 (0)662 842 491
blaue-gans.com

NoMad, Los Angeles
Go west

Downtown LA's NoMad, housed in a beautifully refurbished building from the 1920s, is a little more exotic than its Big Apple counterpart (think peacock and other bird taxidermy and jungle-themed upholstery).

Dining is split into a handful of areas. In the more casual downstairs Lobby you can order cocktails alongside fava bean hummus or a steak. Upstairs, Mezzanine is the ideal spot for a long meal, with a vegetable-heavy menu that might include broccoli variations with black rice, confit egg yolk and lemon.

649 South Olive and 7th Street
+1 213 358 0000
thenomadhotel.com

Hotel Sacher Wien, Vienna
Belle époque beauty

The Hotel Sacher Wien has plied its trade since 1876 and been under the control of the Gürtler family since the mid-1930s. Inside the imposing belle époque shell there are 150 rooms (some snug, others palatial) and a fifth-floor spa.

For food we recommend Rote Bar, a swish affair with excellent Viennese dishes, and the Blaue Bar for aperitifs. Then there's the Grüne Bar restaurant, which serves traditional recipes made with local produce and reinterpreted with a modern twist, and the informal Sacher Eck café for a slice of *Sachertorte* (chocolate cake).
4 Philharmonikerstrasse
+43 (0)1 514 560
sacher.com

Hotel Brummell, Barcelona
Set in concrete

Sandwiched between the city, sea and mountains, Brummell is a seemly 20-room affair that's (fairly) central but feels a world away from the touristy throng. Concrete walls frame fronded plants and an edible garden.

Owner Christian Schallert fell in love with the then derelict building in 2015 and asked architect Inma Rábano to fix it up. The menu in the pretty courtyard at Brummell Kitchen moves from huevos rancheros with chipotle to eggs Benedict with pastrami. Weekend brunch is a delight, from açai bowls to pancakes with syrup and berries.
174 Nou de la Rambla
+34 (0)93 125 8622
hotelbrummell.com

Hotel Skeppsholmen, Stockholm
Military precision

Many of the pastel buildings that make up this 78-room hotel are former military barracks built in 1699. Södermalm firm Claesson Koivisto Rune has preserved the finishes and dimensions of the listed space (hence the modular bathrooms incorporated into the rooms without permanent walls).

Several rooms once housed bunks for soldiers but today they afford space and calm, with modern touches such as lamps by Achille Castiglioni and Pio Manzù for Flos. As for the food, chef Magnus Johansson's breakfast is the toast of the town.

1 Gröna Gången
+46 (0)8 407 2300
hotelskeppsholmen.se

Hotel Palisade, Sydney
Harbour highlight

Once a boozy refuge for down-at-heel sailors and "wharfies" (dockworkers), this five-floor, 19th-century space has been transformed into one of the city's hippest hotels. Interior designer Sibella Court looked to the building's maritime history for inspiration, decorating the hotel in shades of the sea: lots of greys, blues and whites.

On the top two floors the Henry Deane cocktail lounge is a highlight, offering views of Barangaroo Reserve and Sydney Harbour, as well as a mean coconut daiquiri. On the ground floor there's a pub (which also does a great pie).

35 Bettington Street
+61 (0)2 9018 0123
hotelpalisade.com.au

 The Orange Public House & Hotel, London
Tangerine dream

In 2009, The Orange Public House & Hotel opened the doors to its restored building in Pimlico, offering a tastefully country-rustic design and menu. With sash windows, lofty ceilings and the original wood flooring throughout, there's nothing stuffy about the space.

The four compact rooms each have a king-size bed and Aesop toiletries. Downstairs, a bustling bar and dining rooms offer seasonal modern European fare. All produce used here is locally sourced from independent suppliers.
37 Pimlico Road
+44 (0)20 7881 9844
theorange.co.uk

 Grand-Hôtel du Cap-Ferrat, Saint-Jean-Cap-Ferrat
Riviera icon

Opened in 1908, the Grand-Hôtel du Cap-Ferrat is a priestess of the French Riviera. Its plot on the rocky peninsula of Saint-Jean-Cap-Ferrat commands stunning views and is so vertiginous that its guests ride a glass funicular down to the 1930s swimming pool.

The Michelin-starred Le Cap restaurant serves Provençal and Mediterranean delights such as *émincé* (thinly sliced) sea bass fillet, or fricassee of lobster with black garlic from Var, on a terrace shaded by Aleppo pines.
71 Boulevard du Général de Gaulle
+33 (0)4 9376 5050
fourseasons.com/capferrat

 14

Babylonstoren, Franschhoek, South Africa
Homespun hospitality

Consisting of whitewashed cottages, suites and a manor house that dates back to 1777, Babylonstoren farm hotel is simple and superb at pretty much all it does.

Almost everything is made on-site: the wine comes from the vineyards and the garden supplies the restaurants. The Greenhouse café serves salads and sandwiches and the main restaurant, Babel, dishes up colourful, vegetable-focused plates. The Bakery, meanwhile, serves Italian-inspired dinners and makes fresh bread.
Klapmuts Simondium Road
+27 (0)21 863 3852
babylonstoren.com

 15

Wanås Restaurant Hotel, Skåne, Sweden
Down on the farm

The medieval estate of Wanås is famed for its park that's peppered with the work of A-list sculptors. In 2017, Kristina Wachtmeister turned two 18th-century buildings into a hotel with 11 guest rooms and a farm that supplies the Wanås Restaurant.

With a menu fed from the teeming forests, the plates brim with wild mushrooms, foraged berries, homegrown vegetables and game. There are plenty of *fika*-focused delights in the form of fresh-baked bread, cinnamon buns and ice cream made with milk from the farm.
Hässleholmsvägen
+46 (0)44 253 1581
wanasrh.se

Hotel SP34, Copenhagen
Great Dane

Copenhagen doesn't want for cosy cafés and diners serving first-rate grub, so the fact that Hotel SP34's in-house Väkst restaurant has won a loyal following is testament to its quality.

The menu is Nordic, vegetables often take centre stage and it's the dinner rather than the breakfast that shines. The restaurant is also a functioning greenhouse and features pots overflowing with verdant foliage hanging above diners. Fresh lunches and three-course dinners with wine pairings see the restaurant swarm with locals – fair praise in a city full of good food.

34 Sankt Peders Straede
+45 (0)33 13 3000
brochner-hotels.dk

La Mirande, Avignon
Cardinal virtue

Avignon was once the papal seat and this was the former cardinal's mansion, not far from the Palais des Papes. Twice a week, in the hotel's 19th-century basement kitchen, head chef Florent Pietravalle cooks produce from the Grau-du-Roi market for a select table d'hôte.

Cooking classes hosted by some of the region's best chefs are another draw and you can learn to make Provençal classics on a wood-fired stove. Restaurant meals are served on a leafy terrace or, in winter, in the panelled dining rooms in front of roaring fires. Bon appétit.

4 Place de l'Amirande
+34 (0)4 9014 2020
la-mirande.fr

Ottmanngut, Merano
Bucolic breakfast

The restaurant in Merano's Ottmanngut hotel is *the* place to start your day. Breakfast comes as a three-course meal that changes daily. Homemade sourdough bread with jams and cheeses, Bircher muesli, and poached eggs on toast with stracchino cheese feature regularly. Most of the ingredients come from South Tyrol and some from the hotel's orangery, which yields lemons, tangerines and plump Valencias.

The garden is a great spot in which to sip a cappuccino while leafing through the international selection of magazines and newspapers.
18 Via Giuseppe Verdi
+39 (0)473 449 656
ottmanngut.it

Conservatorium Hotel, Amsterdam
All the right notes

This neo-gothic building designed by Dutch architect Daniel Knuttel began life as a bank in 1897 and a century later was home to the Conservatorium van Amsterdam. When the music school outgrew it, the Set Hotels group transformed it into a 129-room hotel. Now occupying the former drum room is restaurant Taiko led by chef Schilo van Coevorden.

The menu is Asian, with a peppering of Dutch produce. Highlights include locally farmed veal *tataki* with mango, coriander and peanuts and king red crab in a spicy red curry.
27 Van Baerlestraat
+31 (0)20 570 0000
conservatoriumhotel.com

 Albergo Briol, Barbiano, Italy
On a high

Since 1928 the Briol has been proudly in
the hands of women for three generations. Its
current owner Johanna Von Klebelsberg (*pictured*)
continues the tradition and even cooks for her
guests when the chef has the day off.

Lounge on wooden Lanzinger chairs and gaze
over the Isarco Valley as you sample a plate of
doughy *Knödel* (dumplings) stuffed with cheese,
speck ham, spinach, stinging nettle and herbs.
For dessert, try the *Kaiserschmarrn* (shredded
pancake) served with cranberry marmalade.
1 Via Briol
+39 (0)47 2165 0125
briol.it

 Condesa DF, Mexico City
Hidden wonder

From the outside, Condesa DF looks like any
other beautiful colonial townhouse in the historic
district that gives the hotel its name. That's
why the inner courtyard, where you'll find the
restaurant El Patio, is such a joy.

The space is modern and kitted out with
bold furniture by French designer India Mahdavi.
Equally surprising is the Mexican-French fusion
menu from executive chef Antonio Balderas,
which runs the gamut from Mexican *chilaquiles*
(fried corn tortillas) to a take on a salade niçoise.
102 Avenida Veracruz
+ 52 (0)55 5241 2600
condesadf.com

 22

Drake Devonshire, Wellington, Canada
Lake escape

In 2014, a decade after converting a former flophouse into the Drake Hotel in Toronto's west end, hotelier Jeff Stober set his sights east to Prince Edward County. Tucked along the shores of Lake Ontario, the hotel's restaurant has lake views and a menu that celebrates the region's rich soils and waterfront location, courtesy of chef Alexandra Feswick.

The farm-and-lake-to-table fare is a nod to Ontario's pastoral history. The limestone-heavy soil has also nourished some of the country's top wines, which can be sipped on the beach below.
24 Wharf Street
+1 613 399 3338
drakedevonshire.ca

 23

Hoshinoya Kyoto, Kyoto
Yes we ryokan

Hoshinoya Kyoto is a modern reinterpretation of Japan's traditional ryokan. Located on the Oi River in the forested Arashiyama district, the property had been operated as an inn for about a century before Hoshino Resort Group bought it and gave it a judicious makeover.

Chef Ichiro Kubota's *kaiseki* (Japan's haute cuisine) menu changes almost daily and incorporates a few modern touches. In spring he uses bamboo shoots, foraged plants, minnows and young sweetfish, while during the rainy season he serves a Japanese escargot.
11-2 Genrokuzan-cho
+81 (0)50 3786 1144
hoshinoyakyoto.jp

 24

Small House Big Door, Seoul
Seoul food

When Seoul-based studio Design Methods converted this 1960s storage space into a pared-back four-storey hotel, it devoted the ground floor to a bar and bistro. The industrial-style space is kitted out with design classics such as Cite Lounge armchairs by Jean Prouvé and iconic Callimaco floor lights by Ettore Sottsass, as well as tables and chairs by Design Methods.

Small House Big Door is open to guests and non-guests from 11.30 to 23.30 and serves simple western-style food such as hearty burgers, jam-packed sandwiches and well-dressed salads.
6 Namdaemun-ro 9-gil
+82 (0)2 2038 8191
smallhousebigdoor.com

 25

Hotel San Francesco al Monte, Naples
Mamma's pride

Any hotel with a view like San Francesco al Monte's, spanning from Mount Vesuvius to Capri, would be doing a disservice to its guests by not focusing on the surroundings in its kitchens too.

Luckily, chef Vincenzo Stingone is committed to Neapolitan tradition at his fourth-storey La Terrazza dei Barbanti. Inspired by watching his mother cook for the family, he's kept dishes simple to let the produce shine. This place is at its best in summer; sit on the terrace and order clam spaghetti with courgette flowers and lemongrass.
328 Corso Vittorio Emanuele
+39 (0)81 423 9111
sanfrancescoalmonte.it

Lobby group
Hotel bars

There's something about a hotel bar that captures our collective imagination. Are we extras in a James Bond film or at least sitting next to a spy? Might an attractive stranger slip us a room key and a smile? We can't guarantee it. But the allure and the intrigue endure and, if you're a guest, you're only a short shuffle from your room, making the commute a breeze.

Our rundown of drink spots ranges from leafy Floridian courtyards to London champagne bars, rooftops overlooking Ipanema Beach and, ahem, bar-raising hotels in the Big Apple. Each is different but all share a certain liveliness, irreverence, charm and a touch of mystery. All are worth a visit, whether or not you bond with Bond or find yourself propositioned by a beautiful stranger.

The Langham, London
Bank on it

The Langham features two top stop-ins: Artesian and The Wigmore. The latter is located in an old banking hall reimagined by Martin Brudnizki Design Studio into a lush, art deco-style tavern. On the menu you'll find British pub fare prepared with great attention to detail.

And the drinks? The team behind Artesian offer true gems, including cocktails such as the Corpse Reviver No 1 – made with calvados, cognac and a vintage barolo – and Wigmore Saison, a beer from the tavern's own brewery.
15 Langham Place
+44 (0)20 7965 0198
the-wigmore.co.uk

Crosby Street Hotel, New York
The long view

The hotel may be located on Crosby Street but its block-wide bar stretches all the way through the lobby to Lafayette. The Crosby Bar makes it easy to belly up to the long pewter counter, which is well accented by green and orange barstools.

With large windows letting natural light filter in from the garden, it's a lovely daytime stop. Try the signature cocktail – with vodka, mint, pineapple juice and a splash of elderflower liqueur – that goes down swimmingly on a sunny day in the Big Apple.

79 Crosby Street
+1 212 226 6400
firmdalehotels.com

Krafft Basel, Basel
Swiss precision

Across the cobbled lane from the 60-room Krafft Basel hotel is Consum. This laid-back, light-filled wine bar in a former corner shop on Rheingasse is under the same management as the hotel (some rooms are nestled a few floors above).

In winter, Consum is a cosy retreat, with its wooden bar and leather banquettes. In summer, punters spill onto the pavement, enjoying rosés and cold beers under cream parasols. There are more than 100 European wines, a sharp selection of cocktails and plenty of cheese and charcuterie.

19 Rheingasse
+41 (0)61 690 9130
consumbasel.ch

The Battery, San Francisco
Recharging point

The Battery is a private members' club but you can get around that by staying in one of its 14 rooms (or the penthouse). This gives you full membership privileges, including access to the library and the four bars.

Start at the light-filled House Bar (open from 07.00, should you need a stiff drink to start the day) then move on to the intimate and more formal Living Room bar. If the sun's out, have a beer on the terrace of the Garden Bar. The Musto Bar is the club's biggest draw, while the wine cellar is stocked with 600-plus bottles.
717 Battery Street
+1 415 230 8000
thebatterysf.com

Kettner's Townhouse, London
Plenty of bottle

Soho House & Co is behind the revival of this much-loved 1867 restaurant, champagne bar and now hotel. The layout is mostly unchanged from the days when it welcomed everyone from the Rothschilds and royalty to Winston Churchill and Oscar Wilde.

A tiled 1920s floor in the lobby leads to a marble-topped champagne bar with a homely feel. To the right there's another light-filled bar that, in turn, leads to a grand dining room encircled with 35 Grade II-listed 1920s mirrors.
29 Romilly Street
+44 (0)20 7734 5650
kettnerstownhouse.com

Hotel Viu, Milan
Drink in the view

As the name hints, this hotel's best feature is its view of Milan's skyline. The terrace hosts one of the city's few rooftop pools, and the eighth floor bar is a great spot for a G&T.

Cocktails are suitably light and refreshing but for something more elaborate head back down to the ground floor Bulk bar. Like the rest of the hotel, the bar is kitted out with Molteni&C furniture so decadent velvet upholstery abounds. Barman Mattia Pastori's creations often feature daring ingredients but his reinventions of the classics are notable too.
6 Via Aristotile Fioravanti
+39 02 8001 0910
hotelviumilan.com

Hotel Metropole, Brussels
Fin-de-siècle splendour

Built in 1895, the grand lobby of Hotel Metropole in Brussels is a journey back in time to the belle époque. Head to the hotel's Bar Le 31 to sip cocktails surrounded by mirrored walls, marble columns, gilded bronze, and colourful frescos.

In 2011 the bar was refurbished and the furniture redesigned by French firm Cartisane, staying true to the fin de siècle-style throughout. For the ultimate joie de vivre, the drinks menu offers a careful selection of champagne, decent whiskies and classic cocktails done delightfully.
31 Place De Brouckère
+32 (0)2 217 2300
metropolehotel.com

 8

Freehand Miami, Miami
Heady mix

A bar in a hostel isn't often nominated for a James Beard award (a top US culinary prize) but the Broken Shaker has received rightful acclaim. The concept and bar scheme is the handiwork of partners Elad Zvi and Gabriel Orta, who use herbs and spices from the garden and freshly pressed ingredients to make syrups and sodas.

They'll happily make something to order (though be warned it's mighty busy come Art Basel Miami Beach in December). There are only a few seats inside but the patio has plenty of deck furniture.
2727 Indian Creek Drive
+1 305 531 2727
thefreehand.com

 9

Grandhotel Hessischer Hof, Frankfurt
Old-fashioned taste

Few of Frankfurt's bars can compete with Jimmy's, which is as grand as the hotel it calls home. It's been around for 65 years and hasn't changed a bit (smoking is allowed while electronic devices aren't). The wood-panelled space is furnished with leather armchairs, dim lighting and oil portraits that once hung in Hessian castles.

The drinks menu is vast (we recommend the classic martini) and so is the well-stocked humidor. Once the clock strikes 22.00, Jimmy's pianist starts to tickle the ivories.
40 Friedrich-Ebert-Anlage
+49 (0)69 75400
grandhotel-hessischerhof.com

 10

The Connaught, London
Art deco delight

Consistently voted one of the world's best bars, the Connaught Bar in the eponymous Mayfair hotel is a Gatsby-esque affair. Platinum silver leaf-coated walls, stucco ceilings, leather seats and art-deco details – all designed by the late David Collins – give the bar a jaunty 1920s air.

Being served a cocktail here is a celebratory experience. Try the signature rum-based Vieux Connaught, delivered on a mirrored tray, topped with artistically shaved orange peel and saffron-infused smoke. Any evening spent here is bound to be memorable.
Carlos Place
+44 (0)20 7314 3419
the-connaught.co.uk

 11

Soho House, Istanbul
Care to join me?

A long, white marble bar sits at the heart of the Palazzo Corpi, built by a Genoese merchant in 1873. The gold-frescoed walls and sweeping staircases are almost as handsome as the smart bar staff in their white tuxedos.

Perch on a velvet stool or nestle into a Chesterfield and try a signature Yandan Carkli, which includes coffee-infused raki, or an Eastern Standard made from gin, cucumber, mint and lime. Don't miss the rooftop, where you can sit in a deck chair and watch the sun set over the old city and the Golden Horn.
34430 Evliya Çelebi Mahallesi
+90 (0)212 377 7100
sohohouseistanbul.com

The Peninsula Beverly Hills, Los Angeles
Starry nights

Tucked behind panels of dark birch, The Club Bar at The Peninsula Beverly Hills feels exclusive and offers a drinks menu to suit the tastes of those who frequent it. Expect to see patrons sipping from a glass of a peaty single-malt that's poured tableside.

If you'd rather sample something a little more local, try La Drama, Tito's Vodka base with crème de mûre, a splash of grapefruit, fresh lime and jalapeño garnish. Come awards season, The Club Bar is the hottest ticket in town.
9882 South Santa Monica Boulevard
+1 310 551 2888
beverlyhills.peninsula.com

Bannisters by the Sea, Mollymook, Australia
Shore thing

In the quaint town of Mollymook, frequented by Sydneysiders for long weekends and holidays, are Bannisters Pavilion and Bannisters by the Sea. The latter sits on the oceanfront and features the relaxed Bannisters Pool Bar (as well as Rick Stein's slightly more upscale restaurant).

Try the local seafood sharing plates and either sip on a cocktail or choose a bottle from the long list of Australian wines. If you're walking into Mollymook proper, be sure to stop at Pavilion's Rooftop Bar and Grill too.
87 Tallwood Avenue
+61 (0)2 4455 3044
bannisters.com.au

Botanique Hotel & Spa, Campos do Jordão, Brazil
Garden variety

Located in the mountainous region of Mantiqueira in São Paulo state, Botanique Hotel & Spa has only 17 rooms and prides itself on its laid-back, colourful "Brazilian-ness" (for want of a more fitting term).

All the hotel's interiors are by local designers while the highlight of the restaurant and bar, Mina, is the selection of national cocktails and wines from southern Brazil. We recommend the Rangpur Caipirinha, made with limes picked from the hotel's own garden.
4000 Rua Elídio Gonçalves da Silva
+55 (0)12 3662 5800
botanique.com.br

Park Hyatt Sydney, Sydney
Crack open a frosty one

Park Hyatt Sydney isn't weighed down by the stuffiness of some of its five-star competitors. It reopened in 2012 after an extensive refit but remains uncommonly relaxed, despite its position snaking along a waterside berth near the southern base of the Harbour Bridge.

The 155 rooms and suites offer views towards the high-rise CBD and Sydney Opera House. The palette is muted and homely (as if to prove this the lobby bar is called The Living Room) and guests (sorry, no walk-ins) wanting to unwind can enjoy a drink by the rooftop pool.
7 Hickson Road
+61 (0)2 9256 1234
sydney.park.hyatt.com

 16

Hotel München Palace, Munich
Bavarian boozer

The Hotel München Palace is a family-run affair in the Bavarian city's borough of Bogenhausen. The five-star abode is within walking distance of the English Garden, a park known for its beer gardens. But who needs that when you have the Palace Bar?

Managed by Roland Kuffler of the eponymous catering imperium, the wood-panelled bar is a homely space with a glass-roofed Winter Garden. As well as expertly mixed cocktails, the bar serves a melange of western and eastern cuisine, concocted by chef Walter Jenny.
21 Trogerstrasse
+49 (0)89 4197 1821
hotel-muenchen-palace.de

 17

Park Hyatt Milan, Milan
Welcome respite

For a bar whose terrace is a few steps from the ever busy Galleria Vittorio Emanuele II, Mio Bar is surprisingly intimate. Surrounded and shielded by a row of gently fragranced Mediterranean plants, the outdoor area is open through the summer and autumn. In winter, guests retreat to the stools surrounding the bar's marble counter.

Aperitivo here honours Milanese tradition, with well-executed vermouth and bitter classics, but the ambitious cocktail menu also features 12 types of Bloody Mary. Snacks comes courtesy of Michelin-starred chef Andrea Aprea.
1 Via Tommaso Grossi
+39 02 8821 1234
hyatt.com

 18

Hôtel Providence, Paris
Divine providence

Perched between La Porte Saint-Martin and the Canal Saint-Martin, Hotel Providence is the result of the hard work of the owners Pierre and Elodie Moussié. The pair hunted down every piece for their 18-room hotel, bar and restaurant in this 19th-century Haussmanian building.

Each room has a private bar inspired by the design of the traditional Parisian counter. You can either ask a bartender to come to your room to make a cocktail for you or follow the two recipes for making your own, using the shaker provided. That said, the downstairs bar is best.
90 Rue René Boulanger
+33 (0)1 4634 3404
hotelprovidenceparis.com

 19

The Standard High Line, New York
Hit the high life

Suspended above New York's Meatpacking District, the Top of the Standard (which shares an investor with MONOCLE) has the views you'd expect from this aptly named watering hole. While the main attraction is the nightlife (the bar was once called the famous Boom Boom Room) it's mellowed with age, with more emphasis on jazz.

For the best views, take the lift to the top for afternoon tea and in warmer months you can even step out onto the roof one floor up. Space up here is limited though, so be sure to book in advance.
848 Washington Street
+1 212 645 7600
standardhotels.com

NoMad, New York
One to wander to

The lovingly restored turn-of-the-century building that houses the NoMad sits in the heart of the recently branded district of the same name, just north of Madison Square Park. The stars of the show are the restaurant and bar run by Daniel Humm and Will Guidara.

The bar has its own kitchen, which turns out an informal menu of pub-food-inspired dishes. The cocktail list, courtesy of bar director Leo Robitschek, is heavy on classics with a twist but also features special concoctions of rare spirits.

1170 Broadway & 28th Street
+1 212 796 1500
thenomadhotel.com

Imperial Hotel, Tokyo
In the spotlight

In a city that craves novelty, the Old Imperial Bar is a beacon of continuity. Located in the Imperial Hotel, Tokyo (*see pages 64 to 65*), the bar has changed little since 1970 and its history stretches back even further. Inside is an original mural and wall tiles saved from the 1923 incarnation of the hotel designed by Frank Lloyd Wright.

Old-school bartenders in bow ties have decades of experience between them and serve all the classics, including the perfect Martini or a Mount Fuji, the signature cocktail since 1924.

1-1-1 Uchisaiwai-cho, Chiyoda-ku
+81 (0)3 3539 8088
imperialhotel.co.jp

 22

Hotel Fasano Rio de Janeiro, Rio de Janeiro
Going up in the world

After you've pressed the lift button for the top floor and emerged onto the Fasano's upbeat outdoor bar scene, here's what you do.

One, look at the beautiful view (and people) of Ipanema. Two, decide whether you want to get into the pool, which will probably be packed with preeners (perhaps best to wait). Three, secure a spot in the shaded bar and order yourself a hearty Caipirinha. This can be heaven on a hot evening as the sea and cachaça hazes collide.
80 Avenida Vieira Souto
+55 (0)21 3202 4000
fasano.com.br

 23

Fairmont Hotel Vier Jahreszeiten, Hamburg
Golden oldie

Dating from 1897, the Jahreszeiten Bar at this Fairmont establishment on the western shore of the Alster is grand yet rustic. Visitors enter through a 16th-century church door and perch on leather benches salvaged from a vintage Rolls-Royce – a convivial spot for a drink or two with views of the river.

Enrico Wilhelm and his team are on hand to mix any variety of drinks from noon until 01.00 each day. The Old Fashioned suits this haunt best but whatever you order will be good.
9-14 Neuer Jungfernstieg
+49 (0)40 349 40
fairmont.com/vier-jahreszeiten-hamburg

 24

Badrutt's Palace, St Moritz
Get piste

The Badrutt family brought the first tourists to St Moritz for winter sports and their legacy is here at the historic Renaissance Bar. With its elaborate fireplace and cosy velveteen chairs, this elegant hotel bar transports you to another era.

Patrons still refer to Renaissance Bar as Mario's, after the bartender who invented the famous San Moritzino cocktail. For a more casual retreat we recommend the hotel's Bar Carigiet, known for its murals by the Swiss illustrator and designer Alois Carigiet.
27 Via Serlas
+41 (0)81 837 1000
badruttspalace.com

 25

The Beverly Hills Hotel, Los Angeles
In the Pink

Inside the "Pink Palace" you'll find Bar Nineteen12, its name giving away the year it first opened. This bar offers a quintessentially LA vibe: lean silhouettes toast against the backdrop of palm trees on the breezy terrace, which leads to a handsome indoor lounge and bar.

From its list of signature cocktails, try the Frontier Eclipse: Bulleit Rye bourbon with Cherry Heering liqueur. This beauty is sweetened with a strawberry-lemon agave, balanced with walnut bitters and garnished with star anise – perhaps not the only one you'll spy on your visit.
9641 Sunset Boulevard
+1 310 273 1912
dorchestercollection.com

Acknowledgements

CHAPTER EDITING:
Monocle 100
Josh Fehnert

The perfect hotel
Josh Fehnert

50 elements
Josh Fehnert

The hotel team
Josh Fehnert

How I opened a hotel
Matt Alagiah

Hotel schools
Marie-Sophie Schwarzer

Essays
Melkon Charchoglyan

Lives lived in hotels
Ed Stocker

Three survivors
Melkon Charchoglyan
Josh Fehnert

Nine lives of the hotel
Chloë Ashby

Hotel architecture through the ages
Sophie Grove

Hotel restaurants
Josh Fehnert

Hotel bars
Josh Fehnert

**The Monocle
Guide to Hotels, Inns
and Hideaways**
EDITOR
Josh Fehnert

ASSOCIATE EDITORS
Chloë Ashby
Melkon Charchoglyan

DESIGNERS
Loi Xuan Ly
Kate McInerney
Maria Hamer

PHOTO EDITORS
Matthew Beaman
Shin Miura
Victoria Cagol

Monocle
EDITOR IN CHIEF
& CHAIRMAN
Tyler Brûlé

EDITOR
Andrew Tuck

CREATIVE DIRECTOR
Richard Spencer Powell

BOOKS EDITOR
Joe Pickard

ASSOCIATE EDITOR
Chloë Ashby

ASSISTANT EDITOR
Mikaela Aitken

WRITER
Melkon Charchoglyan

DESIGNERS
Loi Xuan Ly
Kate McInerney
Maria Hamer

PHOTO EDITORS
Matthew Beaman
Shin Miura
Victoria Cagol

PRODUCTION
Jacqueline Deacon
Dan Poole
Rachel Kurzfield
Sean McGeady
Sonia Zhuravlyova

Special thanks:
*The hoteliers that hosted
us around the world*
Louise Banbury
Tom Edwards
Pete Kempshall
Amy Richardson
Rachel Sampson
Giulia Tugnoli

Writers:
Mikaela Aitken
Liam Aldous
Chloë Ashby
Luke Barr
Robert Bound
Jessica Carmi
Ivan Carvalho
James Chambers
Guy Delauney
Lyse Doucet
Josh Fehnert
Leiah Fournier
Henry Foy
Megan Gibson
Nolan Giles
Janine di Giovanni
Sophie Grove
Ted Henken
Daphné Hézard
Mary Holland
Tomos Lewis
Kurt Lin
Gaia Lutz
Hugo Macdonald
Charles McFarlane
Tarajia Morrell
Andrew Mueller
Fernando Augusto Pacheco
Dan Poole
Joann Plockova
Thomas Reynolds
Marie-Sophie Schwarzer
Jayson Seidman
Carlo Silberschmidt
William Brian Smith
Ed Stocker
Matthew Sweet
Saul Taylor
Junichi Toyofuku
María Ulecia
Annick Webber
Fiona Wilson
Jacob Wirtschafter
Gregor Wöltje
Zayana Zulkiflee

Research:
Dan Einav
Audrey Fiodorenko
Will Kitchens
Aliz Tennant
Ceinwen Thomas
Zayana Zulkiflee

Photographers:
Martin Adolfsson
Serra Akcan
Yayoi Arimoto
Rodrigo Cardoso
Brett Carlsen
François Cavelier
Terence Chin
Silvia Conde
Emanuele Cremaschi
Alex Cretey-Systermans
Rose Cromwell
Jimmy Dabbagh
Daniel Dorsa
Sean Fennessey
Luigi Fiano
Alex Fradkin
Stefan Fürtbauer
Daniel Gebhart de Koekkoek
Pedro Guimarães
Lindsay Lauckner Gundlock
Shimpei Hanawa
Benya Hegenbarth
Mariano Herrera
Tina Hillier
Shinichi Ito
Eugene Ivanov
Katrina James
Tetsuo Kashiwada
Martin Kaufmann
Tali Kimelman
Simon Koy
Jacob Langvad
Anthony Lanneretonne
Jason Larkin
Wilson Lee
Lit Ma
Lasse Bech Martinussen
Trent McMinn
Luca Meneghel
Thomas Meyer
Lianne Milton
Conny Mirbach
Ye Rin Mok
James Mollison
Claudio Morelli
Valerie Narte
Dunja Opalko
Cristobal Palma
Jun Michael Park
Ian Patterson
Jussi Puikkonen
Ben Quinton
Robert Rieger

Rocco Rorandelli
Tom Ross
Putu Sayoga
Mark Sommerfield
Jan Søndergaard
Carlos de Spinola
Paulius Stanius
Kohei Take
Marc Tan
Alicia Taylor
Jöel Tettemanti
Brad Torchia
Tanya Traboulsi
Gianfranco Tripodo
Kenneth Tsang
Clara Tuma
Nathanael Turner
Andrew Urwin
André Vieira
David de Vleeschauwer
Weston Wells
Simon Wilson
Dan Wilton
Christopher Wise
Norito Yamauchi
Fuminari Yoshitsugu
Samuel Zeller
Marvin Zilm

Images:
Ake Eson Lindman
Alamy
Paul Barbera
Nicole Franzen
Getty Images
Hotel Parco dei Principi
Metrixell Arjalaguer Nacho Alegre
Nacása & Partners
Felipe Neto
Juan Felipe Rubio
Annie Schlechter
Tiberio Sorvillo
Shutterstock
Herbert YPMA

Illustrators:
R Fresson
Satoshi Hashimoto

Index

About Monocle

In 2007, MONOCLE was launched as a monthly magazine briefing on global affairs, business, design and more. Today we have a thriving print business including a radio station, shops, a website, cafés, books, films and events. At our core is the simple belief that there will always be a place for a brand that is committed to telling fresh stories, good journalism and the kind of experience that only paper delivers.

Our team

We're London-based and have bureaux in Hong Kong, Tokyo, Zürich and Toronto, with Bangkok and LA added in 2018. It seems our team have developed a keen eye for a smart city pied-à-terre and a good hotel bar. You'll find all their picks throughout this book, plus a few specific tips from some of our editors (*see opposite*).

Monocle magazine

Monocle magazine is published 10 times a year, including two bumper double issues (July/August and December/January). We also have three annual specials: THE FORECAST, THE ESCAPIST and a drinking and dining directory. Look out for our seasonal weekly newspapers too, which cover everything from politics to fashion.

Monocle 24 radio

Monocle 24 is our round-the-clock internet radio station that was launched in 2011. It delivers global news and shows covering foreign affairs, urbanism, business, culture, food and drink, design and print media. You can listen live at *monocle.com/radio* or download via iTunes, SoundCloud or from our own site.

Monocle books

Since 2013 we've been publishing books – like this one – together with Gestalten, as well as a series of city guides that are perfect for both seasoned travellers and first-time visitors. Our 30-plus guides take you off the tourist path and show you the sites beyond the obvious. Buy today at *monocle.com/shop* or *shop.gestalten.com*.

Monocle Café and Kioskafé

We don't just write about hospitality and pert service either. We also have cafés in Tokyo, London and Zürich serving excellent coffee, breakfasts and lunches. And if you're passing through London's Paddington, be sure to visit our pioneering newsstand and coffee shop: Kioskafé.

A sample of shows to listen in on

1. **The Briefing:** Weekdays, 12.00, London time
2. **The Globalist:** Weekdays, 07.00, London time
3. **The Monocle Weekly:** Sundays, 12.00, London time

6
Get involved

A subscription to MONOCLE means you never miss a copy. Subscribers gain access to our archive and product collaborations at *monocle.com*, benefit from a 10 per cent discount at our shops (including online), and receive offers and invitations aplenty.

Choose your package
Premium one year: 10 × Monocle, The Escapist + The Forecast, The Monocle Drinking & Dining Directory, Porter Sub Club bag

One year: 10 × Monocle, The Escapist + The Forecast, Monocle Voyage tote bag

Six months: 5 × Monocle, The Escapist OR The Forecast

Subscribe now:
monocle.com/subscribe or
subscriptions@monocle.com

7
Where our editors stay

Tyler Brûlé, *editor in chief*
Work: Park Hyatt Tokyo, Tokyo

Weekend: Grand Hotel a Villa Feltrinelli, Gargnano (*see page 127*)

Holiday: Schloss Elmau, Krün, Germany (*see page 100*)

Andrew Tuck, *editor*
Work: Crosby Street Hotel, New York (*see page 287*)

Weekend: Hotel Albergo, Beirut (*see page 22*)

Holiday: Belmond Copacabana Palace, Rio de Janeiro (*see page 80*)

Robert Bound, *culture editor*
Work: Fairmont Hotel Vier Jahreszeiten, Hamburg (*see page 293*)

Weekend: Kinloch Lodge, Isle of Skye

Holiday: 137 Pillars House Hotel, Chiang Mai

Chloë Ashby, *associate editor, Books*
Work: Hotel Henriette, Paris (*see page 62*)

Weekend: Babington House, UK

Holiday: Micasaenlisboa, Lisbon (*see page 45*)

Sophie Grove, *senior correspondent*
Work: Hotel Locarno, Rome (*see page 34*)

Weekend: Splendid Palace, Istanbul

Holiday: Parco dei Principi, Sorrento (*see page 84*)

Tomos Lewis, *Toronto bureau chief*
Work: Hotel G, San Francisco

Weekend: The Harbourmaster, Aberaeron, Wales

Holiday: Casa Mosquito, Rio de Janeiro

Join us

There are lots of ways to be part of the ever-expanding MONOCLE world, whether in print, online or on the radio. We'd love to welcome you on board.

Read the magazine

You can buy MONOCLE at newsstands in more than 60 countries around the world – or get an annual subscription at *monocle.com/subscribe*.

Listen to Monocle 24

You can tune in to Monocle 24 radio live on our free app, at *monocle.com* or on any internet-enabled radio. You can also download our shows as podcasts from iTunes or SoundCloud to stay informed as you travel from nation to nation.

Subscribe to the Monocle Minute

Sign up today at *monocle.com* to receive the Monocle Minute, our free daily news-and-views email. Our website is also where you will find a world of free films, our online shop and regular updates about everything we're up to.

MONOCLE – *keeping an eye and an ear on the world*

Thank you